CRYPTO DECRYPTED

CRYPTO DECRYPTED

Debunking Myths, Understanding Breakthroughs, and Building Foundations for Digital Asset Investing

JAKE RYAN
JAMES DIORIO

WILEY

Library of Congress Cataloging-in-Publication Data

Names: Ryan, Jake, author. | Diorio, James, author.
Title: Crypto decrypted : debunking myths, understanding breakthroughs, and building foundations for digital asset investing / by Jake Ryan and James Diorio.
Description: Hoboken, New Jersey : John Wiley & Sons, Inc., [2023] | Includes index.
Identifiers: LCCN 2022057666 (print) | LCCN 2022057667 (ebook) | ISBN 9781394178520 (hardback) | ISBN 9781394178544 (adobe pdf) | ISBN 9781394178537 (epub)
Subjects: LCSH: Cryptocurrencies.
Classification: LCC HG1710.3 .R935 2023 (print) | LCC HG1710.3 (ebook) | DDC 332.4–dc23/eng/20221201
LC record available at https://lccn.loc.gov/2022057666
LC ebook record available at https://lccn.loc.gov/2022057667

Cover image: Wiley
Cover design: © Vit-Mar/Shutterstock
Author photos: Courtesy of the Authors

SKY10044637_031723

Contents

Foreword

You're about to delve into one of the most fascinating technological innovations ever devised – and I'm a little jealous. You see, when I first heard about bitcoin in 2012, it was still quite new, and I certainly wasn't looking for it. It kind of . . . found me. It was easy to dismiss the notion of "digital money" as a fad or a fraud – and that's precisely what most people did way back then.

Come to think of it, most people are still dismissing it. What a huge mistake – one that you're not making, judging by the fact that this book is in your hands. Unlike most people, you're ready for the knowledge you're about to obtain. Good for you!

You might not yet understand what bitcoin is, or the blockchain technology that underlies it – but that's okay. At least you won't get quizzical glances when you tell friends and family what you're reading about. Come to think of it, the fact that there's a book you can read on the subject is a huge advantage I didn't have back in 2012. So, yeah, I'm a little jealous.

Since you're still in the book's foreword, you're to be forgiven if the subject still makes little sense. A perplexed expression was certainly on my face the first time I heard of bitcoin, despite (or because of) my knowledge and experience in the financial field. Digital money? *What is that?* I wondered. And more to the point, why do we need it? It took me about a year to fully understand the answers. It wasn't easy to get the information; there weren't any books available. And as I'd talk about crypto, most people dismissed the idea as a fad or fraud.

They're wrong, of course. As you'll discover in this fine book by Jake Ryan and James Diorio, blockchain technology and the digital assets it makes possible are revolutionary – the most profound innovation in commerce since the invention of the Internet. Unfortunately, most people don't yet realize this – giving those who do a distinct set of advantages.

By learning about this new tech, you'll be able to incorporate it into your life sooner than others – giving you both career and investment opportunities that evade others.

If there's a downside to this tech, it's the fact that most people still don't get it. And over the past decade, I've found that those with the greatest disdain tend to be the people with the least amount of knowledge about it. Unfortunately, that still includes most financial professionals. As a group, financial advisors are as uneducated about crypto as everyone else – and that's a problem, considering that they collectively manage two-thirds of all American investors' money.

What's an investor to do when their advisor knows nothing about this new asset class? Take control: learn about it yourself – and find an advisor who did the same.

And this book is great place to start. By the time you finish, you'll have a better understanding of blockchain and digital assets than most people. Along the way, you'll discover that Jake and James are great guides. Their passion pops off these pages, thanks to their knowledge and training as computer scientists, along with their expertise in AI and hedge fund management. They link AI, IoT, and robotics to blockchain technology; the result will be autonomous systems used in every industry and by every government to boost productivity and generate, transfer, and store value.

This technological revolution is just getting started, and the convergence of AI and blockchain will change how we live, work, and play. That makes *Crypto Decrypted* essential, and, by choosing to read it, you're taking an important step toward the future.

Ric Edelman
Founder, Digital Assets Council of Financial Professionals
Host, *The Truth About Your Future* podcast

Acknowledgments

Crypto Asset Investing in the Age of Autonomy was a Herculean effort. When the opportunity presented itself for a follow-up, Jake and I agreed that the only way to do it would be together. To say it's an effort is an understatement and, in accordance with the concept that it takes a village to raise a child, it seems to also take a village to write a book. With that in mind, there are far too many people who deserve to be acknowledged but we'll do our best below.

Together we would both like to acknowledge the following:

We would like to thank the entire Tradecraft Capital team. You tirelessly shucked and jived, picked up slack, and filled any gaps required in operating our fund while we were furiously putting pen to paper. Carissa Posch and Albert Perez, thank you for all you do in getting our message out to the masses via our newsletters, TikToks, and podcasts. And, to Sofia Koo, for keeping the firm running when we had to focus on the book, thank you so much!

We also want to acknowledge Ron Levy and METaI International and the Crypto Roundtable, the group of brothers really helped in our distribution strategy and more.

We would also like to thank Herb Schaffner. Herb, you brought not only wisdom and guidance but also tremendous contribution and encouragement to this work. Herb, brother, you are the best! Thank you!

And we would also love to thank and acknowledge Bill Falloon for his tireless stand for the authors and we really appreciate you!

We would also like to thank Susie Frank for your amazing work in helping us write our vision.

We would like to thank Ric Edelman for your ongoing partnership and for the fantastic Foreword in this book, as well as Don Friedman of DACFP.

We also would like to thank Michael Terpin, for your wisdom and collaboration; John Durrett, for your confidence in what we are creating; and Anurag Shah, for your insight.

We would also like to thank Josh Hong. Josh, you were among the first with whom we collaborated in this space. We've learned much from you, and you've been a true friend as well as a colleague. Thank you!

In addition to the above, Jake has the following acknowledgments:

I would like to thank, again, my mom, for her support and tireless effort in helping us edit and review the material that goes out. I'd like to thank and acknowledge my ex-wife Onkar, for her support in raising our beautiful son Rome; and my son, who gives me the inspiration to build a better world for him. And to Ellie Ruple, who is an amazing connector and someone who's helped me get my books in the hands of many influential people.

Finally, James has the following acknowledgments:

I'll start with Jake Ryan. I acknowledge you, Jake. You are truly a thought leader and a visionary, and it has been my absolute honor not only to build Tradecraft with you, but to collaborate on this new tome. You started me on this journey into the world of digital assets – little did I know that we'd be partners and co-authors. I appreciate and cherish our partnership. Thank you!

I would like to thank my mom, Patricia Diorio. Mom, you not only have given me the gift of life but have always believed in me no matter what. Thank you!

I also thank OJ Zeleny. OJ, you've been a backstop and a grounding rod for many years and have always provided an environment for me to be creative and produce my best. Thank you!

I want to thank my family – my huge extended Italian family (you are too many to name, and you know who you are). You have been with me through the most difficult of times, and I thank you for your steadfast encouragement and staunch support of a lifetime of entrepreneurial musings. Thank you!

I'd like to acknowledge Maureen Charles. Maureen, as an author, coach, and friend, your mentorship has guided me in so many areas of my life, not the least of which is this one. Thank you!

I'd like to extend a special acknowledgment to Sofia Koo – far more than just my life partner, you're an incredible business colleague and a tireless advocate. I'd not be here without you. Thank you.

Finally, I'd be remiss not to acknowledge my late daughter, Bella Diorio. Bella, it was an honor and a privilege to be your dad. You inspired me to be my best in the world and bring that back home to our family. I know you looked at me funny when I started this crazy blockchain journey, but you were an enthusiastic supporter nonetheless. I wish I could have shared more of it with you. I miss you. Thank you for the years we had.

Note from the Authors

We're excited to present this work to you. A little about us – we both come from the technology sector. Both of us have degrees in computer science and worked in the software development industry for the first 20 years of our respective careers, moving from developers to managers to, ultimately, business owners together. We worked together as partners from 2001 to 2004 and then went our separate ways, although we always kept in touch. The partnership worked and it's a little bit of kismet that we're here together again bringing you this book.

(From Jake) I started angel investing in 2014 and made my blockchain startup investment in 2015. From those 15 angel investments made, I've had four exits and hold one investment that turned into a decacorn. I've worked with two VC accelerator firms, as well as being a strategic advisor for a private equity firm and an advisor to several venture-backed startups. Although I'm a technologist, my passion has always been investing. I bought my first mutual fund at the age of 15, my first stock at the age of 17, and started trading options at 22. It was in 2016 that I bought my first bitcoin for roughly $475, and that led me to thinking a lot about this new industry. I love crypto, because it's the intersection of tech and finance and I knew it was time. I had the notion to start a crypto hedge fund in 2017, ultimately leading to Tradecraft Capital, which I soft piloted in 2018 and then opened to private investors in 2019. It has been quite a ride. I'm proud of what we've accomplished and prouder to share this work with you. I hope you enjoy it.

(From James) My story starts the same as Jake's but takes a few different turns. It's true that I'm a computer scientist. As a programmer I enjoyed the challenge of developing complex applications and, although my early career was during the rise of the Internet, I really was so focused on my work that I missed the bigger picture as it was unfolding.

I missed the forest for the trees, if you will. It was in 2012 while I was growing a Software-as-a-Service company that my lead architect came to me and said, "Jim, I'm going to start bitcoin mining." I thought he was nuts and was embarking on a fool's errand, and I thought no more of it. Then, in 2016, Jake told me about bitcoin. I didn't really understand it and when I saw the outlandish price of $674 a coin, I was clear that I missed the window, told Jake he too was nuts, and ignored the whole crypto thing. Boy, was I wrong.

After an exit in 2017 I thought to myself, maybe *I'm* nuts. From there, my journey began. After a few years of traveling from Dubai to Toronto, New York to San Francisco, and everywhere in between, digesting every piece of information I could find, I became convinced. I became an early investor in Tradecraft and was thrilled when Jake asked me to be an advisor and help him shape the *Age of Autonomy*® thesis. I knew he was on to something. I also knew that many people were participating in this ecosystem without a real understanding of it or, worse, were ignoring it just as I had. It was then that I made it my goal to educate as many people as I could so that they didn't let this opportunity pass them by. I began with the concept of *Crypto Decrypted* as a way to educate, which ultimately turned into a monthly blog, and never looked back. I suppose that is what led us here, and why I'm so excited to share this with you. It's been an amazing ride – but from our view, we're still at the very beginning of one of the most exciting technological breakthroughs the world has ever seen.

Our goal is to take a different point of view about crypto and digital assets. Most books talk about the technology of blockchain, but lean heavily into the investment potential of bitcoin and digital assets. Similarly, it seems the majority of articles written focus on tokens or coins and their price. They contain headlines like "bitcoin is up $10,000 this year" or "bitcoin fell to $20,000 from its peak of $68,000." While we certainly want to highlight the investment potential that digital assets can be, we also want to be sure you understand the technology and innovation that's occurred over the past few decades and the profound impact this will have on society. We're now able to do something we couldn't do before, and that's why blockchain technology is important. That's ultimately why any blockchain-based digital asset has any value at all.

The purpose of this book is to explain the technological innovation that's occurred and to try and unpack the *what, how,* and *why* from a technology viewpoint. Just as the Internet was the backbone of the Age of Telecommunications, blockchain technology is the backbone of a new wave. We hope that after reading this book you'll have a much better understanding of what digital assets are, what crypto and blockchain tech is, and why this breakthrough is so important.

Crypto is a wild ride. The volatility — the change and impact of that change — occurs at breakneck speed. Many events over the past few years have destroyed value and investment by bad actors. Some events have destroyed value because we are still in an experimental phase and the technology is not yet mature. This happens during any technological revolution, as we're in the early stages of this technology adoption cycle. The vision of what we see as possible doesn't yet match what we can actually achieve. But it will.

After reading this book, we hope you have a better understanding of what's going on and why it's so revolutionary.

We hope you enjoy this book; moreover, we hope that by the time you're done with it, you have the same wonder and excitement about this new age that we do. Enjoy!

From our Legal Team

Introduction

The world of decentralized finance, cryptocurrencies, and blockchains has changed dramatically since I wrote my first book, *Crypto Asset Investing in the Age of Autonomy*, in 2019. When I was researching and writing that book, you could still buy a bitcoin for less than $11,000, and most people had never heard of an NFT, much less the metaverse. The years since then have seen exponential growth in crypto projects, fans, and naysayers. My fund has expanded as well and this time I'm collaborating with my business partner, James Diorio, to bring you something a little bit different.

For those of you who are familiar with *Crypto Asset Investing in the Age of Autonomy*, we will touch on these concepts and also some of the fundamentals for the first-time reader. That book, however, was primarily about establishing the foundational thesis and providing a general broad perspective about how to build a crypto portfolio. We've written this book with a slightly different goal, particularly that of understanding – we noticed that there are plenty of books that discuss *how*, but often without real context of the *why*. To that end, this work will provide investors as well as the curious amateur with an in-depth understanding of blockchain, crypto, and emerging digital assets like NFTs and, importantly, *why* they are so important (the breakthrough). We will also clear up common misconceptions about blockchain and crypto (the myths) and, ultimately, walk the reader through the essentials of making crypto a profitable and reliable instrument in savings, retirement planning, and active and passive investing activities (the foundations for investing).

It's easy to mistake bitcoin and other digital assets as just another new investment opportunity. Yes, it is that – but it's so much more. It's really the beginning of an entirely new economic infrastructure and technological foundation. We are eager to share not only our knowledge of this emerging technology and economy, but a vision of how it can be used to improve people's lives.

These benefits are not just about making crypto millionaires. What if a Venezuelan struggling with a 2,719% inflation rate could put money into a cryptocurrency account to protect themselves from hyperinflation? Or a musician could sell a fraction of a digital music file and receive royalties every time their song was resold?

Wishful thinking? Not at all. It already exists. The technology is there, and the marketplace is already forming around it. And those are just two examples of a fascinating new world that blockchain makes possible. After reading this book you will understand the innovation, properties, and promise of crypto in all of its many manifestations.

Is investing in crypto scary? Yes. But what's scarier is continuing to use financial infrastructure that requires trust to complete a transaction. If you have to trust a bank or a counterparty to complete a transaction, you're taking on invisible risk that you no longer need to. When people get a taste of being able to use public financial infrastructure that is trustless, that doesn't require trust to complete a transaction, they're never going to want to go back to trust-required financial infrastructure. Just ask anyone from Lehman Brothers to Bear Stearns to MF Global to the Cyprus Bank to BlockFi to FTX to Celsius. Investors and customers alike all either had to go through a bankruptcy process or are currently in line with a bankruptcy process to try and get their pennies on a dollar.

Once crypto and blockchain technology is really understood by the public, everyone is going to want to use trust-minimized, peer-to-peer public financial infrastructure to complete their economic transactions – that's what this whole crypto revolution is about. Removing counterparty risk. Removing the middleman. Removing the guy you have to trust with your money. Let's end this and build an economy that's transparent and can grow on sound money principles. That's what this is all about.

We've written this book to provide both serious investors and the curious amateur with an in-depth understanding of crypto foundations and emerging assets like NFTs and to clear up common misconceptions about crypto. Most of all, the book walks the reader through the essentials of making crypto a profitable and reliable instrument in savings, retirement planning, and active and passive investing activities.

We will provide factual, informed, razor-sharp analysis of blockchain and cryptocurrency and other crypto assets and explore their value to the investor and the economy at large. We will acknowledge where risks lie, how to get started safely, and will debunk the unfounded myths around crypto. We'll look at crypto history, its place in the economy, unpack the fundamentals of this technology and, drawing on facts, lay out the details you can use. No pom-poms. No gibberish. No jargon.

A word about style. As two of us are writing this, you, as the reader, will get well-rounded insights. We each have had our own experiences and you'll find storytelling throughout. So, when you see a reference to a personal experience it might be Jake, it might be James. For read-ability we don't distinguish who the writer is, because that's not what is important. What *is* important is that the concepts have been delivered in a way that makes sense to you, and that both of us are of a common thought process on the content you'll find inside.

We'll tell you why these financial innovations matter to the world and to you. We'll share a huge basket of developing opportunities as this new world of money evolves. Now, let's go!

PART I
THE PRIMER

In Part One of this book, we cover the basics of the technology and innovation of blockchain, tokens, smart contracts, smart contract platforms, and digital assets. We aim to give you a basic understanding, a primer into the world of digital assets. Once you have a better understanding of the technology and innovation of digital assets you will be better equiped to understand the breakthrough, follow the debunking of the myths, and you'll see why investing in them is something every investor should consider.

1

What's the Big Deal About Blockchain?

Everyone is talking about crypto, the colloquial term for digital assets. Love it or hate it, it seems to be on everyone's lips. The fact is that crypto is now mainstream. From Main Street to Wall Street, your street to our street, everyone has an opinion. We would often go present to different groups, ranging from trade shows to investor summits, and even as little as three years ago people looked at us like we were aliens. Truly — aliens bringing some unfathomable concept and, clearly, not of this Earth. Things have changed quite a bit over the past few years.

Bitcoin is the most popular and well-known of the crypto assets built on a blockchain. Yet Bitcoin is only one of thousands of crypto networks, applications, and protocols empowered through blockchain technology. Stories of teens driving Lamborghinis, or businesspeople who invested, then lost, all of their bitcoin by throwing away their wallet accidentally or forgetting a password permeated throughout. Riches were made and riches were lost, and everyone seemed to know about this volatile new asset. During this process, crypto has become somewhat of a dirty word. There is *so much baggage* around it that it's hard to actually cut through the noise and, with all the hype about making money, we see that the fundamentals and foundations of this amazing technology are generally overlooked and misunderstood. So let's start by understanding that blockchain technology is a breakthrough.

Blockchain, recently made possible through decades of computer science and mathematical innovations, enables computers in different locations to access, verify, and share their data. By doing so, blockchain technology overcomes one of the biggest computer software challenges of all time: how to share information quickly and reliably among separate, unaffiliated entities without the involvement of a centralized gatekeeper. This is known as the Byzantine Generals Problem and is discussed thoroughly in Chapter 12.

The breakthrough in solving this problem cannot be overstated, as it allows peers to transact business without an overlord. That may seem rather ho-hum to you, but consider the simple act of handing your friend a 20-dollar bill. You don't need to go to a bank or get permission; you can just do it. Well, before blockchain the only way to digitally exchange something was to go through that central third party. Now, you can just do it directly – like handing your friend a 20-dollar bill. Four unique characteristics make blockchain revolutionary. Blockchain is:

1. Decentralized: No central authority controls transactions occurring over the network.
2. Immutable: Posted transactions are there forever and can never be deleted or changed by anyone.
3. Transparent: Every transaction on the blockchain is public record and can be viewed by anyone on the network.
4. Authenticated with cryptography: Blockchains use complex mathematical codes to store and transmit data to ensure the legitimacy of each transaction and participant, just like an old-school signature. Every participant in the cryptoverse, via their crypto wallet, has a unique digital signature that's impossible to forge.

These features of blockchain position this technology as the biggest technological disruptor since the Internet. Blockchain, however, unlike many technology breakthroughs, is actualized by and empowers those who use it. As Vitalik Buterin, co-founder of Ethereum, said, "Whereas most technologies tend to automate workers on the periphery doing menial tasks, blockchains automate away the center. Instead of putting the taxi driver out of a job, blockchain puts Uber out of a job and lets the taxi drivers work with the customer directly." This is what we mean by peer-to-peer. To start giving this context let's look at Bitcoin, which is a blockchain that is a worldwide peer-to-peer financial network.

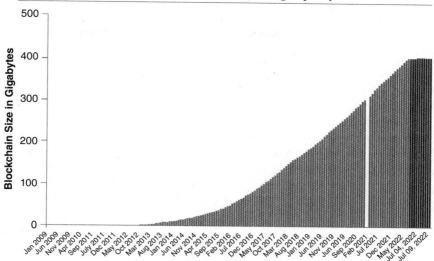

Figure 1.1 Bar Chart of Bitcoin Blockchain Size
Source: Blockchain © Statista 2022.

It's the network and interaction directly between two people that is really important, and, as noted in Figure 1.1, the Bitcoin blockchain has grown significantly since its inception in 2009.

A Blockchain Is a Specialized Database

Google began when two graduate students in computer science and mathematics at Stanford, Larry Page and Sergey Brin, prototyped their search engine called BackRub (seriously). Page and Brin weren't planning on launching one of history's most successful companies. Rather, as computer scientists and academics the two friends saw the World Wide Web as a system of citation. In the world of academia, credible research is valued by how the author's work responds to citation (or reference), and by how future projects and publications cite the author's article or book. Well, the web to Page and Brin was simply a vast catalog of articles and information, but, without a way to cite (reference) other works, it would not realize its true potential. To Page, "the entire Web was loosely based on the premise of citation – after all, what is a link but a citation?,"

John Battelle wrote in his landmark book *The Search*. If Page could "divine a method to count and qualify each backlink on the Web, as Page puts it, 'the Web would become a more valuable place.'"

This may be strange now, but Page, Brin, and other computer scientists at the time saw the Internet as a graph. Each computer was a node, a data point, and each link on a web page connected the nodes. The result: "a classic graph structure." Brin and Page envisioned a search engine as perfecting the academic citation model.

"Not only was the engine good, but Page and Brin realized it would scale as the Web scaled," Batelle wrote. "Because PageRank worked by analyzing links, the bigger the Web, the better the engine. That fact inspired the founders to name their new engine Google, after googol, the term for the numeral 1 followed by 100 zeroes. They released the first version of Google on the Stanford Web site in August 1996 – one year after they met."[1]

We tell this story to make a point about innovation breakthroughs. In our daily lives, as we go about doing our jobs and getting stuff done, Google can seem like a utility service that mysteriously materialized on our computers. Of course, if we take a moment and think about it, we can dredge up a few relevant facts about how search engines came into our lives. Maybe inventing the wheel was an exception, but most technological breakthroughs happen as discoveries rooted in well-established systems begin to take hold. Jared Diamond observed that technology has to be invented or adopted. We say it is almost always both. Blockchain technology, then, was first invented, then adopted.

Decentralized

It can be easier to start understanding blockchain as a new kind of database where data is stored on individual, independent computers that exist in locations all over the globe. This makes a blockchain network *distributed*, because it consists of many computers that are not all in one location. That's pretty easy to grasp.

Decentralization is a little different, however, because blockchains are also decentralized. The best way to think about decentralization is to think about your photos on your laptop. If you drop your laptop in the ocean, you've probably lost your snapshots of vacation on the Big Island sipping a frothy, fruity rum drink. You may retort "not so!" because you have a backup somewhere.

That's great; however, if that backup goes kaput, then, once again, your pictures of that mai tai in Hawaii are gone. A next step, of course, would be to have all your photos uploaded to "the cloud" – a central location – which then allows us to download to multiple devices. In this, we're getting closer, but we still have that pesky central location. If that location falls into a sinkhole, the means to synchronize across all devices fails. What if there were another structure that didn't rely on single points of failure? In this example, what if there were 100,000 computers that all had copies of your photos (for some of you, that's a scary thought, so let's just pretend it's only the photos you want people to see), and every time you take a new photo, *every* computer gets a copy. That is decentralized. No single point of failure, no point more important than any other. That is decentralization. Blockchains are decentralized because every computer can access all of the information on a blockchain, which makes them very robust. There is no central entity controlling any given blockchain interaction; it's all kept on track with ingenious cryptography and computer software.

Immutable

Almost every database technology in use today allows transactions to be altered or overwritten. This includes everything from bank balances to health records. In a blockchain, by contrast, once a transaction is written into a block it is there forever and can never be deleted or changed by anyone. Period. So, if Bob sends Sally one bitcoin (BTC), once that transaction is confirmed, Sally has one BTC. That transaction is irrefutable, written in stone, and can never be changed. It's written on the blockchain. The computers in the network validate it (agree), and everyone has access to that transaction record. If Bob says it didn't happen – and even if Bob takes Sally to court (that BTC may be worth $1 million someday!) – we could look for the transaction on the chain and know the facts. There are few places in the world where this kind of certainty exists, and it's essential not only for currency transactions but also for transactions of any type.

Immutability becomes very interesting when you're keeping records over long periods of time or conducting business that depends on a shared idea of value, title, ownership, or scarcity. Our current tradi-tional economy requires trust at every turn. You trust the credit card machine company to debit the correct amount from your bank account when you are at the grocery store checkout counter. It would be best if you trusted that the store's bank and payment systems will operate as expected. You need to trust that the banks will honor their agreements. And so on and on and on. It's the whole reason brands are so valuable. They are marks of trust.

In the future crypto economy, trust will be less critical because you won't need a third party to facilitate and settle transactions. When you can deposit money into your cryptocurrency wallet, you're assured that the blockchain keeps track of everything. If you are interested in a work of art, you can see its provenance (the whole history of ownership and origin) on the blockchain. No third parties needed. No need for trust. Instead, everything is authenticated cryptographically. With applications built on blockchains and cryptocurrency, transactions occur peer-to-peer.

Before Google, the citational credibility of a web page was a black box; the Google search brings scientific transparency to the question of trust – it allows you to find and reference data all over the world. The blockchain provides its own brand of transparency into the custody of currency, supply chains, and sensitive data such as medical records.

Transparent

Another seminal quality of a blockchain is transparency. Everything that is ever written on the chain is visible to anyone at any time. This, in and of itself, is a marvel. You see, almost every other database in the world is exactly the opposite. Data is stored and you only get to see whatever the owner of the database wants you to see. In the blockchain world it is the opposite, and that is one of the great strengths of this technology.

Let's say that Fred sends one bitcoin to Mary. This will be written on the blockchain, and no one can ever deny that this occurred. When you combine this with the concept of immutability, this becomes a powerful recordkeeping system and an unalterable chain of title. Whether used for tracking products from farm to table, validating the ownership of any physical good, from art to autos, or affirming accounting entries and money transfers, there is no question of the activity that has taken place and, importantly, it is visible to anyone.

We want to be clear at this point that it is the transaction that is visible; your identity is not. I was recently sending a friend a transaction using Venmo, which has this feature that your transactions can be publicly visible. That's weird. I don't know about you, but generally I don't want the whole world to know when I send money to someone. So, in the Fred/ Mary example, we don't have to worry about this because blockchains are pseudonymous, meaning that while your transactions are visible, your identity is not (unless, of course, you disclose it publicly, but that is your choice). Everyone can see that a transaction happened, but they do not necessarily know who the parties on either end of the transaction are.

No, this does not make blockchain a hotbed for criminals. As we will learn in Chapter 9, money has to come on to the chain somewhere and off the chain somewhere. It's possible to trace the flow of money to these endpoints, which tend to be tied to humans. In almost all cases your activities can be traced back to you. Frankly, we want this to be the case because this allows us to confirm ownership, chain of title, transaction activity, and so on. All of this and more will be discussed further as you dive into this work, but the important part is that this is the best of both worlds. You can transact while generally maintaining anonymity and yet there is still a permanent record that can be traced if needed.

Cryptographically Secure

Our current economy still relies on the power of our unique signatures. We put our "John Hancock" on something and that is our bond, our agreement. Signatures have been so important up until now that some states, like Texas, still require a "wet" actual physical signature on important documents like mortgages. The challenge with digital signatures has always been the concern that they can be copied. Enter cryptography.

Cryptography is the art of using technology to secure data so that it can only be accessed by the desired party, and such parties have what is known as a "key." Think of cryptography as a lock on your data that can only be accessed with the right key. Blockchains like Bitcoin also require signatures in order for transactions to occur. The reason we can trust them is because blockchains use cryptography techniques and the only ones who can authorize a transaction are the ones who hold the specific keys. Bitcoin uses complex mathematical codes to store and transmit data to ensure the legitimacy of each transaction and participant. They are unique, just like an old-school signature is unique. This brings us to your wallet. A wallet is a place where crypto assets can be stored. They are cryptographically secure addresses (just like your house has an address) that anyone can send assets *to*. But the only way to transmit assets from a wallet is with your key. When you enter your key, you are "signing" a transaction. Every key/wallet combination creates a unique digital signature that's impossible to forge. We discuss wallets in more depth later in Chapter 2.

The unique digital signature in a blockchain is authenticated and can't be repudiated; the hash is unique to origin, so one can't later deny sending a message. The mathematical nature of the hash can't be reversed, and no two or more messages have the same coding. Each is locked, like a chain, bearing an invisible tag like a barcode that cannot be removed.

We all know that natural scarcity and rarity create value. Cryptography not only makes it easier to establish the authenticity of someone conducting a transaction, it can also create verifiably rare digital assets that mimic scarcity rarity in the natural world, like gold and diamonds.

Crypto apps built on a blockchain, like Bitcoin and Ethereum, require a "consensus mechanism" to settle transactions and secure the network. Bitcoin uses a proof-of-work (PoW) consensus mechanism that involves using powerful computers (aka bitcoin miners) running nonstop. Right now, it takes an enormous amount of energy and a certain amount of expertise and dedication to mint a bitcoin, for example. Just like a one-of-a-kind, handmade couture gown takes more time (and costs more) than a mass-produced gown, bitcoins are not easy to make. Bitcoin's creator engineered scarcity by designing the software to stop making bitcoin at 21 million coins.

But PoW is only one consensus mechanism. Another is proof-of-stake (PoS) – and it is not energy-intensive. Instead, it's based on users staking their crypto assets (and risking losing them) to secure transactions on the blockchain. For example, the popular blockchain Ethereum is transitioning to PoS. Once Eth 2.0 is fully in production, Ethereum will be the second-biggest blockchain, and it will be running on PoS. In Chapter 11, we'll explore the ongoing evolution of these two technologies for forging coins.

Nonmoney Examples of Blockchain Technology

Bitcoin is the king of blockchain and everyone knows it. Bitcoin is a money use case; that is, it is designed to be currency and do the things currency would do. We'll dive deep into this in Chapter 2; however, the fact that bitcoin is money is a big part of the reason many people think that all crypto is money. The fact is, there are endless applications for blockchain technology. We'll discuss this throughout the book but just to get you started, the following are three examples, which we find compelling, that are in use today.

Decentralized Finance

One of the first successful uses of blockchain technology is decentralized finance, known as DeFi. We discuss this more fully in Chapter 4, but as an overview, DeFi platforms allow people to lend or borrow funds from others, speculate on price movements on assets using derivatives, trade cryptocurrencies, insure against risks, and earn interest in savings-like accounts. DeFi makes it possible for anyone with a smartphone to put money into a savings account, get a collateralized loan, and make or receive a digital payment. DeFi platforms are basically software programs that run 24/7 and allow anyone to use them – a far cry from the protocols at most banks. This makes DeFi a free-market playground of crypto apps that many are enjoying and, in the process, making money. As a caution, however, if you choose to explore this world of protocols, we just want to send a word of wisdom to always be prudent with your money, never invest more than you are prepared to lose, and always be aware that scammers are out in force, just as they are in most other marketplaces.

Supply Chain Management

Blockchain technology is already being adapted into our supply chains, markets, information technology systems, and points of purchase. There are growing cases where this technology reduces fraud in the counterfeiting of luxury brands and high-value goods, helps companies recognize how ingredients and finished goods are passed through each subcontractor, and lessens losses from counterfeit and gray-market trading.

"Major brands have already begun partnering with tech firms and other entities in response to rising demands for improved brand protection. LVMH (Louis Vuitton SE), for instance, working closely with Microsoft and ConsenSys, has created Aura Ledger to provide proof of authenticity of luxury items and trace their origins from raw materials to point of sale and beyond to the used-goods markets," reports Global-Trade, the trusted logistics and global trade outlet. Pretty soon, when you see that Louis Vuitton bag that should be $10,000 for sale for the bargain price of $1,500, you won't just need to rely on your gut and logic to determine that it's not real – you'll be able to use blockchain technology to verify this very thing.

It's not just luxury brands that are stepping in, but the biggest business drivers on the planet. The buttoned-down blue-chip giant, IBM, for example, has an entire practice devoted to blockchain supply chain solutions. Consulting giant McKinsey & Company is urging clients to consider integrating blockchain. According to the none-too-radical business analysts at Deloitte, "Blockchain-driven innovations in the supply chain will have the potential to deliver tremendous business value by increasing supply chain transparency, reducing risk and improving efficiency, and overall supply chain management." Among many examples, companies have integrated blockchain to track the responsible sourcing of tuna in Indonesia, secure digital media usage and sharing rights, and manage business-to-business (B2B) trade and supply chain finance products.

The Society for Human Resource Management documents how blockchain can verify identity, credentials, education details, and payroll management. And we have insider reports that media companies are adopting blockchain technology to eliminate fraud, stop piracy, and protect intellectual property rights of content.

Ultimately, this is where the power of a peer-to-peer, immutable, decentralized network comes into play. Transactions are permanent, traceable, and aren't subject to manipulation. This makes them perfect for this job.

Additional Examples

This is just the beginning. Blockchain technology is the foundation for Dapps (decentralized applications), platforms, and protocols, which in turn make it easy to send and receive money across borders, clear and settle financial transactions, manage supply chains, enable device-to-device transactions in the Internet of Things, create more reliable property and asset registries, and improve record-sharing in health care, among others. The benefits – greater speed, transparency, lower cost, and ease of access and control of one's own data – offer tremendous opportunities for expanding global commerce and improving the lives of everyone on the planet. All of this can be a little dry, but we believe it's important to understand the fundamentals – this will make it much more valuable in later chapters as we explore the breakthroughs. Rather than stay theoretical, in the next few chapters, we will introduce the most important applications for blockchain technology that are already proving useful and effective without controversy.

Blockchain Technical Components

In order to really understand Bitcoin or any blockchain, we need to have a fundamental understanding of how a blockchain works. Unfortunately, most people skip this step and simply want to jump on the bitcoin train, but understanding how a blockchain works will shape your entire investment strategy. These are the fundamentals that most skip, so this is where we are going to start.

A blockchain is software that runs on a computer server just like any other server-based application, just like a web server hosts a website, for example. The software components of a blockchain are programmed in code. These include blocks, which store transactions (data), the hashing function, which organizes the transactions and allows for searching/sorting, and the consensus mechanism, which keeps all the nodes in the network synced and accurate and allows transactions to be approved. The software also includes any functionality to create a wallet or sign (approve) a transaction.

The server is the computer hardware that may run one or more instances of the blockchain software. An instance of the software is a node. The network is merely the connected servers, each of which may have one or more nodes running on it. Since anyone can run the blockchain server software, the network is a globally decentralized network that runs on the Internet, just like other server-based software.

Transactions

A transaction is a single entry on the public ledger. It's broadcast to all the nodes in the network. Any time a user sends a token from one wallet to another, that's a transaction. A transaction is data that is recorded inside a block, and a block will have one or more transactions stored in it.

The most important function, and where the big innovation lies with blockchains, is consensus. Consensus is the process of all of the nodes agreeing on whether a transaction is valid or not. In order for a transaction to be considered valid, 51% of all the nodes must agree. If they do, the transaction is grouped together with other transactions and permanently stored in a new block, which all nodes then have a copy of. This process is called *gaining consensus* and we'll discuss this in more detail in the Consensus Mechanism section later in this chapter. The critical part is that consensus allows blockchains to stay in sync, protect the data, and know that all the other nodes and copies of the public ledger are identical within the entire system. This is unprecedented and allows us to have a peer-to-peer system without requiring a trusted third party like a bank or a company. As peers, the nodes can agree and confidently confirm that the transaction is valid. We'll unpack this further in a later section.

Blocks

A block consists of a collection of ordered transactions, and each block is then connected to the last minted block. This is why we call it a blockchain, because it is an ever-growing linked set of blocks. Now, we mentioned ordered transactions. Order is important because if Sofia sends Bill one bitcoin and Bill sends Otto one bitcoin, Sofia's transaction must happen first. That may seem basic, but it's really a fundamental point.

The software only allows the creation of a block, which it then links to the previous block. It cannot alter transactions once the block is written, so the entire data structure has the property of being immutable – that is, it cannot be changed over time. This is a compelling characteristic because it allows the software to enforce the committed information. We can know with certainty that no one came in and tinkered with any element of the system to change any amounts or other aspects of the transaction. This is very different than a traditional data structure like a database, where records can be edited or deleted by design. Pretty much all data that we store is in a database of some type, and as such one has to trust the company, the database system administrator, the company that made the database, and so on. There are many layers of trust required. With a blockchain, the environment does not require trust of a third party. It is *trustless*.

In the traditional/legacy economic system we've had since the beginning of time, every participant in an economic transaction would require some form of trust. In the new decentralized economy, trust is no longer required.

Hash/Hashing Function

A hashing function isn't as scary as it sounds. Put simply, the hashing function provides a number that helps data be structured. This is called a hash, and delivers several features. First, the data can be encrypted and cryptographically secure. We're not going to dive into cryptography here but let's just say that a cryptographically secure number is very hard for other computers to guess. This level of security is where "crypto" comes from, and it is a distinguishing factor of blockchain technologies. Second, the hash maintains the proper order of block-chain transactions, and it also connects the blocks together, creating a chain of blocks (blockchain).

The specific implementation of the hashing function and the ability to create cryptographically secure data sets is what makes blockchain technology so unique, and it solved the Byzantine Generals Problem (BGP). Solving this problem is the breakthrough that you need to understand, and which we discuss in Chapter 12.

Miners and Proof-of-Work Consensus

The consensus mechanism is a critical component to the blockchain, as the trusted third party cannot be removed without the ability to have all the participants agree on the order and status of such a dynamic system. This agreement is called consensus.

In the case of the original blockchain, Bitcoin, Satoshi Nakamoto applied an innovative upgrade to previous research in this area by creating the proof-of-work (PoW) consensus mechanism. Under PoW, computers run software that is working to create the next valid hash. These computers are called miners. A miner must spend resources, such as energy/electricity, to do this, as unique, cryptographically secure hashes are hard to find! The first miner who does this wins the block reward and earns the right to mint, or create, the block. Blocks on the Bitcoin blockchain are minted roughly every 10 minutes, although the timing is dynamic as we don't exactly know when a new hash will be found.

It's then required for the other miners to verify the block – where they agree that all of the transactions are correct – and update their own public ledgers. This ensures that all copies of that ledger are identical.

At this point we do want to note that there are a couple of risks that could compromise a blockchain. If a hacker could successfully attack a blockchain's consensus mechanism, they might be able to alter the order of transactions and/or *double-spend*. Double-spending is when a user within the system, a hacker, spends the same token twice (or more – sometimes many more – times). Imagine going into a jewelry store, buying a $2,000 ring, or a $2,000,000 ring, and using the same $100 bill 20 times, or 20,000 times. That would be theft on a grand scale and is one of two main ways a blockchain could be hacked.

Another risk is what's called a 51% attack. A 51% attack is when one (or more) miners gain control of more than 50% of the mining hash rate. If an attacker controls more than 50% of the network's hash rate, they can control and interrupt the recording of new blocks in that blockchain. This prevents other miners from completing blocks and allows for repeated double-spending. It's a big deal! Thankfully no major blockchain, like Bitcoin or Ethereum, has ever had a successful 51% attack. This is what makes blockchains so unbelievably secure. A miner would have to spend an enormous number of resources, making a 51% attack economically infeasible.

Now, a successful 51% attack has occurred. In 2018, the blockchain Bitcoin Gold (BTG) incurred enormous losses. That blockchain was a fork (copy) of the Bitcoin blockchain during the "Bitcoin Blocksize War," which resulted in many different blockchains competing to be the best Bitcoin. This was possible because all of the software is publicly available: anyone can make a copy and make changes to it. Many did this, but just making new software doesn't mean that it's going to be accepted. There were dozens of forks of the Bitcoin open-source software and tons of "Bitcoin innovators" (we say this while stifling a chuckle) who were trying to "improve" Bitcoin by creating their own version. We might couch this a little differently and say that there were many opportunists who wanted to control the evolution of Bitcoin because, in doing so, they would then have a greater chance of growing wealth with their version. There is a book, *The Blocksize War,* that covers this period and set of events in detail if you'd like to know more. It was a key time when many decisions were made and the idea of Bitcoin Maximalism (those who only believe in bitcoin and eschew all other variants) was encapsulated and coalesced. Suffice it to say, the other Bitcoin variants were unsuccessful. The only version I can think of that still exists is Bitcoin Cash and I hope we can all agree that blockchain is worthless, although I suppose Roger Ver, its creator, would disagree. Back to the point. BTG was a blockchain that was created, but it wasn't adopted by the same number of miners that run the current Bitcoin blockchain. Because of that, a group was able to control over 51% of the nodes, and thereby "hack" the chain. Think of it like this. It's possible to bribe a jury of 12 — all you need are seven people to align. It's difficult, however, to bribe a jury of hundreds of thousands or millions. Worth noting, the other successful 51% attacks of any note that occurred were on the Ethereum Classic and Verge blockchains. We would never invest in any blockchain that has had a successful 51% attack for obvious reasons.

Block Rewards

So, why are miners spending incredible amounts of energy to find the next cryptographically secure hash? Well, this is another ingenious part of the network. In the case of bitcoin there is a fixed number of 21 million that will ever exist. The bitcoin is held in a reserve pool, however, and it is not available for use unless it is released to the Bitcoin network. The reason there is so much buzz about mining is that the first miner to create the next valid, cryptographically secure hash earns some bitcoin! This is called a block reward and it's the whole point. Currently there are approximately 19.2 million bitcoin in circulation out of the 21 million that have been created. Every time a miner earns a block reward, a small amount of bitcoin is released and becomes publicly available. Importantly, the miner that earns the block reward has initial control of these coins and, with the price of bitcoin, it's easy to see how this can be very profitable.

Note that every miner is important, and if a miner wasn't the one to create a new hash and win the block reward, then they'll perform a *verification*, which is the process of confirming the transactions, specifically the order of transactions within the newly minted block. They help reinforce that the original miner ordered the transactions. This is how all copies stay in sync in the decentralized environment wherein they all operate. If a miner goes offline for a period, they can come back online, obtain the hash number for all the blocks they missed, and update their ledger to the latest state.

Aligned Incentives

Another aspect of the new digital, decentralized economy is that all participants, from creators to miners to users, have aligned incentives. Since no one person or collection of people "owns" a blockchain outright, it's the groups of participants who work together who ensure the proper running of the blockchain and its ecosystem. The reason they do this is that they all want to "win."

The three primary groups are the users (the blockchain's functional users), the miners, and the developers. Each group is incentivized to work in the best interest of the blockchain and its ecosystem. Miners win by earning block rewards. The creators of the blockchain win if their blockchain is used by users. Users win if they can participate in the blockchain to accomplish whatever that blockchain is designed to accomplish. Generally, each of these groups will hold tokens and (simplistically) and want those tokens to increase in price. We could do an entire book on the study of tokens and their fundamental economics (tokenomics), but that's for another time. For purposes of this discussion, we're going to simplify and focus on value. If a blockchain provides value, just like if a business provides value, then it will garner usage. The more users in a system, the more value that system will have and the more demand for tokens there will be. In general, if a blockchain has more demand than supply of tokens, that token price will increase. We do have to say that this economic alignment is important, but too many people are caught up in price increases for price increases' sake and are missing the point. Successful ventures are the ones that provide value. Those that do will win and grow. Those that don't, over time, won't.

Other Consensus Mechanisms

Bitcoin has come under fire for its energy usage in its PoW consensus mechanism. While we don't expect it to change, we do want to highlight that many other blockchains use different, more efficient mechanisms.

This is part of the evolution of Satoshi Nakamoto's original work. Different mechanisms include proof of stake (PoS), proof of capacity (PoC), proof of history (PoH), and proof of activity (PoA). We're not going to unpack the differences in each of them here, but suffice it to say that they all require nodes that must reach some sort of agreement in order for transactions to be confirmed and blocks to be written. The one additional mechanism we do want to highlight is proof of stake.

Proof of stake (PoS) is a consensus mechanism that is used by many new blockchains and has a very different way of coming to agreement. Instead of miners, PoS chains have validators. Validators aren't spending energy trying to find the next hash, as in PoW systems. Instead, validators become a part of the network by pledging some of the tokens. They stake the native token of the blockchain, which means that the token is locked up and cannot be otherwise used. In exchange for this, they get to participate in the functioning of the network and can earn rewards just like in PoW.

Validators are responsible for the same tasks that miners do in a PoW chain. There is still a primary validator who confirms that a transaction is correct, writes the block, and receives the reward, while the rest validate that transaction. The difference here is that the validator who gets the privilege of writing the block is selected randomly, with a higher weighting generally given to those validators who have staked more of the token. There is risk, however, as nodes that are dishonest may lose their staked tokens.

As of this writing Ethereum has just completed "The Merge," which was their conversion from a PoW consensus mechanism to a PoS consensus mechanism. Anyone can be a validator if they stake 32 or more ether, the native token of Ethereum. Those who are taking more risk by staking more ether have a greater chance of getting selected to write the next block and earn the reward. This was a huge technological feat and accomplishment and sets the stage for additional improvements to the blockchain, namely increasing speed and reducing cost, over the coming years.

PoS has gained popularity due to its energy efficiency and accessibility to more validators. Whereas bitcoin mining using PoW requires a significant investment in computing power, almost anyone can run a validator by pledging some of the native currency of the blockchain. We believe PoW consensus is required for cryptocurrency, or coins that are providing the money use case. It's required because there needs to be a cost of production when it comes to minting new money. We've learned from history that it cannot be free to mint new money. However, we believe all other blockchain use cases can be built on top of a blockchain using a PoS consensus mechanism. As time goes on, we expect more innovative consensus mechanisms to make their way into this growing ecosystem.

2

Bitcoin, the First Application of a Blockchain

We won't overlabor Bitcoin as there are plenty of books that dive deep into this origin story. Because Bitcoin is Bitcoin, however, we have to start here. Bitcoin was the first crypto superstar, created in response to the chaos of the 2008 financial crisis. During this time lenders failed consumers in a public way, feeding a growing distrust of big banking. Banks received far more than just bailouts. Profits were allowed to stay private while losses were socialized—the public, instead of the banks, shouldered the burden. Bitcoin, by far the most well-known and trusted token, was born out of destruction.

Bitcoin's pseudonymous creator, Satoshi Nakamoto, responded by creating an alternative digital currency that did not rely on too-big-to-fail central banks and other murky authorities such as the Securities Investor Protection Corporation (founded and funded by brokers to more or less insure investors who lose money at financially troubled member firms). Nakamoto's whitepaper influenced developers and investors worldwide. He proposed a peer-to-peer (P2P) payment system that did not require third-party confirmation. Banks, governments, and other central authorities aren't required to settle every transaction, noting that "what is needed is an electronic payment system based on cryptographic proof instead of trust, allowing any two willing parties to transact directly with each other without the need for a trusted third party." Given the distinctions identified in the previous chapter, perhaps this section of the Bitcoin whitepaper makes more sense now:

> Transactions that are computationally impractical to reverse would protect sellers from fraud, and routine escrow mechanisms could easily be implemented to protect buyers. In this paper, we propose a solution to the double-spending problem using a peer-to-peer distributed timestamp server to generate computational proof of the chronological order of transactions. The system is secure as long as honest nodes collectively control more CPU power than any cooperating group of attacker nodes.[1]

Nakamoto defines a token or electronic coin as "a chain of digital signatures," where each owner transfers the coin to the next by digitally signing a hash of the previous transaction and the public key of the next one and adding these to the end of the coin: "A payee can verify the signatures to verify the chain of ownership." We are stressing this because the origin and intent were important, and blockchain is the breakthrough upon which Bitcoin was built.

How to protect privacy and identity, and maintain crypto security? Nakamoto identified the tradeoff found in the traditional banking model. Sure, our information is private, relatively, but the companies and entities that facilitate the bank's transactions are behind closed doors. The bank is a black box that we cannot see into. Nakamoto's answer was to make everything transparent so that "the public can see that someone is sending an amount to someone else, but without information linking the transaction to anyone."

A blockchain opens the closed doors with the hash we discussed in Chapter 1. Hashes are put together to form a chain, with each additional timestamp reinforcing the ones before it. This is our blockchain. The blockchain identifies each participant and their action so all can see. Imagine if you received a record and timestamp of the investors and service fees and vendors that benefit from or participate in each Venmo transaction.

And so crypto's first hero, Bitcoin, was born. Fourteen years later as we write this, hundreds of millions of people worldwide, particularly the younger generations, trade and trust bitcoin and other cryptocurrencies (while the U.S. savings bonds their parents trusted aren't seen as spectacular savings vehicles because − well − they aren't). Bitcoin is considered by many to be a viable, alternative digital currency. It can be used at

Starbucks and Home Depot, has been endorsed by seminal investors Paul Tudor Jones and Stan Druckenmiller (to name just two), has earned favor at big banks such as BlackRock, and is even legal tender in some countries. Bitcoin is available to anyone around the world with a smartphone and can be sent halfway around the world in a matter of minutes for a fraction of the cost to wire or transmit funds otherwise. Bitcoin was the first successful blockchain. Thanks to its success, there are now thousands more digital coins and tokens. Some will survive; most will not.

Crypto assets, the tokens that are used by blockchains for various purposes, represent a new asset class for investors. They are not correlated to stocks, bonds, or gold, although there can be periods of high correlation. They can increase in both price and value without the economy growing. They can be used to generate real interest income or to represent real goods or digital goods. Owning crypto assets helps an investor diversify by providing an asset class that is not solely U.S. dollar–denominated. Crypto assets are, of course, still new and therefore still volatile, as 2022 reminded us, but as the market matures, we foresee that they will become increasingly attractive to more and more people.

As of February 2021, according to numerous sources, Bitcoin had a market capitalization of more than $1 billion, with over 300 million people having used or owning cryptocurrencies. The leading nation for crypto users is India, with about 180 million users in 2021, while the United States was second with 27 million crypto owners. More than $110 billion is traded in cryptocurrency per day, according to Blockchain.com.

Most U.S. adults have heard at least a little about cryptocurrencies like bitcoin or ether, a Pew Research study found in 2021 (see Figure 2.1), with 16% of people saying they had invested in, traded, or otherwise used one. Nearly 9 in 10 Americans told Pew that they had heard at least a little about cryptocurrencies; about one quarter said they had heard a lot about them. Men ages 18 to 29 were particularly likely to have used cryptocurrencies (see Figure 2.2).

We cite these numbers to illustrate the rapid growth and scale of the crypto markets but, look, they are still young, and these can be risky investments, as noted by the 46% of investors in the survey who have done worse than expected. That's where this book comes in, to add some context and clarity. "An investment in knowledge pays the best interest," Ben Franklin said. And if you are uncomfortable in this new world, that's good news, too, because, in the words of investor Robert Arnott, "What is comfortable is rarely profitable."

Crypto Still Popular Despite Crash

Share of U.S. respondents that have invested/plan to invest in cryptocurrency

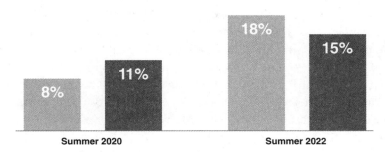

Currently invested in cryptocurrency

Plan to invest in cryptocurrency*

* "Very likely" in the next two years (including expansion of current crypto investments).
Survey of 1,000+ U.S. adults (18–64 years old), of which 789/708 owned investments (2020/2022).

Figure 2.1 Crypto Chart of U.S. Investors

Source: Statista Global Consumer Survey © 2022, Statista. / Public Domain CC BY 4.0.

42% of American men ages 18 to 29 say they have invested in, traded, or used a cryptocurrency

Among U.S. adults who say they have ever invested in, traded, or used cryptocurrency, % who say each of the following is a ___ they have done so

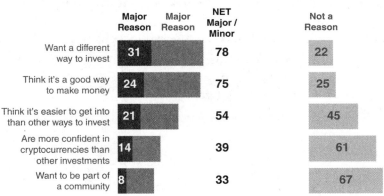

Figure 2.2 Exposure to Crypto

Source: Statista Global Consumer Survey © 2022 Pew Research Center.
Additional information: Pew Research Center. Note: Those who did not give an answer are not shown.

What's Unique About Bitcoin

While there are thousands of crypto assets, Bitcoin is the granddaddy of them all. It possesses many characteristics that give it unique importance to the investor. Following are the essentials:

- **Bitcoin's supply will never exceed 21 million bitcoin.** The anti-inflationary nature of Bitcoin bears even more importance as we experience sustained inflation in the global economy. For every 210,000 blocks that get produced, which occurs roughly every four years, the reward for mining a bitcoin is halved. This means that the inflation rate decreases by half because the only way for bitcoin to get minted into the system is through the block reward to miners.

- **Bitcoin is akin to digital gold.** Bitcoin is not a traditional investment like a stock, but a currency in and of itself and is classified as a commodity by the Commodity Futures Trading Commission (CFTC). As with any commodity, bitcoin is produced and used. Bitcoin miners expend work by labor, equipment, and energy to create bitcoin. There is a cost of production just like with gold or any other precious metal and, unlike fiat currency, is not an attempt to create value out of thin air. It retains its traded value no matter what governments do with their monetary systems. It does not have counterparty risk and is not a liability on another party's balance sheet.

- **Bitcoin is validated by triple-entry accounting.** This is a fancy way of saying that every transaction is audited as it is written, something that is now only possible because of blockchain technology.

- **Bitcoin is sound money,** which means its value has been set by the marketplace and it performs the functions of money well by having the six characteristics of good money:

  1. Divisibility
  2. Durability
  3. Portability
  4. Uniformity
  5. Acceptability
  6. Scarcity

What's important to consider here is that bitcoin far outperforms gold in these characteristics. Bitcoin is more *divisible* than gold. Bitcoin uses eight decimal points of precision, meaning the smallest amount of bitcoin (BTC) transferable is 0.00000001 BTC. Gold can't get to that level of precision for divisibility. Bitcoin is more *durable* than gold; it is merely letters and numbers that form a public key that can be stored in a computer or even on anything physical. If desired, a person could etch the key into gold. Bitcoin is more *portable* than gold. We can send 10 billion dollars' worth of bitcoin around the world in 15 minutes, and it would cost up to a few dollars. There is no need for an army of planes to transport 24 tons of gold with bitcoin. One key to bitcoin's intrinsic value is the built-in payment and storage network. A bitcoin is a bitcoin is a bitcoin. It's math and, therefore, highly *uniform*. There is no purity test for bitcoin. Bitcoin is *accepted* at exchanges worldwide, thousands of stores, and places of business. No one can buy a plane ticket or cup of coffee with gold, but they can with bitcoin. Finally, it's *scarce* – even more scarce than gold. There will only ever be 21 million bitcoin mined. Gold continues to be mined and will continue to grow its supply.

Bitcoin as digital gold will allow us to build credit, currency, lending, financing, and equity ownership just as gold allows us to build these things in traditional finance. Bitcoin as gold is key to building stable-coins, decentralized finance, and a host of digital financial infrastructure needs we will discuss throughout this book.

A Global, Public Payments Network

Bitcoin, at its core, is a worldwide public payments network. It's public infrastructure that allows anyone in the world to pay anyone else, without a bank account, without approval from a central authority, and without the need to worry about borders or trust or any of the past barriers. That's the innovation! This is a breakthrough from the past. It's this innovation that allows us to do something we couldn't do prior to the invention of Bitcoin.

Prior to Bitcoin, the only real way to send a payment internationally was through a set of middlemen, all taking their cuts and adding friction (cost) to the process. Ask anyone who's tried to send remittance or wires to another country. It can cost anywhere up to 20% in fees and take days. Even wires can take days.

Back in the 2000s, I ran a software services company. We were headquartered in LA, but we had acquired a software developing company in Monterrey, Mexico, that had a few dozen developers. The service was called nearshore, distinct from offshore. With offshore software development, you're connecting with a team in India or Russia, someplace that's on another continent, as the name implied. Nearshore is done in the Americas, where you're connecting with a team in another country, but you're using the same time zones. There are a lot of benefits to nearshore over offshore. Invariably, I'd be sending a wire every month to our development center down in Mexico. The wire might take only an hour (or two) to send, but the settlement typically took over a week. There was human intervention throughout the review process and with both banks. We were charged wire fees and even though we had a bank in Mexico with the account in U.S. dollars, our Mexican counterparts would need to convert U.S. dollars to Mexican pesos at some point to pay expenses and salaries. Of course, foreign currency transactions take 5–8% when converting so right off the bat they were losing money just on conversion to local currency. The transactional pipeline was like a clogged artery due to intermediaries and fees throughout the process. Conversely, with Bitcoin, the transaction and settlement process can happen, typically in under 2 hours. In 2022, we're coping with currency fees and big volatility with the price of bitcoin in various sovereign fiat currencies, but we can envision a day when most transactions can stay within the Bitcoin ecosystem. Even with those conversion fees, Bitcoin doesn't require a bank account or permission from anyone to use. Anyone can create a wallet for free, thus reducing friction and inefficiency. More simply put, if you have a smartphone or a computer, anyone can send money to anyone else elegantly and efficiently.

Public versus Private

We discussed in Chapter 1 the pseudonymous nature of Bitcoin, which is a public blockchain. This means that anyone can use it and all data is visible. Public blockchains, for example, include Ethereum, Solana, and Curve. But there are also private instances of blockchains. You can think of an analogy to the Internet where the Internet is a public network of computer networks and an intranet is a private network. A company intranet is only accessible by individuals in that company. Public means anyone can access it; private means only a limited number, generally defined by a company, group, or organization, can.

Private blockchains, such as Hyperledger from IBM, create private solutions for supply chain management, cross-border trade, banking solutions, and digital ticketing solutions. It's permissioned, meaning you'll need to create an account and get company permission to use the system.

Consider the similarity of the analogy to that of private intranets and the public Internet. Which of the previous made the biggest difference to society during the Age of Information, intranets or the Internet? The answer is that the Internet's public infrastructure made the biggest difference. Like public blockchain, the Internet doesn't require permission to use. It significantly reduced friction in communications, for it's the Internet that allows anyone to send an email or post a web page and communicate nearly freely with anyone else in the world. That was the power of the Age of Information. Well, we have another amazing technology here, and understanding these fundamentals will make you a better investor.

Economic Empowerment and Bitcoin

We're going to unpack this later in Chapter 15; however, it's worth noting that, in the same way that billions of human beings from Calcutta to Cape Town to Chicago carry an affordable cell phone, Bitcoin is leveling access to digital money transactions for humanity.

With Bitcoin, anyone with a smartphone can put money into a savings account, apply for a loan, and make or receive a digital payment. This is revolutionary, especially in countries where it's almost impossible for ordinary people to obtain a bank account, credit, or loans. A Nigerian who lacks access to a bank account but wants to receive money from relatives abroad without paying exorbitant fees can do so easily, quickly, and cheaply with Bitcoin. There are thousands of other commercial applications that can improve the lives of billions of people.

This isn't just in emerging markets, either. As noted in a *Forbes* interview with the always eloquent Chris Giancarlo, affectionately known as Crypto Dad for his early support of cryptocurrencies as former commissioner of the Commodity Futures Trading Commission,[2] and current president of the Digital Dollar Foundation:

In the online world, the digital dollar gets more interesting. Basically, if you shop online today, you can't use fiat currency for peer-to-peer payments. You must go through intermediaries. A digital dollar, however, would give you the same ability to make direct peer-to-peer payments online with digital dollars that you can in the physical world with paper currency. And not just for online shopping.

Take a grandmother working in Philadelphia who has a granddaughter in the Philippines, for example. The granddaughter back in the Philippines sends her grandmother a text message with pictures of her birthday party blowing out birthday candles. That photo is received by the grandmother in an instant. But when the grandmother wants to send $100 back to her granddaughter as a birthday gift, it takes days and costs anywhere between $7 to $17 dollars in transaction fees. With a digital dollar, the transfer would be the same as a text or a photo, all in an instant of time. And when the money arrives, it is $100 worth of immediately spendable U.S. money, and no intermediary is needed to verify the funds or charge processing fees. A digital dollar would be very effective as a means of greater inclusiveness for communities whose needs historically have been underserved by retail banks and financial service providers.

Chris is referring to a digital dollar here, which is on the agenda of the U.S. government, but the same analogy holds true for bitcoin as well as stablecoins and any other crypto asset today. In fact, one could argue that we wouldn't even be talking about a digital dollar had Bitcoin not jumped onto the scene and grown into the juggernaut it is today.

A Regulatory Head Start

It's important to acknowledge that Bitcoin and Ethereum, the two most popular crypto assets, have already passed regulatory scrutiny with officials from both parties, the CFTC and the SEC.

The CFTC monitors virtual currencies for fraud and risk and publishes substantial guidance for the investing public. As stated by the CFTC, "While its regulatory oversight authority over commodity cash markets is limited, the CFTC maintains general anti-fraud and manipulation enforcement authority over virtual currency cash markets as a commodity in interstate commerce." We applaud the CFTC for its inno-vation and leadership in bringing legitimacy to Bitcoin and Ethereum. At times, the SEC and CFTC have effectively coordinated oversight, monitoring, and enforcement in cracking down on fraud and Ponzi schemes. A great deal of what will happen with the regulation of crypto protocols will unfold over the next few years.

We saw one of the more promising 2022 bills was sponsored by Senators Debbie Stabenow (D-MI) and John Boozman (R-AR), giving the CFTC the leading role in overseeing the two largest cryptocurren-cies and the platforms on which they are traded. The bill passed the Senate in August 2022; this bill or parts of it are likely components of what will ultimately become law.

In the bill, "oversight of the remaining cryptocurrencies would be divided between the CFTC and the Securities and Exchange Commission though the process for making those determinations is not yet clear," the *Washington Post* reported. "The two agencies have been jockeying for more authority over digital assets, contributing to confusion in Washington over how to classify and regulate cryp-tocurrencies and the economy that has sprung up around them. The bill aims to provide some clarity by deeming as commodities both bitcoin and ether which together account for roughly two-thirds of the cryptocurrency market."

Bitcoin versus bitcoin

A quick note on capitalization. While we all know the rules for capitaliza-tion in writing, the rules are a little different for the world's most popular digital asset. In writing, you'll often see references to Bitcoin and also references to bitcoin. I can say that when I first saw this, I was quite con-fused and thought the inconsistencies just to be mistakes (that everyone seemed to make). Nope! As it turns out, these two things are distinct.

Bitcoin refers to the actual blockchain, a network of hardware running specific software. It's the whole enchilada. We don't often think of it this way, but it is really the most correct way to view Bitcoin: as a worldwide payment network. The other use, "little b" bitcoin, refers to the actual asset. So, when you see "Jim sent Jake one bitcoin," you can be sure that the reference is to the actual coin itself, not the entire network.

Getting Started with Bitcoin

Okay, so maybe at this point you've done all your due diligence and you want to actually own some crypto for yourself. We know that this can be daunting, so for those looking for a step-by-step checklist, this section is for you.

Exchanges

To begin with, let's look at purchasing directly off of an exchange:

- **Do your homework and pick an exchange.** If you invest a modest amount, you must choose a cryptocurrency exchange or trading service. You can buy, sell, and hold bitcoin and other cryptocurrencies through the exchange. We recommend using an exchange that allows you to withdraw your crypto to your online wallet, which is the most secure option. While there are many trustworthy exchanges, Coinbase, Kraken, and Gemini are the most user-friendly, with reasonable fees and robust security. Binance caters to a more advanced trader, offering more serious trading functionality and a better variety of altcoin choices but is not available to citizens of the USA and many others. CNET and *Forbes* are credible sources for updating your list of exchanges. CNET recommends Bitflyer, Gemini, Coinbase, Kraken, and crypto.com as the "best crypto exchanges let[ting] you easily trade coins and tokens while keeping your assets safe and your fees low." *Forbes Advisor* cites Gemini, Bityard, Kraken, crypto.com, and Coinbase as their "best for beginners," and adds KuCoin to their best exchanges list. We expect that this list will evolve over time, so be sure to check in with a reliable source to see who is currently recommended.
- **Register on the exchange.** You will generally need to provide the same personal information and payment details that you would for a brokerage or bank account. While the philosophy of anti-authority and anonymity behind crypto is essential to some, the reality is that to use a major exchange and to ensure that your funds don't get lost or locked up, you'll need to go through a know your customer/ anti–money laundering process, also known as KYC/AML. This process allows you to be identified while at the same time allowing the

exchange to confirm that you are not a bad actor. We recommend that you avoid exchanges that do not require your identification, as these are far more likely to be security risks.

- **Place an order.** After choosing an exchange, you will need to put money into your account before beginning to invest. When you've funded your account, you're prepared to make your first purchase. Various platforms have slightly different protocols. Some, like Coinbase, are designed for the beginner and walk you through step-by-step; it's very much like buying a stock through an online broker. Others, like Coinbase's pro edition, allow you to view charting and create more complex types of orders, and have lower fees. Unlike a stock, you can purchase any amount of crypto. If you have $100, you can buy $100 worth of bitcoin, ether, or any other crypto. The exchange will do the math and you will have crypto deposited in your wallet on the exchange. (More on wallets in a second.) We recommend that you start with the basics, then move up to the more advanced exchanges where you can take advantage of market, limit, and stop-limit orders. It's also worth noting that many exchanges provide ways to set up recurring investments, allowing clients to dollar-cost average into their assets of choice.

Your Wallet

That should be pretty straightforward, but now you have some options. You can keep your funds on an exchange, or you can move them off the exchange and into your own wallet. A wallet is a cryptographically secure address that *you* control, and this is one of the main points of blockchain technology as it allows you to hold your funds directly and outside of an exchange. This personal wallet ensures that you have control over the private key to your funds.

If your funds are in your wallet, then you are the responsible party and, importantly, no one can take them from you. This of course requires a certain level of responsibility, just like keeping cash in a safe in your own home, so you will need to keep that in mind. When you open a wallet, you will get a public key and a private key. The public key allows anyone to send funds to you; the private key should be kept secret and safe, and this key allows you to send funds from the wallet. Always keep your private keys safe, for if you lose your key, you lose access to your funds. This doesn't mean that you actually lose the money, but it would be inaccessible.

You want to be sure to understand that exchange-based wallets, like wallets on Coinbase, are only as secure as the exchange itself. "Exchange wallets are custodial accounts provided by the exchange. If the exchange is hacked, investor funds are compromised," *Investopedia* explains. This is because, just like with your money at a bank, the exchange is a *counterparty*. Of course, this risk exists in any situation where someone is holding your funds, such as those who were nipped in the savings and loan crisis where approximately 1,043 out of the 3,234 savings and loan associations in the United States closed from 1986 to 1995, some leaving depositors without recourse to access their funds.[3] This leads us to the phrase "not your key, not your coin," which is heavily repeated within cryptocurrency forums and communities.

When first considering this concept, we were confused ourselves. How do my funds get transferred into a digital wallet? The answer is that they don't. Wallets don't actually hold your tokens. Instead, they hold your keys and allow access to your funds on the blockchain. Wallets can be "hot" (software-based) or "cold" (hardware-based and not connected to the Internet). Think of a hot wallet as a software wallet that resides on your computer or phone. These wallets generate the private keys to your coins on these Internet-connected devices and store them for you so you don't have to keep remembering them. A cold wallet is hardware-based, resides offline, and holds your private key on a software-protected file inaccessible to the Internet. There are many popular software wallets; Trezor and Ledger are the two most well-known. The big advantage of a hardware wallet is that your private keys at no time encounter a network-connected computer or potentially vulnerable software. For those who want to simplify this process, there is one other option, known as a "paper wallet," which prints your public and private keys on paper, which can then be laminated and stored. A big disadvantage of paper wallets, however, is that you are required to enter your private key every time you wish to send funds, and any time you type your key into a computer or phone there is risk, either from Internet threats or nosy neighbors. We don't recommend paper wallets.

Wallets have one failsafe to recover private keys. When a wallet is created you will be presented with a *seed phrase*. A seed phrase is a list of 12 to 24 words that are unique to the wallet. This is the one artifact that you must save when creating a wallet, which many people store on paper and leave in a hidden or secure location. There are metal kits that can be purchased that allow you to store your key (literally, the words printed in metal) so that they cannot be destroyed by fire, water, and so on. If you ever lose access to your wallet, you can recover the wallet with your seed phrase.

Wallets, just like the wallet in your back pocket, require a certain amount of responsibility. If you lose your physical dollar-bill wallet, you lose the money inside it. This is the same for your crypto wallet, but this is the trade-off that we have. If we want to control our own money, then we have to take the proper safeguards. Such is the price of autonomy!

PayPal and Other Secure Options

Bitcoin, ether, litecoin, and bitcoin cash can be purchased directly through PayPal, and Venmo. Crypto purchased on Paypal may be transferred off Paypal, however crypto purchased on Venmo must, for now, stay on Venmo. According to Venmo's website: "At this time, it is only possible to buy, sell, and hold crypto on Venmo. Venmo does not currently support using crypto as a way to pay or send money on Venmo, using crypto as a way to make purchases, or peer-to-peer crypto trades." So your crypto will reside on the Venmo network until such time as you choose to convert it to cash.

Bitcoin ATM

We collectively marveled back in 2018 when, upon driving down the street, we saw a "Bitcoin ATM" sign in our local liquor store. Sure enough, these machines exist, and they function much like your regular ATM, except that instead of dispensing cash, a Bitcoin ATM requires you to insert your cash into a machine, which it processes, then converts it to bitcoin, which is then moved to your online wallet. As of this writing, about 200 Walmart stores have these machines at their coin kiosks. The machines charges you a purchase and conversion fee for exchanging your money to bitcoin. It is worth noting that both fees are pretty steep compared to those of other options, but these machines allow cash to be converted without going through an exchange. Ah, how the world has changed.

On Risk

Many years ago I was an avid skydiver, and over the years I've amassed 320 jumps, including some 20 with a wingsuit. Skydiving is one of the most exhilarating and, strangely, peaceful experiences I have ever had. Once I leave the plane and surrender to the pull of gravity, for me, it's like feeling one with everything in the world. Regular skydivers will generally share their version of this, but it all just comes down to one thing: the awesomeness of being in the air. In order to skydive you have to sign a waiver because, the fact is, throwing yourself out of an airplane is risky. It turns out the actual incident rate is much lower than for things we do every day, like driving in a car. In fact, you are over 4,000 times more likely to be in a fatal car crash than a skydiving accident. You don't need to sign a waiver for getting into a car, but, let's face it, that's commonplace and stepping into an uncommon environment such as skydiving is just unusual, so it gets people's attention. A death from skydiving could be from the cause of equipment malfunction, an error during the skydive, an error of the pilot of the plane, someone running into you and knocking you out, a dust devil (tiny tornado), a rock falling out of the sky, and so on. The point is, when you arrive at the skydive, you'll sign a waiver, which is a very scary piece of paper letting you know that this is risky and if anything happens to you, regardless of what it is, then it's on you. If you want to jump, you take the responsibility. If you don't, you don't.

Know Your Risk Envelope

While investing in crypto assets is not fatal, of course, none of this is risk free. You need to be aware that money could be lost because of market conditions, your error, counterparty error, technology error, and so on. It is important to keep this in mind. Should you choose to invest, and many do, be aware that you could, for a variety of reasons, lose all of your investment. This is also true of just about any kind of investment, but because crypto is new and still maturing, it gets a lot of press, mostly about the bad things that happen. In alignment with this, the CFTC put together an advisory that is not dissimilar to that skydiving waiver, designed so that you can make an informed choice. Here is an excerpt of this advisory:

Virtual currency is a digital representation of value that functions as a medium of exchange, a unit of account, or a store of value, but it does not have legal tender status. Virtual currencies are sometimes exchanged for U.S. dollars or other currencies around the world, but they are not currently backed or supported by any government or central bank. Their value is completely derived by market forces of supply and demand, and they are more volatile than traditional fiat currencies. Profits and losses related to this volatility are amplified in margined futures contracts.

For hedgers – those who own bitcoin or other virtual currencies and who are looking to protect themselves against potential losses or looking to buy virtual currencies at some point in the future – futures contracts and options are intended to provide protection against this volatility. However, like all futures products, speculating in these markets should be considered a high-risk transaction.

What Makes Virtual Currency Risky?

Purchasing virtual currencies on the cash market – spending dollars to purchase bitcoin for your personal wallet, for example – comes with a number of risks, including:

- Most cash markets are not regulated or supervised by a government agency.
- Platforms in the cash market may lack critical system safeguards, including customer protections.
- Volatile cash market price swings or flash crashes.
- Cash market manipulation.
- Cyber risks, such as hacking customer wallets.
- Platforms selling from their own accounts and putting customers at an unfair disadvantage.

It's also important to note that market changes that affect the cash market price of a virtual currency may ultimately affect the price of virtual currency futures and options.

When customers purchase a virtual currency-based futures contract, they may not be entitled to receive the actual virtual currency, depending on the particular contract. Under most futures contracts currently being offered, customers are buying the right to receive or pay the amount of an underlying commodity value in dollars at some point in the future. Such futures contracts are said to be "cash settled." Customers will pay or receive (depending on which side of the contract they have taken – long or short) the dollar equivalent of the virtual currency based on an index or auction price specified in the contract. Thus, customers should inform themselves as to how the index or auction prices used to settle the contract are determined.

Entering into futures contracts through leveraged accounts can amplify the risks of trading the product. Typically, participants only fund futures contracts at a fraction of the underlying commodity price when using a margin account. This creates "leverage," and leverage amplifies the underlying risk, making a change in the cash price even more significant. When prices move in customers' favor, leverage provides them with more profit for a relatively small investment. But, when markets go against customers' positions, they will be forced to refill their margin accounts or close out their positions, and in the end may lose more than their initial investments.[4]

The bottom line is this: Investing has risk, so ensure that you operate inside of the parameters you are most comfortable with, and never invest more than you are willing to lose

3

What Makes a Smart Contract Smart?

In this chapter, we cover smart contract and smart contract platforms. Smart contracts are programs that are executable and live on a blockchain. Smart contract platforms are the actual blockchains themselves. We'll distinguish the difference between the two and give you a better understanding about each concept and why they're so important to the technological revolution – they create an entire new world for what's possible.

What Is a Smart Contract Platform?

With Bitcoin handled, we're now going to explore one of the most exciting features of blockchain technology, and that is the concept of a smart contract. It's so important that there is a special group of blockchains known as smart contract platforms that are specifically built to facilitate the use of this simple but amazing feature. The smart contract platform is a blockchain that provides the backbone for building decentralized applications. The ecosystem consists of wallets and tokens, as you would expect, along with a programming language that allows developers to build blockchain applications. Such applications are known as Dapps or decentralized applications, and they are entirely functioning systems that are peer-to-peer, generally with all of the standard properties of a blockchain. Smart contract platforms are known as "Layer 1," while the applications that are built on top of them are denoted as "Layer 2." Smart contracts can be built into the applications and will run when predetermined conditions are met and are thus paramount to the operation and flourishing of decentralized finance (DeFi) and other blockchain applications. Unlike databases, where administrators maintain and update records, smart contract platforms rely on contributions from the network – hundreds of thousands of participants – to validate transactions.

Earlier this year I was preparing to travel and the day of my trip, my flight was canceled, which required a whole lot of logistical juggling to reschedule. Naturally I have travel insurance; however, making a claim is never simple. Imagine instead that, when a flight is canceled, that data is automatically sent to an insurance smart contract as an input and, if the flight was covered, the contract would automatically issue a refund as an output. This idea, posed by TrustRadius, could happen automatically, cost effectively, and securely, and minimize effort and expense. This is only one example. The types of Dapps that use smart contracts that we will see are limited only by the imagination of the developers, and we believe that this technology will touch every area of commerce. Smart contract platforms empower them to set up and manage private and public blockchain networks instead of building from scratch, saving them money.

In the view of the Securities and Exchange Commission (SEC), smart contract platforms can carry different regulatory risks than other crypto classes. If platforms have their network functioning, are in production, and are sufficiently decentralized, the SEC views these as less risky assets, akin to legal contracts. Smart contract platforms require tokens – their own crypto – to function, and the whole point of a token such as ether, which is associated with the Ethereum blockchain, is to allow transactions to occur. This makes a smart platform contract its own crypto class.

Smart contract platforms are the gateway to burgeoning DeFi systems (we explore DeFi in the next chapter) and can be used for almost any agreement between two parties. As a DeFi platform, they make financial products accessible to anyone with Internet, regardless of their status and nationality. Additionally, users can hold their money any way they want and control where it goes without any interference. The DeFi system also allows peer-to-peer transactions without intermediaries, providing a sustainable alternative to the tightly controlled traditional banking system.

In addition to this, smart contract platforms can be used to create tokenized assets, NFTs (discussed in Chapter 5), and even other blockchains. They are the foundational layer to the implementation of this next technological wave.

The Foundation of the Age of Autonomy®

Twenty years ago, the Internet began to play a major role in our life. We remember growing up during this exciting time, excited about the ability to send information across the world nearly instantaneously (email), get information about businesses instantaneously (web pages), and began to explore this idea of doing business on the web (ecommerce). It was hard to imagine then what a cell phone would evolve into; however, fast-forward a few years and smartphones such as iPhones began to take society by storm (creating anxiety for all of us who were left behind). Now, it is blockchain technology that is seeking to transform current business structure, communication, and internal processes, and also the nature of money. Big-name companies such as IBM, Walmart, Home Depot, and Toyota are all implementing blockchain technology, generally smart contract platforms. What we find so interesting is that with artificial intelligence (AI), IoT, robotics, and blockchain converging, we're seeing automation and autonomous systems playing an ever-increasing role in industry. Industries across the board are seeing dramatic increases in efficiency, product tracing, and security, and it's just begun.

We call this convergence the Age of Autonomy®, which we review in Chapter 11; however, as a sneak preview, consider that IoT will provide sensors and networks to measure and communicate data. AI will process this data into something actionable, and robotics can translate this into the physical world (such as a self-driving car). Blockchain technologies and, notably, smart contract platforms govern and enforce the transfer and store of value from work produced. We're moving to an age of self-driving cars to one of self-driving businesses.

Smart Contracts and the Supply Chain

We discussed supply chain and blockchain innovation earlier, but this example is intriguing as it involves one of the top smart contract platforms and the most unpretentious brands of all time, Walmart.

When a contamination issue arises in the supply chain, identifying where it occurred can be a complex and lengthy process. For example, it took two months for Walmart to identify the source of a salmonella outbreak in Mexican papayas and to recall them. Walmart recognized this issue. The company announced that it would partner with IBM to run two proof-of-concept projects to test a new way of tracking food. One of those projects was centered around tracking mangos in U.S. locations.

Walmart started by creating a benchmark. First, a project member bought a package of sliced mangos and asked his team to identify the farm from whence it originated. It took seven days to trace it back. Given the benchmark, Walmart investigated its own processes and began to digitalize and store food safety processes and product information on the Hyperledger Fabric blockchain. Suppliers used new labels and updated their data through a web-based interface. This action created a single historical record for the produce. By the end of the project, Walmart found that it was able to reduce its product traceability time from seven days to 2.2 seconds. That is a mind-boggling improvement. Now Walmart has vastly expanded its supply chain tracing using IBM blockchain, built on top of Hyperledger Fabric.

As you can see, smart contract platforms are building autonomy throughout the entire production cycle. Robotics will automate production in the physical world, while sensors and data will move through the Internet of Things. Through bots, agents, and cryptocurrency, software will generate, transfer, and store the world's value. Artificial intelligence will provide the brain power to learn, execute, measure, and adapt each component within the decentralized system. We're bullish on companies that understand this dynamic.

The Evolution of the Contract

Contracts are agreements and have been around since the days of ancient Mesopotamia and Sumeria, around 2300–2600 BC. That's a long time ago. Over the years, we've seen contracts evolve; this is a fundamental basis for our legal system – enforcing agreements. Smart contracts permit transactions and agreements to be carried out among disparate, anonymous parties without needing a central authority, legal system, or external enforcement mechanism. The terms of the agreement between buyer and seller are directly written into lines of code. The code and the agreements contained therein exist forever on the blockchain. The code controls the execution, and transactions are trackable and irreversible. A smart contract is self-executing, meaning that once the smart contract can see that the conditions for the contract have been met, it automatically executes. And, because it's on the blockchain, it is unalterable. No chasing payments, no renegotiations, no escrow companies.

As authors, we'd love to see the publishing industry consider smart contracts, as they take away ambiguity or bias. Our literary agent, Herb Schaffner, remembers when the first Kindle prototypes were being passed around publishing offices to the great skepticism of many. Eventually, however, publishers adapted, as readers loved ebook devices and piled up stacks of digital books in their reading queues. Often, new technologies are not quickly embraced; however, let's look at how a smart contract could impact the world of book publishing. In terms of author agreements and author royalties, smart contracts could be coded as part of the overall author–publisher agreement to make royalty deposits into the agent's or author's bank accounts when book sales thresholds are reached. The conditions and executions would be transparent to the author, publisher, and agent, so no longer does the agent have to waste time asking the editor to waste time asking the royalty department to waste time to send a statement. Royalties are already managed on a financial database; plugging that into a smart contract could open up time for everyone involved.

This could easily apply to any kind of royalty and remove all need for interpretation. Another obvious example is home buying. Once the buyer has deposited funds and the seller checklist has been fulfilled, deeds and funds could automatically be transferred without requiring an external escrow agent.

Smart contracts will change law and commerce fundamentally by removing bias, and once you understand how smart contracts work, you will understand how the crypto revolution reaches far beyond digital currencies. Smart contracts will boost our economic engines with the three great lubricators of technological progress: transparency, data protection, and cost reduction. *What bitcoin is to the monetary system, smart contracts will be to the legal system.*

Think of an invoice: it's a simple legal contract. We can already create a smart contract for an invoice that would autonomously transfer money to the designated party once the conditions are met. In the coming decades, we'll be able to create smart contracts as complex and subtle as any legal contract today. The smart contract is a fundamental structure at the basis of the innovation – going forward.

In the following sections we discuss a few selected applications of an emerging digital economy built on smart contracts. These systems promise to be more efficient and safer than previous technologies while protecting your financial and data identity.

How Can We Benefit from Smart Contract Applications?

Several IT experts and scientists have published journal articles analyzing the benefits of smart contracts, including Tharaka Hewa, Mika Ylianttila, and Madhusanka Liyanage in a 2021 article in the *Journal of Network and Computer Applications*. The authors note: "Many applications [that are] already notoriously hard and complex are fortunate to facilitate the service with the blessings of blockchain and smart contracts. The decentralized and autonomous execution with in-built transparency of blockchain-based smart contracts revolutionize most of the applications with optimum and effective functionality."[1]

The researchers confirm smart contracts' beneficial features such as accuracy: "The programmed conditions in the smart contracts are immutable and verified prior to the deployment in nodes in the blockchain network. The execution is automatic once the condition is met. The accuracy is guaranteed without any human or other error on the exception."

The authors also conclude that smart contracts prevent fraud or other noncompliance. In fact, smart contracts will facilitate the enforcement of contractual agreements across many industries and use cases with in-built transparency and resilience against crisis. Next are a few examples.

Banking "Know Your Customer" Regulations

Know your customer is a crucial function in the financial services industry. If you've onboarded at a crypto exchange, you have experienced the many checks, ranging from identification submitted to an actual photo, to prove you are indeed you. These checks get more robust in larger scale and worldwide transactions such as the ones we have with our fund. The reason is simple: to minimize crime, fraud, and money laundering.

This seems straightforward enough; however, the extensive paperwork also presents a liability for bankers and customers. People can conceal their identities in money-laundering activities and, if not caught, banks can be criminally liable. In addition to that, customers submitting information are now releasing their personal data to a third party. What if, instead, your identity information was stored in a nonmodifiable and verified crypto asset (a special form of NFT – we'll discuss this later) that you controlled. A smart contract could look at that asset and verify that you are you without requiring additional information submitted and without requiring you to transmit information over the Internet. As the owner of the data, you would have the ability to disclose as much of your data as desired or required but not more than that. All can be verified by a smart contract. The smart contract makes it easier for the institution while allowing you to have control of your data. This is where we are going as a society.

Real Estate Transactions

Selling and leasing real estate, homes, and commercial space involves lawyers, actuaries, and brokers, and each transaction has extensive processing, verification, and documentation needs. If you've purchased or sold a home, you remember the hundreds of pages of various documents requiring signatures (and if in Texas you need to show up in person to sign on actual paper!). Finalizing major deals can take weeks, months, or even years and is subject to interpretation and, especially, a third-party escrow to confirm whether the transaction is viable or not. A smart contract eliminates most of these delays.

Paper agreements are replaced by a programmed smart contract residing on a blockchain. These contracts contain deal terms as electronic protocols so that each set of data provided to the contract triggers the next step in the process. Once a certain set of criteria is met – say all inspections are done, for example, and all monies have been submitted and verified – the contract can then execute the transaction. Further, all transaction data is stored in the distributed ledger.

Smart contracts also provide the mother of all backup systems, reproducing all transactions, so even if data is lost on one device, the data will still be available via the ledger. These innovations are already happening in companies such as Propy, which uses smart contracts for cross-border real estate transactions, removing the risk and headaches for buyers in different countries and regions, and, as another example, Seattle-based SMARTRealty is applying smart contract technology to everyday real estate rental, purchase, and sale transactions and deploys smart contracts for every deal done. These are just a few of the early adopters. Many more will come and many will rise and fall, just as in the early days of the Internet, but, ultimately, we see a world where real estate and smart contracts go hand-in-hand.

Insurance

We may not always articulate it, but most of us have a sense of the inefficiency of insurance claims processing. Insurers maintain an army of fraud investigators and claims adjusters to monitor claims for lying and misrepresentation, as insurance fraud is rampant. On the other side, policyholders know the frustration of waiting for claims to be processed and paid. Meanwhile, on the governmental end of things, state law enforcement and the FBI actively investigate and prosecute fraud, which the FBI estimates at more than $40 billion per year, which costs the average U.S. family between $400 and $700 per year in the form of increased premiums.

Blockchain technology will save insurers and the insured billions of dollars by minimizing the potential for fraudulent activity.

Not surprisingly, U.S.-based insurers are eager for greater adoption of smart contracts, as smart contracts can automate claims and validation through the decentralized ledgers of the blockchain network, eliminating the bulk of the time-consuming and tedious claims process. Consider automobile insurance. Say you are involved in a car accident, and it was the other driver's fault. You submit a claim to your insurance company to recover your loss. Your insurer begins investigating the claim, as does the other insurance company, both companies doing duplicate work that is subject to delays and possible human error. If insurance claims are placed on a blockchain, different insurers, reinsurers, brokers, and other parties can access the same shared data. Governed by a smart contract, the policies will automatically execute programmed claims-processing actions that can automate information transfers between insurers and other parties and release payments to policyholders seamlessly.

This is only the beginning, however, as smart contract solutions to complex farming issues are gaining traction in many African agricultural regions. In one example, farmers in Ghana receive crop insurance through a smart contract that is triggered when certain pre-set conditions are met, enabling farmers to secure their farms and family livelihood in case of extreme climatic events such as floods or droughts. Another company provides insurance to small farms in Ghana, Kenya, and Uganda through smart contracts that trigger claims based on intelligent weather predictions. By using this technology wisely, smart contracts will not only streamline claims, they may be able to prevent damage and overall lower cost, pain, and impact to all.

Transparent Auditing

As with aspects of the insurance industry, professional auditing services are labor-intensive, subject to fraud, and dense with paper-driven compliances. Smart contracts provide transparency to stakeholders, board members, regulators, and potential business partners, and can support advanced bookkeeping tools and ensure accurate record-keeping based on the incorruptible and distributed codes in the blockchain network. Since the blockchain can't be tampered with, regulators can trust the smart contract for compliance. Similarly, auditors' work can be far more streamlined, as the smart contract will automatically release approvals and signoffs in the forensic auditing process.

Voting and Democracy

Democracies debate, discuss, and explore advances in secure, trusted electronic voting. Some nations are further ahead than others, and some countries face technical hurdles in implementing electronic voting systems. In the United States, voting integrity came under unwarranted and invalidated attacks during the 2020 elections. However, the firestorm of coverage and numerous controversies raised public awareness of the value of integrity and security in the vote. Some research projects underscore that smart contracts can be part of an overall approach to voting systems "by ensuring decentralization, transparency and eliminating a single point of failure."[2]

Health Care

Smart contracts in health care have the potential to improve a range of processes and outcomes. These include storage and security for health information, more robust controls for patient data, and automation of regulatory compliance requirements. Smart contracts can strengthen patent protection for life-critical clinical research, and expose fake and counterfeit drugs.

Blockchain is having an impact on the provenance and tradability of the pharmaceutical supply chain, fake and counterfeit drugs, and tampering.[3]

The simple fact is that no industry is more circumscribed by compliance and record-keeping than health care. The high cost of American health care is partly about costs of hospitalization and how well insurance companies or Medicaid/Medicare negotiate those fees. Insurance companies and hospitals engage in running battles over the fees hospitals charge. Smart contracts could help unravel the byzantine nightmare of health care "funny money" by incentivizing instant payments for improvements by hospitals in lowering fees and achieving other efficiency targets.

Health care thought leader Dr. Mitchel Schwindt analyzed the benefits of smart contracts on hospitalrecruiting.com:

> As members of society age, interactions grow exponentially with providers and health systems. Surgeries, procedures, consultations, and medication changes quickly become difficult to track. . . . [We know] over 90% of hospitalized patients cannot recall one or more medications. The current system is broken and dangerous. Storing patient data on the blockchain, combined with the power of smart contracts, can grant access to those with permission to view and keep records up to date. Ready access is assured in times of emergency. Authorized parties can add to the medical record and make updates backed up on the blockchain. The days of multiple paper copies of scratched-out meds will end. Changes are viewable to all the patient's caregivers. Smart contracts can remove the friction when multiple parties are processing various aspects of a patient's care. Data is current, verified, and accessible, based on the permissions in the smart contract.[4]

Smart contracts allow records and information to be stored on a digital ledger, so communication will travel with patients more efficiently than ever before without filling out numerous forms. The patient's preferred physician can also view records on the blockchain network. Hospitals and health care companies rely on several databases filled with patient information; however, these can be too restrictive to allow for sharing potentially life-saving insights around the globe. Without blockchain and smart contracts, this information may take a long time to reach the recipient and possibly be hacked. If health records were kept in a smart contract and stored on the blockchain, that information would be available to hospitals and research institutions everywhere.

Intellectual Property and Content Creators

Once you have used Venmo, CashApp, or other instant payment apps, we guess you don't want to go back to sending checks by mail. In fact, the generation born between 2010 and 2024 is known colloquially as Generation Alpha, and it's unlikely that many of them will have ever seen or used a checkbook. Instant payment apps are just the start — we can do better. For artists, smart contracts can provide a foolproof remittance system without the intermediaries (banks and companies) that add costs and fees. Smart contracts allow for consistent and near-instantaneous payments per use of song, video, art, crafts, and so forth through real-time remittance. This adds transparency and will speed up payments to musicians and content creators for whom payments often dribble in. Because of their impregnable security, smart contracts are more likely to be adopted by corporations and platforms such as Spotify or Etsy. Think about it this way: What if we could have a Venmo with all of the functionality of Venmo but without the actual company Venmo — just peers exchanging funds? With blockchain-empowered smart contracts, we can do this.

Integration with the Internet of Things (IoT)

Do you get an email from your car reminding you that the windshield wiper fluid is nearly empty? Or that one of the tires needs to be inflated? You know what we're talking about if your car is a newer model. That's the IoT (Internet of Things) at work. The sensor in your wiper tank talks through the Internet to your customer service account, which autonomously sends you the email. Smart contracts are a pillar of all the decentralized, autonomous operations evolving in many areas of our world.

A John Deere tractor now comes fitted with rear-view cameras, touch screens showing application rates, fuel economy, and input placement, and GPS-powered autonomous guidance that ensures efficient coverage with accuracy down to sub-one-inch specifications. Sensors in the tractor communicate with satellites that talk back to the steering and engine operations. These self-driving, GPS-guided tractors plow on the darkest of nights, leaving the driver with few worries aside from staying awake or the fate of his favorite team playing in a game on the radio.

This is important because data will drive smart contracts. IoT, by its nature, is sensor data. Every day more devices are connected and more data is being collected. With billions of devices connected in every major industry, in many places, the move is happening now. Combined with AI and robotics, the IoT is facilitating major steps forward in automation. This is the Age of Autonomy® and, as predicted in Jake's first book, crypto, blockchain, and smart contracts allow for automated financial transactions, ushering in an economy where autonomous, permissionless software can optimize, make real-time decisions, and move capital 24/7. The smart contract platform is the vehicle to facilitate how many of these financial operations work. We dive further into this later in this book.

The function of the smart contract in our economy marks the first part of this story. We tackle the second part in the next chapter, where we explain how smart contract *platforms* work, boosting a massive swath of financial opportunities of which you should be aware. Finally, if you want to geek out about how smart contracts are designed, developed, and programmed, check out the home of smart contracts at https://ethereum.org/en/developers/docs/smart-contracts/.

4

What Is DeFi?

Decentralized finance, or DeFi, is currently one of the most important use cases of blockchain and it stands to change how we transact money. We only need look at the implosion of Celsius to see the challenges of CeFi, or centralized finance (instruments that are managed by a centralized company or bank). First, let's understand what DeFi is. DeFi contracts are smart contracts that reside on a blockchain. They are not controlled by any central entity and as such are much less prone, if not immune, to manipulation. The two best use cases for DeFi right now are collateralized lending and collateralized borrowing. Collateralized lending is the process whereby anyone can check in collateral in the form of a crypto asset and then generate interest by lending it out (which is, by the way, what banks do with your money when you're not using it). Collateralized borrowing, conversely, consists of you borrowing funds that are secured by your collateral in the smart contract. When your collateral is deposited, it's under certain rules and conditions that are agreed, upon including how interest will be calculated, how loan-to-value will be calculated, and so on. The contract then works, and the software guides it. Now, back to Celsius. Celsius was a company that allowed users to check in their crypto assets and allowed collateralized lending (borrowing additional monies using crypto as collateral) and yield farming (lending assets to others and earning interest). All of this is well and good except that it was all under the control of one central entity, Celsius.

When Celsius got into financial trouble, it appears that they manipulated their own balance sheet by having their own token on it with inflated prices, which made them look more stable than they were. This is a function of management, not software. Ultimately, when the shell game could no longer hold up, the company froze everyone's assets and then, ultimately, went bankrupt. Celsius's financial problems were the result of decisions made by centralized management and resulted in billions of dollars frozen and inaccessible to their users. Conversely, while this was happening, DeFi contracts kept working. What we have here is a fundamental question: Do I trust software that is transparent and consistent? Or do I trust humans who have biases and are not always looking out for the best interest of their constituents when it conflicts with their own best interest? Personally, we're siding with software here.

The Wild West

The Economist regarded the future of crypto as a frontier where contending forces include Big Tech, "big rich countries" that have been testing their digital currencies, and software developers "building all sorts of applications" to empower DeFi.

"Finance is becoming ever less the domain of sharp-suited bankers and credit-card executives. Instead, a ragtag cast of characters is overseeing an explosion of innovation that seeks to cut out the incumbents altogether. From established tech firms and fintech startups on America's west coast to developers of various decentralized-finance applications, they are jostling to reshape digital finance," wrote finance editor Rachana Shanbhogue.[1]

Through smart contract platforms, developers are using blockchain technology to create DeFi platforms that allow people to lend or borrow funds, speculate on price movements on assets using derivatives, trade cryptocurrencies, insure against risks, and earn interest in savings-like accounts. There's a freewheeling, Wild West vibe to the legions of apps presented with a trove of visual data.

"In the DeFi space, there's no central authority to report to," Shirin Bucknam, co-founder of Crypto Witch Club, a Brooklyn-based online education community dedicated to blockchain and Web 3.0, told Time .com. "It's really a radical new way of doing things."

It's radical because DeFi runs on a public blockchain that's accessible to anyone with an Internet connection, creating a truly level playing field market. On the supply side, it allows investors to create new forms of capital. Investors infuse collateral into the system through smart contracts and print a new form of stable currency called stablecoins. On the demand side, investors can take that digital money to provide the first formation of capital, which lends money back to the investors and developers who can take the funds and invest them.

Banking for the Bankless

DeFi is emerging as the vanguard of fresh financial freedom in countries where it's almost impossible for ordinary people to obtain a bank account, credit, or loans. Sixty-nine percent of people living in Vietnam, for example, do not have access to a bank account.

Just imagine the advantage of obtaining a cryptocurrency account in a country like Zimbabwe, where inflation was 622% in 2020. In Venezuela, inflation is so severe that artisans sell handbags made from local currency – the bolivar.

DeFi opens up one of the largest new markets: people who are unbanked and not served by traditional finance. An estimated 4.5% of U.S. households (approximately 5.9 million) were "unbanked" in 2021, meaning that no one in the household had a checking or savings account at a bank or credit union. World Bank data shows that 1.9 billion people worldwide do not have access to a bank account.[2]

DeFi's characteristics of availability and low fees make financial services accessible to all: you only need the Internet and a computing device to access DeFi applications. These minor requirements make fintech platforms relatively easy for anyone to use – to save, borrow, and make payments. Emerging markets are among the areas that are most impacted by the world of blockchain, something we will cover in more detail in Chapter 15.

What about those with bank accounts, mortgages, and stock portfolios? Well, crypto is opening up new possibilities for them, too. Compound, for example, is an app based on the Ethereum blockchain that allows digital asset holders to borrow and lend crypto against collateral.

Let's say you bought $1,000 worth of Ethereum's currency, ether. You could add it to Compound's liquidity pool and immediately start earning compounding interest. No application required – not even a phone call. Just download the app. Compound has already amassed more than $6 billion in its liquidity pools.

DeFi delivers these products in a peer-to-peer format so that there are exchanges and derivative contracts, exchanges, and insurance where you can make different shares or fractionalize a given asset.

DeFi apps fall into dozens of service segments. Exchanges and loans comprise the most popular activities on DeFi by billions of dollars. Decentralized payments and insurance, for example, are much smaller in comparison – probably due to the lack of a practical application for many consumers. We believe this may change as the metaverse develops and real-world items get involved.

DeFi assets as investments themselves provide a familiar roller-coaster ride. One investment, yearn.finance, traded at less than $1,000, ran up to $35,000, then as high as $80,000, and resides now at about $9,500 – all over two years. As with any emerging market, expect wild price gyrations but keep the long run in mind, manage your risks, and invest wisely.

DeFi and CeFi: Odd Bedfellows

While the current DeFi marketplace is a domain where you should place small bets or have a strong appetite for risk, the banking industry and consultants from Deloitte to Gartner to IBM see a huge potential for DeFi and CeFi to work in tandem. CeFi would be any big bank, lender, or other institution that provides monetary services. Think Citibank, BlackRock, Visa, and the like. Blockchain and AI expert Avivah Litan of Gartner blogged that "DeFi has the potential to transform financial services and move into the mainstream, assuming regulatory frameworks are clarified, and technology platforms mature."

Compared to CeFi applications, DeFi lowers transaction costs and improves process efficiencies. Based on open-source protocols, DeFi unleashes the creativity of global developers and entrepreneurs who assemble financial primitives into reusable transformational applications that are not feasible using CeFi.

"There are many shades of gray in between, where CeFi and DeFi work in tandem," Litan said. "For example, DeFi can use assets issued by

CeFi players . . . in which case you just have to trust the company issuing the asset used by DeFi ('DeCeFi'). Alternatively, banks may use DeFi to offer financial services to their customers ('CeDeFi').''

Major players in the traditional banking world are already testing the waters and see digital asset strategies as a critical ingredient for traditional banks to gain more customers. Banks embracing digital assets are the next step in the bridge between DeFi and CeFi. "Financial institutions that can overcome outdated beliefs and leverage . . . approaches to prioritize digital asset strategies will be positioned for growth," wrote Ernst & Young partner Aaron Byrne early in 2022.[3] Some of the most notable of these, at least at the time of writing, include:

- The Bank of New York Mellon developed a digital custody platform for transferring, safekeeping, and issuing digital assets. "BNY Mellon is proud to be the first global bank to announce plans to provide an integrated service for digital assets," said Roman Regelman, CEO of Asset Servicing and Head of Digital at BNY Mellon. "Growing client demand for digital assets, maturity of advanced solutions, and improving regulatory clarity present a tremendous opportunity for us to extend our current service offerings to this emerging field."

- Wells Fargo is offering bitcoin investments to its investing clients through a partnership with DeFi human resources innovator NYDIG.

- JPMorgan Chase partnered with Singapore's DBS Group and Temasek to form a blockchain payments platform to ease cross-border payments, trade, and currency settlements, to reimagine and accelerate value movements for payments, trade and foreign exchange settlement in a new digital era, through a newly established technology company.

- Mastercard and Gemini, a cryptocurrency platform, offer a credit card that provides real-time crypto rewards on purchases made with bitcoin or other cryptocurrencies. Customers can benefit from any appreciation in the value of their currency holdings.

- Commerzbank, Isbank, and LBBW became the first banks to execute a commercial cross-border transaction via Marco Polo, a blockchain-enabled trade finance network. The partnership employs DeFi technology to enhance the efficiency and security of supply chain management and trade financing solutions. DeFi features enable the operation of the platform, with the first cross-border transaction taking place on May 10, 2021, and involved the export of laminated special glass interlayers from Germany to Turkey.

- Binance, a leading international exchange, established a $100 million accelerator fund to support blockchain ecosystem building and better synergize DeFi and CeFi. However individual developers decide to partner or not with centralized banking, the DeFi world is generating financial solutions that work peer-to-peer and without intermediaries.

Decentralized finance is a natural progression of the founding ethos of Bitcoin: traditional financial institutions are too powerful, centralized, and susceptible to corruption. DeFi delivers on this proposition by building open-source, noncustodial tools for the ecosystem. This prototype for open-source financial services holds huge ramifications for the nature of lending and loans: no credit check, personal data, or bank account is required. Everyone can participate.

Lending, Borrowing, and Yield

Collateralized lending is the process of a lender providing funds to a borrower, which are then secured by collateral that the borrower provides to a lender. This is one of the main current use cases in DeFi, particularly since it has taken a while for banks to warm up to the concept of bitcoin and other crypto assets. Let's say Mike has five bitcoin and wants to borrow $20,000 to do some home improvements. Mike can, through a DeFi lender, borrow that $20,000 and secure the loan by pledging some of his bitcoin. If he defaults, the lender gets to keep enough of the collateral to pay back the loan; if he pays it back, he gets to keep his bitcoin. DeFi's lending services are provided in the form of smart contracts that offer collateralized loans in a permissionless environment.

Among the major platforms for DeFi lending are Ethereum blockchain protocols like Aave, Compound, and Maker. As noted by the popular Yield app, "Each one allows users to lock their funds in the platform, but smart contracts govern how they work. No third-party can change the underlying code or contracts. Aave, Compound, and Maker are lending services with a proven track record as reliable and secure platforms with easy-to-use websites for executing these complex transactions."

Another popular use of DeFi is the ability to earn interest on your funds by depositing your funds and generating interest on them, much like a CD or a savings account, except at much higher rates. Ultimately, this is just a teaser, as we'll touch more on these specific cases in Chapter 23.

Decentralized Exchanges (DEXs)

Earlier we discussed how to buy bitcoin using a centralized exchange. Centralized exchanges are common in the crypto and noncrypto world and, basically, they are clearinghouses that host buyers, host sellers, and conduct buy and sell transactions out of the common pool of both. Centralized exchanges are trading platforms that allow sophisticated kinds of buy and sell orders, derivatives, and generally a host of advanced options.

As a result of its peer-to-peer nature, blockchain has brought us another gateway, and that is that buyers and sellers directly trade without having to pledge their assets to a third party. Think of it like buying a car. Perhaps your heart is set on an electric sport sedan but you don't want to pay new car prices and are happy with a one- or two-year-old model. You can go to a dealer and see if they have any on their lot. If they do, then that means that they bought the car from another seller and are now selling it to you, likely at a markup. Let's say your dream chariot is there and you decide to buy. You'll pay the cost of the car, which includes dealer markup, and off you go. Suppose, however, you choose to go through a private party. By researching various trade magazines and Internet sites, sure enough, after a little looking, you see that Michelle has a two-year-old electric sport sedan and she's ready to sell. You buy directly from her. This is an example of a *decentralized* or peer-to-peer transaction. Decentralized exchanges (DEXs) such as Uniswap, Kyber, and Pancake Swap work much the same way. They match buyers and sellers and allow peer-to-peer transactions directly to and from a digital wallet without holding any assets at any time. Instead, assets interact with a set of smart contracts that manage the exchange process between two parties. These smart contracts allow for more privacy and fewer transaction costs than a centralized cryptocurrency exchange and, unlike centralized exchanges, assets are never held by the DEX, reducing costs to the user and liability to the exchange.

This changes the regulatory game as well since DEXs aren't asset custodians. Operators know that they must follow the law's letter and spirit regarding the regulatory checkpoints currently in place; however, we can expect a more mature crypto economy to include regulated centralized exchanges, regulated DEXs, and unregulated DEXs. DEXs are going to provide a world where the exchange of assets happens within smart contracts, and a savvy investor will start taking advantage of this paradigm shift.

Derivatives

Organically, new financial markets benefit by giving investors vehicles such as derivatives to hedge their bets. The DeFi marketplace includes a range of applications or companies offering digital derivatives options. The investing relationship is, of course, governed by smart contracts. Players include Synthetix, Binance, Augur, and many others. If you are in a secure position to buy derivatives, you can explore options on your favorite platform. Synthetix, for example, operates as a smart contract platform for some pretty wild plays, including Lyra, a decentralized options protocol. We wanted to include this concept for completeness, but take your time, as derivatives are not trivial and, used incorrectly, can crush a portfolio. Derivatives are an important aspect of the entire financialization process; however, they should be used by experts who know how to use them to hedge risk or speculate. They do have a place in the market.

DeFi and Governance Tokens

There is one more key element of which everyone should be aware. You see, all of this is well and good, but in this world of DeFi and DEX, of systems that have no central control or governance, the question that comes up is: Who is making the rules? Who decides what lending rates are? What loan terms are? If there's no "company" per se we need a novel way to manage the rules of decentralized systems. The answer is in governance tokens. These often-overlooked tokens have a particular value: a say in what comes next.

In a decentralized, blockchain-based financial system, this process of writing rules is often done through the use of on-chain governance, which is a system that mediates how the rules that govern activity on a particular blockchain are set and revised. Early adopters using a new DeFi service can buy (or earn) governance tokens that give the holder the right to vote on how the blockchain is maintained, upgraded, and managed. One token, one vote. MKR, the token of MakerDAO, is a governance token. If you hold 5% of MKR, you have 5% of the voting rights for initiatives on that platform.

Most blockchain projects start with what's called "off-chain governance," which can mean anything from developers trading emails about how to change the code to founders passing notes in GitHub, the main software source code repository used for open-sourced software projects. The people who build the currency write a founding set of rules. After this is set, many go on to establish on-chain governance and utilize governance tokens. These tokens tend to come into play after a crypto network is established.

On-chain governance is more formal and democratic than off-chain, and it allows every governance token holder the right to vote on decisions and choices that will guide the particular blockchain ecosystem. Some ecosystems may vote on features to be released. The decision could be the setting of monetary policy or the reserve requirements of collateral on a loan. Or, it could be what type of consensus mechanism the blockchain uses, which affects performance, resource usage, and security for that blockchain. The on-chain governance structure is designed to maintain transparency because everyone can see the proposals and see the computation of the results of a vote – and avoid human-led backroom deal making.

While the primary focus of crypto investors has so far been speculation on appreciation, governance tokens will likely become more important – and valuable – as crypto investing matures. The reason is fairly simple: as the value of a crypto network increases, so too does the value of the right to govern it. Because token holders must hold the crypto asset to continue voting in that particular ecosystem's interests, investors will want to obtain and hold more tokens so they can continue participating in the governing. As long as the ecosystem makes good decisions and offers a good and competitive service, the token will likely accrue more value as time goes on.

We have something analogous in the traditional financial system. If traditional equity provides a right or claim to cash flows after all business expenses are paid, then governance tokens are somewhat analogous to equity in that they confer a right to control the direction of a crypto network and its treasury.

We're entering a new world, where more and more is being done with less and less. Part of the reason that's possible is that technology as innovation is at the heart of the economy. The world is becoming more automated and, as that trend continues, we're going to need mechanisms that manage the boundary between man and machine. DeFi's systems of on-chain governance and the use of governance tokens look quite promising. Governance tokens give investors not just a stake but a say. As we've seen throughout history, the right to vote is a powerful thing.

5

The Metaverse, NFTs, and Web 3.0

Keanu Reeves broke out laughing during an interview when asked if he knew about Matrix Resurrection NFTs and the long digital lines of potential buyers crashing the site. The interviewer referred to the demand for tokens that have "digital scarcity," to which Reeves added, "and can be easily reproduced!"

Many of us shake our heads at some of the surreal, virtual aspects of the digital economy, especially where value is not obvious. We're here to address that, demystify NFTs, Web 3.0, and the metaverse, and explain why they are essential for investors or anyone else to understand.

Despite Keanu's chuckle, NFTs are not reproducible. NFT stands for non-fungible token, which are digital assets that are provably unique at the code level: only one ever exists. NFTs allow you to buy and sell ownership of unique digital items and keep track of who currently owns them using the blockchain. Bitcoin, and most general crypto assets, are fungible, which means that they can be exchanged and have equal value. Dollars are fungible. Brand-new pencils are fungible. Anything that can be traded for another thing of the same type that has the same properties and value is fungible. With Bitcoin, each coin is the same and contains the same uses. Every bitcoin is the same as every other, just like a dollar in your wallet is the same as any other dollar. By contrast, NFTs are not interchangeable. No NFT can be reproduced. It's a new data structure that will have a profound impact on us.

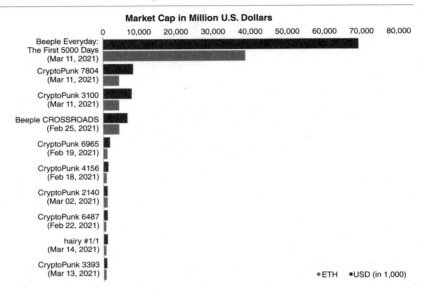

Most Expensive Non-Fungible Token (NFT) Sales Worldwide as of March 16, 2021

Figure 5.1 NFT Sales Worldwide
Source: Various sources, © Statista 2021.

There has been an incredible amount of hype around NFTs and the art world. Mike Winkelmann, aka "Beeple," set the record with the sale of his NFT "The First 5000 Days" for a jaw-dropping $69 million. While not at that level, one-of-a-kind issuances and CryptoPunks, one of the first NFT collections, have NFTs that have garnered thousands each. This is a big reason for the hype wheel. Individuals have spent fortunes to acquire these unique treasures (see Figure 5.1) but, let's face it, just because it's provably unique does not mean that it's the *Mona Lisa*.

The ABCs of NFTs

NFTs are a significant aspect of Web 3.0 and the metaverse because NFTs are digital assets that users can own through blockchain technologies. NFTs have certain benefits that other digital transactions do not, which can be summed up in two main parts. First, because NFT transactions are recorded on the blockchain, they gain all of the blockchain's benefits. Second, each NFT is provably unique, and you can own and buy and sell it. This distinction seems a little confusing, so we'll unpack that further.

If you buy a digital piece of art, in general, you receive a copy of the original file. It's not unique, won't accrue value, and you can't resell it. You may have the right to use it in certain places (privately or commercially), but you don't truly own the digital artwork the same way you would a painting in your home; however, buying an NFT of artwork is pretty much the same as owning a physical piece of art. Using blockchain tech, each NFT is unique at the code level, so we can tell the difference between the two files even if they look the same. Unlike PDFs or JPEGs, which you can't resell after purchase, you can buy and sell NFTs as much as you like because of their uniqueness. Sure, you can make a copy of an image easily on a computer, but that's not the same thing, just like a photo of the *Mona Lisa* is not the same as the original. Provable uniqueness matters, and now it exists in the digital world.

This goes further. Because we can use blockchain transactions to track the history and the creator of NFTs, we can do more with them than with physical assets. For example, anybody who creates an NFT can apply a royalty rate to their digital asset and from then on, any time someone buys or sells the NFT, the original creator would make royalties.

A growing number of influencers and buyers in the fine art world see the promise of NFTs. Willscape Management owner and founder Olivia Kwok Decani – an art investor, consultant, and influencer who created an art fund for a private bank in Switzerland – penned a powerful opinion piece for *World Art News* pointing out the value of NFTs for museums and galleries:

> Before NFTs, digital art was often duplicated, making it almost impossible to separate an original file from a copy. Through the use of NFT and Blockchain technologies, digital artworks can now be identified, authenticated, safely stored on and offline. Distinguishing them from duplicates is easy and convenient. This allows artists to earn money from their digitized artworks by selling original or limited copies.

> NFTs are also now starting to be used in traditional (physical) art. St Petersburg's State Hermitage Museum have created NFTs from some of their artworks – including the likes of Vincent Van Gogh and Claude Monet. ... Art that doesn't exist in a physical form can now

be bought, sold, and collected, opening up many opportunities for artists, collectors, and investors. There are also great benefits to physical
art from NFTs.

Thanks to the introduction of NFTs, art museums and galleries now
have the ability to earn additional revenue from their artworks. Real
paintings can now stay securely in the same places while generating
extra income from the sale of their one-of-a-kind or limited edition
NFT copies. Art museums keep the originals for the public to enjoy,
while their NFTs are sold Worldwide! A win-win.[1]

We are going to see more auctions such as RtisitiQ's selling of digital
NFT versions of the Indian artist Raja Ravi Varma's *The Coquette* and
Reclining Nair Lady, two paintings considered to be national treasures
and not allowed to be taken out of India, but of which authentic digital
editions can now be created.

The Rembrandt Heritage Foundation honored the passing of world-
renowned Rembrandt expert Professor Dr. Ernst van de Wetering by
auctioning off Rembrandt's masterpiece *The Night Watch* in 8,000 digital
pieces (NFTs). This is a whole new provenance for art, and the art world
is the first practical use of NFTs – but this is only the beginning.

Not Just Art

Up until this point we've been discussing art, as that is the most widespread use of NFTs as of this writing; however, an NFT is not an NFT
because it is art; an NFT is an NFT because it's provably unique, one of
a kind, and not reproducible. This means it can represent anything, from
a mortgage, a title to a home or car, a ticket to a concert, health records,
digital goods, birth certificates, to other unique items. Suppose we had a
home title NFT properly implemented so that a court would recognize
it. In that case, we would no longer need mortgage title insurance. The
provenance or ownership history of the home could be proved because
NFTs blockchain entries are immutable. This is just one of the many use
cases we will have.

As another current and non-art example, megabrand Starbucks in
2022 launched its Odyssey experience, which offers members the ability to earn and buy digital collectible stamps (NFTs) that will unlock
"access to new, immersive coffee experiences." Starbucks Odyssey will

be "a new experience powered by Web 3.0 technology that will offer Starbucks Rewards members and partners (employees) in the United States the opportunity to earn and purchase digital collectible assets. ..."

Starbucks is one of the first companies to integrate NFTs with an industry-leading loyalty program at scale while creating a digital community that will enable new ways for Starbucks to engage with its members and its partners. Once logged in, members can engage in Starbucks Odyssey "journeys," a series of activities, such as playing interactive games or taking on fun challenges to deepen their knowledge of coffee and Starbucks. Members will be rewarded for completing journeys with a digital collectible "journey stamp" (NFT).

YouTube announced that it would allow creators to monetize YouTube Shorts using NFTs. CEO Susan Wojcicki said, "We see creators selling their videos and memes as NFTs. We're a platform that distributes content and monetization. If NFTs are an important part of that equation, then we think we should be there."

Nike, famed for its scouts and "cool hunters" who spot youth obsessions—trends before they reach the big mall on the highway, acquired RTFKT Studios, a decentralized corporation of crypto creators, calling it "a leading brand that leverages cutting edge innovation to deliver next generation collectibles that merge culture and gaming." RTFKT collaborated with teenage artist FEWOCiOUS to sell real sneakers paired with virtual ones, selling some 600 pairs/NFTs in just six minutes, netting over $3.1 million at the time, Richard Lawler reported in *The Verge*.

These are just a few examples of how big brands are integrating NFTs today, but this is just the beginning. NFTs will play a key role in the metaverse, virtual words in which we can participate as digital representations of ourselves. If that sounds a little esoteric, then read on and let's explore this together.

The Metaverse

Conversations about the metaverse are *everywhere* but we think the term probably thrown around a lot without any real understanding of what it is or, more importantly, what it can be. The metaverse has been conceptualized for many years, and we've heard many definitions, from "the 3D Internet" (that's not a complete definition) to "digital reality" (words that don't really convey completely). Many of the fundamental elements we've been discussing come together to form the metaverse, including blockchain technology, virtual reality (VR), augmented reality (AR), artificial intelligence (AI), smart contracts, NFTs, and crypto assets, among others.

For our purposes let's consider the metaverse to be an immersive digital world that will allow us to conduct ourselves just as we do in the physical world. We can possess objects, talk to people, read, write, play, work, travel – the list goes on and on. Importantly, this world will allow us to do things that we cannot do in the physical world. Some are pure fun, such as being able to fly or teleport, while others are more practical, such as having face-to-face conversations with people halfway across the world as if they were in our living room with us.

Up until recently we've had to rely on our imaginations, books, movies, and games to give us a sense of what it would be like to operate in an extraphysical capacity. The metaverse, however, will allow us to truly experience a digital world firsthand, through our own senses. In this world you are represented by an avatar, a digital version of yourself. Avatars can be created to look just like you or nothing like you, but they are the digital representation of you, with which you will experience the new frontier.

There have been many films that have represented their versions of what this could be like. In our opinion, one of the best, current representations of what the metaverse could be is seen in Steven Spielberg's 2018 film *Ready Player One*. If you haven't seen it, we recommend it. While you may take or leave the storyline, it clearly shows how we may all one day be jacked into a digital reality and it explores the differences and nuances that it may bring. We'd also add a 2022 Amazon Prime series called *The Peripheral*. In this series, VR and AR collide with quantum physics, where a headset user can link their haptics device directly into their brain, much like how we hear Elon Musk envisions his startup Neuralink. What's interesting about this series' spin on the metaverse is how a player can learn how to play a first-person shooter game, gain those muscle memory skills, and then use an AR headset to make the real world look and feel more like a game – so much so that they can apply their game-playing skill acquired in a VR game directly into the real world with an AR system. Just as *Star Trek* visions are now reality, we see *Ready Player One* and *The Peripheral* as some of the best examples of visualizing what accessing the metaverse could really be like.

Consider that NFTs can also play a role in identity, and we may no longer have logins. Instead, an ID-NFT may authenticate your digital identity, store your data, and allow you to complete transactions in the same space. On top of that, creators can use this much like a resume or portfolio. The immutability of the blockchain will cement and make the authorship of a creator's work transparent. Pirate copies and reshares without credit will be much harder to accomplish.

Technology is tilting the playing field to the advantage of creatives. Imagine communities such as the Amazon Direct Publishing Community, where self-published authors support and share tips and strategies, but each writer has more control and more profit. These are the kinds of decentralized collaborative communities being nurtured by the metaverse.

"Digital artists like Arc are drawn to the technology's ability to confer uniqueness, permanence, and proof of provenance," wrote reporter Terry Nguyen in *Vox*. "Artists and musicians have historically relied on middlemen – auction houses, galleries, and streaming platforms – to sell or host their work. In some cases, they don't earn royalties from future sales. With NFTs, artists can ensure that they receive a predetermined share of royalties (usually 10%) from sales on the secondary market."

MANGA and Mainstream Adoption

In the metaverse via a pair of VR goggles (at least for now), we can visit friends, tour buildings, and even conduct business. Facebook, the social media platform with almost three billion users worldwide, became so convinced of this new world that they changed their name from Facebook to Meta. (As an aside, this resulted in the famed acronym FAANG (Facebook, Amazon, Apple, Netflix, Google) changing to MANGA, the word for Japanese comic books, which somehow seems appropriate when considering the digital world that is the metaverse.

Meta, while it was still Facebook, purchased Oculus VR tech in 2014 (for $2 billion) and subsequently evolved the product and brought it to market. I can remember in the middle of the pandemic donning a headset and meeting friends and family in the VR world Altspace. It certainly wasn't like in the movies but, honestly, it was way better than I expected. The user base is still very small when compared to traditional social networks such as Facebook (see Figure 5.2), but we think it's easy to see its potential and it makes sense that Meta is making this move. The metaverse stands to be the evolution of the social network.

Total Users of Selected Virtual Platforms Worldwide as of October 2021

Characteristic	Number of Users
Web 3.0 Virtual Worlds	50,000
Non-Fungible Tokens	412,578
Blockchain Gaming	2,364,576
Decentralized Finance	3,450,000
Global Crypto	220,000,000
Gaming/eSports	250,000,000
Facebook	2,970,000,000

Figure 5.2 Virtual Platform Usage

Source: Adapted from Nonfungible: Goldman Sachs; facebook; Cryptoslam; Dune Analytics; Crypto.com.

Facebook isn't the only one, however, as the conglomerate market cap of the current Web 2.0 metaverse economy is estimated to be nearly 15 trillion dollars, according to findings by Statista, Bloomberg, MSIV, and Roundhill Investments (see Figure 5.3).

Eventually, using VR and AR technology, the metaverse will feel to many as realistic as the physical world. Using blockchain technology, you'll be able to own property and start companies just like in the physical world. Creators can hold events and meet fans around the world as electropop superstar Grimes did in Decentraland, a metaverse virtual reality where users can buy virtual property (in the form of an NFT plot of land). In late 2021, some major companies, including Samsung, Adidas, and Miller Lite, bought virtual properties, and additional artists like Grimes performed concerts on the platform.

Similarly, in 2019 Marshmello held a concert in *Fortnite*, a battle royale video game that drew 10 million fans, making it Epic Games' largest event. But what caught our attention was Axie Infinity, a video game that allows players to earn a living by playing the game. This is because the game is based on NFTs and has an in-game economy based on Ethereum.

Market Capitalization of the Metaverse, Facebook and Gaming Worldwide as of October 2021 (in Trillion U.S. Dollars)

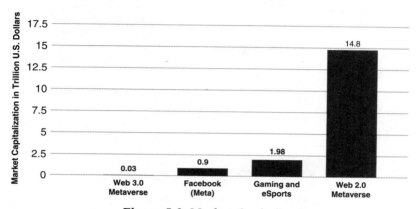

Figure 5.3 Market Capitalization
Source: CoinGecko; Adapted from Bloomberg; MSIV; Roundhill Investments.
© Statista 2022.

In Axie Infinity, players collect and mint NFTs of digital pets called "Axies." Axies can be bred, used to battle each other, and traded on a marketplace using cryptocurrency. "Bosses" loan Axies to players, who grind the game in exchange for a wage.

These types of play-to-earn games have existed on the periphery for a while now. Still, projects like Axie Infinity demonstrate that the opportunity for more mainstream adoption– and for humans to explore engaging and remunerative activities – has arrived. As seen in Figure 5.4, in a 2021 survey of global Internet users, people ranked overcoming obstacles that they were prevented from doing in real life as the biggest benefit of the metaverse. They ranked enhancing imagination and creativity second, and identified the importance of the metaverse for upskilling, education, and exploring new career opportunities.

There are already many ways that people are considering using the metaverse, as illustrated in Figure 5.4, and this market will grow exponentially in the coming years. Citi's 2022 "Metaverse and Money" research report estimates that the metaverse economy could be in the range of $8 trillion to $13 trillion by 2030, with the creator economy driving larger-scale adoptions by fans.[2]

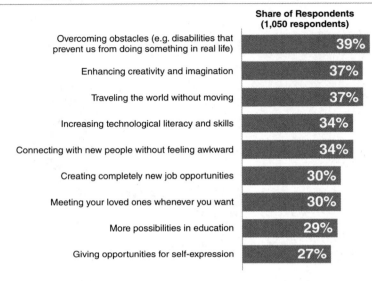

Figure 5.4 Benefits of Metaverse Worldwide, 2021
Source: Tido © Statista 2022.

Web 3.0

We'll take this back to reality now and close this section out with a conversation about Web 3.0. Web 3.0 is a buzzword that is often heard and even more often misunderstood. We'll start by saying that Web 3.0 is a moniker to attempt to describe the next evolution of the World Wide Web. Roughly speaking, "Web1" was the early Internet and mostly consisted of static websites. This period was from the early 1990s through about 2004. This was a period primarily of consumer engagement. The Web evolved into what we can call the "Web2" period, which began around 2004 and continues today. We might consider the Web2 period as the period of big business consolidation and, importantly, one in which consumers simply gave up their data freely to conglomerates in the service of convenience.

Let's consider Amazon, Meta (Facebook), and Google, just to start. Amazon is basically *the* place to go online if you want to buy something. As a by-product of this, Amazon knows a whole lot about your buying habits – something that would not necessarily be possible if you went to smaller storefronts that didn't talk to each other. Similarly, Meta knows your friends, your hobbies, your political interests, your favorite animal, and, well, far too much about you. Google does as well, primarily from searching, but also consider that for those who use Google cloud, *all of your data* is in their hands. This data, anonymized or not, can be used to create powerful profiles of who you are, your interests, and can even be used to predict behavior. We give this information up for convenience and, for the most part, since Facebook and Google are ostensibly "free," why not? Well, Warren Buffett has been known to say, "If you've been playing poker for half an hour and you don't know who the patsy is, you're the patsy." Similarly, if we're not paying for the service, then we, indeed, are the product.

The price we pay for this convenience is freedom. Our digital footprints are managed and monitored by a few, and this information can be used for the benefit of the corporation, and not necessarily for our own best interests. It can be crunched, processed, and utilized specifically to drive corporate profits, often with little consideration of our own personal needs.

Here's where this gets really troublesome. I listened to an excellent podcast some years ago that had Dr. Pippa Malmgren speak on this topic of big data, and her example stuck with me. Let's say a couple is going to get a divorce. To compound it, one of the partners, we'll call her Jane, is pregnant. We would argue this is private information (and, indeed, it is). Let's say, however, that Jane wants to get a home loan or some kind of credit. The credit company, however, through the use of AI and big data crunching, noticed many online searches about "divorce," as well as "baby", "birth," and "crib." This data then gets cross-referenced with a recent Amazon purchase of an actual crib and other baby furniture and it confirms that there was a subscription purchased to an online legal service specializing in divorce. The AI may come up with the conclusion that our heroine, Jane, is indeed about to have a baby and is indeed about to become divorced.

Here's the problem: What happens if this information is then used to conclude that Jane is a higher credit risk, may have additional financial burdens, and then, ultimately, this conclusion is used by the lending company to deny Jane's loan? What if it's used by a potential employer and factors her into not getting a job because she might be taking maternity leave and it was concluded that, as a new mother, she would not be able to function as productively, as she would be distracted? This may seem far-fetched, but this kind of social profiling happens more and more every day.

The impact of this is already being seen in China, where a "Social Credit" system launched in 2014 ranks every person on "trustworthiness" and, in turn, may put them on a blacklist.[3] Blacklisted individuals may be denied travel by plane or train, the ability to vote, attend certain schools, or rent vehicles, or even deny the ability get fast Internet. All of this is, of course, in the name of creating a more "trustworthy" system, but it's really just big data being crunched to force social compliance according to the desires of a central party. All of this is possible because of the vast amounts of data given freely to centralized entities who then share that data for profit.

Web 3.0, a term coined by Gavin Wood in 2014, proposes the opposite of this system. Instead, it's a World Wide Web that is built incorporating blockchain technologies and is, in essence, *decentralized*, with all of the advantages therein.

One of the best ways to consider Web 3.0 is as a decentralized Internet, where all parties get to interact but where data is owned and shared at the individual level, peer to peer. We need only to look to artists for an example of how this could play out. Right now, plenty of entrepreneurs – artists, writers, musicians, and content creators, among many others – make a living using various digital platforms. The rise of Web 3.0 can make this infinitely easier to do. Cryptocurrencies, blockchains, smart contracts, and NFTs will provide these entrepreneurs with the tools they need for security, privacy, independence, and stability. In the music industry, for example, not only do artists battle with music labels over rights, but they also face piracy. Musicians currently might only see payments of less than $0.05 per stream on platforms like Spotify, Amazon Music, and YouTube Music, but if they issue an NFT for their music then every time someone plays that song the artist can automatically get paid without relying on a middleman. What's more, unearthing new revenue streams is a real possibility with Web 3.0, and companies are cropping up that aim to aid creators.

In Web 3.0 no central conglomerate has all the data, and no central conglomerate approves transactions. Instead, peers interact, creating trusted transactions with the agreement of other peers in the community. As a quick reminder, this is exactly how blockchains are designed to work. We learned earlier that when Sally sends a bitcoin to John, this transaction is observed by a computer in the Bitcoin network (a miner). Once a majority of the miners agree that the transaction is legitimate, the transaction is confirmed and written permanently on a new block, of which all miners have a copy. No central bank, central authority, game, business, or agency has to approve this and, importantly, no central bank, authority, game, business, or agency gets *paid* to ensure that transactions occur. Everyone who uses the Bitcoin blockchain can control their own coin and where it resides, and if it is in a wallet to which only you have the keys, no one can take that bitcoin without your consent.

Consider then, that Web 3.0 is the extension of this, *not* just for the exchange of money, but for the exchange of all data. This ushers us into the realm of sovereign data, which is data that each user owns and controls. We're early in this concept right now and we'll explore what the future of sovereign data might look like in Chapter 24; however, for now just consider what the world would look like if you controlled your data, you decided whom to share it with, and then how much to share. This would turn the world on its head and shift power away from the Googles of the world and back into the hands of the autonomous individual.

Overall, Web 3.0 is amping up to be the next hub of the creator economy. The reaction to data misusage is strong, and controversial revenue streams are pushing creatives to jump ship from legacy platforms and notice the benefits of Web 3.0. The legacy Internet forces creators to create content that accumulates social engagement, but with costs. In contrast, Web 3.0 will arm creators to produce content they can own and monetize. With it, the future of the creator economy is looking ever brighter.

PART II
DEBUNKING MYTHS

Part Two is dedicated to debunking common myths and misconceptions about crypto. During any new technological revolution, a period where a cluster of new innovations drives a new long-wave economic cycle, there are always some of the same types of observations and myths. We both remember, during the early adoption phase of the Internet Age, pundits who remarked that the Internet was just used for theft or crime or porn. Or people who said that there is no real functionality or application that would ever hit the mainstream. During the early days of the Internet, "the establishment" was noted for saying that the Internet was only used for games by nerds. Well, we all know how the Internet turned out. We argue the same thing is happening right now in the world of blockchain and crypto. Real vision is rare. People need to step back and consider that it takes decades for true innovation to get developed, built, and distributed globally.

Mobile phones back in the late 1990s were weak, but entrepreneurs could envision a world where everyone would have PCS (personal communication services) devices, a.k.a. smartphones, that would enable movies to be piped over the Internet to directly to the device. Music could be enjoyed on the device. Users could access the web through this PCS device, allowing anything that was done on a computer to be done on a mobile device. PCS devices obviously were the pre-vision of smartphones. The first hardware that brought this type of functionality to market was Nokia and BlackBerry. But it took a decade for Apple to come out with the iPod and then the iPhone. It was that product that really brought the original vision of a PCS device to the market and by 2007–2008, just about everyone had a mobile device on their person, and was accessing the web, playing music, and using their phone in a way originally envisioned in that notion of a PCS device a decade earlier. It takes time.

While we wait in those early years, it's the vacuum of real products that makes way for myths that weave stories of concern or fear – stories that misrepresent what's really possible with innovation.

It happened in the early days of the Internet, and this time around is no different. With crypto and blockchain, the stories and articles that get the most "clicks" are stories of fear and concern about how crypto is bad for X, Y, and Z. Those of us in the crypto industry have a term for it: FUD. People spouting stories with fear, uncertainty, and doubt. FUD articles hit the mainstream far more than articles about the innovation and the groundbreaking products and services that are getting built. The average person is far more likely to read an article about how bad crypto is for the environment or how much money has been stolen using crypto than to read a story about how new services using blockchain technology can revolutionize how we do business, or articles that explain what the technological innovation actually is and what we can do now that we previously couldn't.

In this section, we aim to address some of those myths and provide a compelling counterpoint to consider. Sometimes – actually, most times – with technological innovation that's early in its adoption cycle, things may not be what they seem at first blush.

6

Myth – Regulation Will Kill Crypto

The crypto winter only intensified the buzz about the popular myth that the U.S. government will regulate crypto out of existence (therefore, there's no point in investing in it). We strongly disagree. We've already seen signals from the Commodities Futures Trading Commission (CFTC), the Internal Revenue Service (IRS), the Securities and Exchange Commission (SEC), Congress, and the White House that, while regulation is coming, it's not intended to strangle crypto in any way. In fact, it's the opposite. Policymakers want crypto to thrive. To do that, they want to curb excesses and ensure more transparency.

Chair Gary Gensler at the SEC can sound like a regulatory hawk, but as legislation has moved forward, he and the SEC emphasized early cooperation far more than excessive enforcement. The crypto industry broadly supports the two major bills likely in some form to become law.

So far, the SEC has cracked down on fraud, as it should, but the SEC fundamentally wants crypto entities and assets that act like securities to have some rules. For Gensler, if a token barks like a security, walks like a security, and talks like a security, it's a security. As of this writing, we're confident of a strong bipartisan law and new funding for the CFTC to handle its new legislative assignments. The parties on Capitol Hill, the White House, and the agencies want a steady, progressive, regulatory structure. It's essential to know the fundamental conflicts inherent in this transition.

But we'd like to wave a little bit of caution here. Regulation too fast, too hard can kill innovation. Just look back at the Red Flag Act of 1865. During the oil and automobile revolution, the UK government came out with legislation that required every car to have at least one person walking in front of the automobile to have red flags out to let people know that a car was coming. The intent was safety. However, the knock-on effects were disastrous. That legislation killed the automobile revolution in the UK. Let's not let history repeat itself here in the United States, where it appears we're doing everything we can to kill innovation.

You'll want to note that by the end of 2022, only three of the top 15 blockchain protocols are headquartered in the United States, whereas during the Internet Age 10 of the top 15 Internet companies were headquartered here.[1]

Investing is about making good bets. Good bets require knowing the odds, and knowing the odds requires having reliable information. If you bet on an NFL game, we suspect you know who is starting at quarterback, who is injured, what the team's record is, and a plethora of transparent stats. The legendary futures trader Larry Hite observed, "There are just four kinds of bets. There are good bets, bad bets, bets that you win, and bets that you lose. Winning a bad bet can be the most dangerous outcome of all because a success of that kind can encourage you to take more bad bets in the future when the odds will be running against you. You can also lose a good bet no matter how sound the underlying proposition, but if you keep placing good bets, over time, the law of averages will be working for you."[2]

The Sticking Point

Part of the difficulty with regulating crypto assets is that they can evolve. There are times in the lifecycle of a crypto asset when it acts more like security and others when it acts more like a commodity or even something else altogether. Because of this, there is confusion about what body has the jurisdiction to regulate it. Our greatest concern is that some regulatory bodies here in the United States may become short-sighted and damage the chance innovation has to benefit our society and our economy. And frankly, if we get regulation wrong here, the innovation will simply go to wherever in the world it's treated best.

Regulating too expansively would be like regulating the Internet before we understood how online commerce would function in the world. That would have been bad, indeed. Ideally, regulation will be strong enough to protect investors from fraud but not so strict that it will stifle entrepreneurship, innovation, and investment. Moreover, good crypto regulation should reflect U.S. values, including privacy, security, freedom, and sovereignty. If we leave it up to other countries, such as China, we could be tied to a system built on entirely different values – tracking, surveillance, central authority, and lack of public transparency.

Like the Internet in the early 1990s, the crypto sector is still in its infancy. We don't know what a flash-in-the-pan will be (Google Reader, anyone?) or what will become fundamental to our lives, like social media or the iPhone. In the early days of the Internet, Congress could not have predicted the role that personal data mining and political disinformation would play, much less how to protect consumers against them. At the time, the industry was pushing for an open Internet, where anyone could create a web page.

As it turns out, it may be that both the SEC and the CFTC are correct: there are times in the lifecycle of a crypto asset when it is more like a security and others when it is more like a commodity. There are also times when it may act like something else altogether. Because of this, there is confusion as to what body has the jurisdiction to regulate it. This is a critical issue being wrangled over by Congress, the White House, and the industry. Another complicating factor: many people are under the impression that crypto assets are all the same, but this is incorrect. Several distinct classes and models range from cryptocurrencies to utility tokens to governance tokens. We have a detailed exploration of each asset class in our book *Crypto Asset Investing in the Age of Autonomy*; suffice it to say for this book that each comes with unique risks, governance, purpose of use, ways of accruing value, and roles in the larger ecosystem. Cryptocurrencies were designed to be a store of value and a medium of exchange. An investor can buy them, sell them, purchase things with them, and lend them out to generate yield through an interest rate like sovereign currencies. In contrast, governance tokens (discussed more fully in Chapter 17) give the holder the right to vote on managing, upgrading, and governing a crypto network. Regulators need to recognize this complexity and tailor new rules to the distinct types of crypto assets.

Indeed, we support the idea of "temporality" that the SEC has considered: that an asset can begin as a security and change into a commodity over time. Tokens from an initial coin offering (ICO) where the builder is looking for an up-front investment are securities. Once the crypto network is built and is sufficiently decentralized, the assets become commodities.

Crypto Classification: Security versus Commodity

So then, let's unseal this whole "Is crypto more like a stock or a pork belly?" debate and figure out where we are as regulation is coming into view.

In 2017, many in the market started to declare the idea of a utility token and to distinguish it from a security token. A security token represents a tokenized version of a financial security. You can think of real estate or equities that are tokenized assets as security tokens. In contrast, a utility token is a token used to power a blockchain network — to provide "use." Many protocol coins and tokens use a utility token to transact on their network. Ethereum and Solana are examples of blockchains that use utility tokens. In this case, in order to complete a transaction on each of these respective networks, you need to use a little bit of their respective tokens, ETH and SOL.

Howey Test

The basic framework used to determine whether something is a security or not is called the Howey Test, which refers to a court case between the SEC and the W. J. Howey Company. It consists of three questions:

1. Is there an investment of money with the expectation of future profits?
2. Is the investment of money in a common enterprise?
3. Do any profits come from the efforts of a promoter or third party?

Securities produce a return to a common enterprise, which we say is a central organization. It's ownership in the enterprise's capital structure, whether equity or debt. The spirit of the law is to capture an agreement: "I'll give you some money for a percentage of the potential profit the enterprise generates."

That is not what's happening with most crypto utility tokens. They are not generating a return that is then divided by the owners via dividends or share repurchase. Although some tokens do split returns generated from fees, most expectations of future returns are generated by scarcity of supply and demand. There may be an expectation of profit, but that's where it gets tricky, because that's not inherent in their design.

Consider Similar Analog Assets

We can point to plenty of assets people buy with this expectation of a return. Most of them revolve around scarcity of the asset playing into a tight market of supply and demand. While not necessarily understood by all investors, this is a key factor to generating profit with crypto assets. It's much clearer to see in the analog world, where rare and scarce items often demand a pretty penny. Examples include:

- Numismatic (rare, collectable) coins
- Precious metals
- Collectibles
- Concert tickets
- Rare art

None of these assets, are considered to be securities, yet they accrue in value. It's really important that you understand this distinction. Scarcity drives value, and not everything that grows in value is a security. All three factors of the Howey Test need to be considered collectively.

Commodities – Looking at "the What"

Commodities are goods, property, or assets that can be bought or sold on an exchange, typically raw materials or agricultural products. They don't produce a return from a common enterprise, they are goods or property that are mined or grown, and their intrinsic value is based on market supply and demand. This is what distinguishes commodities from securities. Commodities aren't characterized by their fundamental nature but by prices and availability. Milk is a commodity. So is oil, lumber, corn, and raw coffee. Commodities of the same grade are fungible, meaning they can be swapped with each other, no matter who produced, mined, or farmed them. So a coffee broker buying "specialty grade" green coffee beans from two different growers in Hawaii isn't concerned for the most part with the grower but with the quality and purity of the beans.

As with other commodities, bitcoin can be traded on the futures market overseen by the CFTC through exchanges, including the Chicago Board of Trade and the New York Mercantile Exchange. Through these exchanges, traders close a deal on when a trade will happen, agreeing on a fixed price and future delivery date for the goods being traded. On that date, the commodity is sold, and money exchanges hands. The price at that time is the one in the contract, no matter what the current price of the commodity on the open market is.

The Punchline

At the end of the day, this all boils down to one thing. Regulators are getting their hands around this in a way to promote crypto, not kill it. The EU has taken bit steps with their 2022 Markets in Crypto Assets (MiCA) law, which is groundbreaking. As of this writing, all language has been agreed upon and overwhelmingly accepted by a vote of 28–1. The law is expected to go into effect in 2024 and provides regulatory clarity and guidance regarding consumer protection, money laundering, and stablecoins. One highlight regarding stablecoins is that the EU wants to promote euro-backed stablecoins and limit the use of U.S. dollar–backed stablecoins. They are now looking ahead and getting ahead of the digital asset wave that is on the horizon. The United States should take note for a couple of reasons, notably that this points to a world that may be less and less dollar-based in the future.

Regulation like this provides clarity, and clarity will promote adoption. We're already seeing big players like BlackRock partner with Coinbase in anticipation of regulatory clarity. From our view, this clarity will facilitate growth and does not hamper it.

7

Myth – Crypto Is a Bubble

Yes, during the crypto winter of 2022, all markets took a beating, and crypto took a serious beating. In June, bitcoin was down approximately −55% year to date (YTD) and the widespread crypto markets were down roughly −70% YTD. There was a ridiculous amount of fear in the markets; much of it came from centralized finance companies like Celsius blowing up, along with actions the Federal Reserve was taking to unwind previous actions they'd taken during the pandemic to boost the economy.

Many investors acted out of fear. We were coming out of a pandemic. Interest rates were rising notably, with the Fed hiking rates by three-quarters of a percentage point in June, then again in July, again in September, and an additional three-quarters of a point in November. In summer 2022 the Fed laid out its agenda of pain, which eliminated uncertainty. "In a further sign of the Fed's deepening concern about inflation," the Associated Press reported, "it will also likely signal that it plans to raise rates much higher by year's end than it had forecast three months ago – and to keep them higher for a longer period. Economists expect Fed officials to forecast that their key rate could go as high as 4% by the end of this year. They're also likely to signal additional increases in 2023, perhaps to as high as roughly 4.5%."[1]

Federal Funds Effective Rate

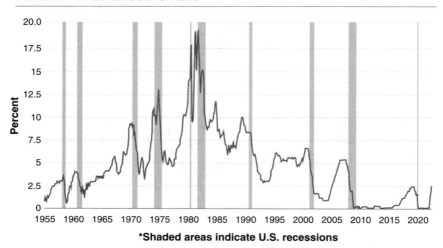

Shaded areas indicate U.S. recessions

Figure 7.1 Fed Funds Rate
Source: Board of Governors of the Federal Reserve System (U.S.).
Additional information: fred.stlouisfed.org.

During the summer of 2022, inflation was at a 40-year high. Many believed a recession was imminent. It was a scary time if you were long on crypto because there is so much volatility in its trading. Unless, perhaps, as we said at the time, you've lived through this before (see Figure 7.1).

In 2014 and again in 2018, we saw the market pull back in similar trends, with bitcoin being 70% and 80% off its all-time high before rocketing to 1,200% and 1,800% gains, respectively. We've seen this pattern. It's a cycle! We were at the exact same kind of bottom. Market conditions were unusual but that didn't change the fact that for those who want massive gains, well, bottoms are the best time to deploy.

These trends did provide investors with generational buys on select assets, opportunities that may never happen again, and, although this manuscript was sent off to the editor before the upswing, we fully anticipate it, just like in other cycles. While 2022 reminded us that crypto hype and volatility can be excessive, that doesn't mean crypto is, by default, a bubble. It's a new technology that will be valuable for endless purposes. It means smart investors look for the signals in the noise. Our philosophy is based on our belief in technology and the norms of functioning markets – that they experience cycles.

Carlota Perez offers essential insights in her book, *Technological Revolutions and Financial Capital: The Dynamics of Bubbles and Golden*

Ages. Going back hundreds of years, she shows how any technological revolution will go through a bubble or mania phase. It's happened five times in the past 200 years, from the Age of Industrialization through the Age of Information.

We are at the beginning of a new crypto economy. As the technology evolves, we will see more use cases emerge. We can remember how during the Internet Age in 1995, early adopters of home computers, many who had Internet connections to AOL (AmericaOnline!) and the Internet, were talking about how these technologies were going to revolutionize communications. I remember being excited myself, running around to local businesses in Austin to try and sign them up to build websites. I would tell them that anyone would be able to find out about their product or service and they could have a website explaining and presenting their business online. They would ask me, "Great, how's anyone going to find me?," and I didn't have a good answer. Why? Because search engines hadn't been widely adopted yet, so few knew how to go to a search engine (remember, this was eight years before Google was widely used, in 2003) and look up whatever they wanted to search!

So, the sale of new websites kind of died right there when I couldn't answer that simple question of "how are they going to find me?" It's similar now in the Age of Autonomy®. We've got a lot of early adopters running around saying how great crypto and blockchain are, but we don't have all the basic tools built yet to make wide adoption easier and more compelling. We still need to build the "search engines" for crypto.

Spring Follows Winter

Who doesn't enjoy a beautiful summer's day on our favorite beach or lake, wearing short sleeves and sipping a cold drink? And when we have a portfolio of assets, we love when they're hot and the arrows are trending up. Crypto is fun; like any other investment, when the markets are roaring, the fanfare is loud and pronounced. When crypto is cold and in a deep downturn, the naysayers and skeptics emerge.

There's an adage, "Buy low; sell high." Well, we know crypto prices crash really, really low during crypto winters. It's difficult to compete with human psychology, however, and when things are down, we are in a state of fear. What if it goes lower? It could certainly go lower, just as we had a falling knife in March 2020, but trying to catch the bottom of a bottom can be as challenging as trying to catch the top of a top. Timing the market is a fool's errand, so it's worth looking to see if value is present. We see an upside for 2023 and beyond, with crypto markets down approximately 85% of all-time highs as of this writing in September 2022. A quote from Warren Buffett, the famed investor, comes to mind: "When people are fearful, be greedy. When people are greedy, be fearful." According to Mr. Buffett, this would undoubtedly be a good time for greed.

We are here to provide perspective, particularly as it relates to the crypto markets, and to shed some light on why the top investors in the world remain bullish on crypto. Quoting Paul Tudor Jones, "It's hard not to want to be long crypto."

Do You Believe in Technology?

During 2022, many commented about the strength of our convictions in crypto. What we said then is what we continue to affirm. We're crypto bulls in both balmy summer and ice-cold winter. My fellow investors, the question is not "Will crypto go up?," the question is "Do I believe in blockchain? Do I believe in the technology?" If the answer is yes, the first question is best restated as "When will crypto go up?" Blockchain is a technology play.

Institutional and financial players continue to lean into blockchain and crypto investments and haven't backed away. In fact, early big-bank naysayers are now scrambling to get their blockchain strategies in order. This is because it's now a given that this technology is here to stay. Paradigm-shattering technologies are rare, but they exert their influences in diverse, unpredictable, and frankly thrilling ways when they arrive.

We can look back to the last long-wave economic cycle, during the Information Age, when the Internet was invented in 1969. It was called Arpanet back then and originally consisted of just four nodes (i.e., computer servers networked together). For decades, it was primarily a product of academia with some repurposing by the government, then by large online companies for the first retail use cases (CompuServe, anyone?). It wasn't until 1994, when Marc Andreessen and James Clark founded Netscape, that the Internet began to take off. That was due to the World Wide Web – the information superhighway, as it were. It's the reason web addresses started with "www." It was the first web browser, Netscape Navigator, that allowed everyone to "go online" and opened the door to the Internet as a technology for the masses that everyone could access and benefit from.

On that timeline, it took 25 years from its inception for the Internet to gain any kind of real accessibility, and another five before it became usable. It was then another 12 or so before we started to see the first instance of smartphones, which have made us all quasi-cyborgs. In the Netscape era, we were just figuring this Internet thing out. Businesses were formed. Some survived (Amazon), and some collapsed spectacularly (AltaVista, Pets.com), but, as history unfolded, it was the technology that carried the day.

At the same time in 1995, just as the Internet was gaining traction with a paltry 16 million users, opinions were everywhere, one famously stating that the Internet was a fad and would not make it past 1996. (I'll just let that sit and pause for a moment for dramatic impact ... Okay, good.) There was even a famous *Daily Mail* article on December 5, 2000, that was titled, "Internet 'may be a passing fad as millions give up on it.'" Yes, that article was published in 2000!

We're way past the fad point with blockchain and crypto. Companies will come, and companies will go. During this crypto winter, Luna took a spectacular belly flop, Celsius filed for bankruptcy, and BlockFi stock investors got wiped out and FTX bought it to save it (and get a great deal), then promptly imploded a few months later. Three Arrows Capital, one of the top five largest crypto hedge funds at the time, managing $10 billion, shuttered. Many rich people lost money. Many smart people lost money.

That's what happens in growing markets during a new technology adoption cycle. Not every business is going to succeed. In fact, most don't. Indeed, not every company will be Amazon, and it took Amazon nine years to make any kind of profit at all, with plenty of naysayers along the way.

Any new technology adoption is rife with challenges. So, when we talk about crypto, we're talking about technology. From an investor standpoint, it is a technology investment. Blockchain, having solved one of the top 10 computer science problems of all time, the Byzantine Generals Problem, allows us to transact in a peer-to-peer way without a central authority. This impact cannot be measured now, just as it would have been impossible back in 1994 to imagine the effects of smartphones and how they would shape our lives. If you're not clear on what the Byzantine Generals Problem is, you're not alone. This is *the* breakthrough and one that we will discuss completely in Chapter 12.

Blockchain is not going away. As one more data point, college campuses, such as the one at University of Texas at Austin, are now combining their computer science and blockchain programs. This sends a clear message not only about the relevance and projected future of blockchain, but also where the talent will be focused in the coming years.

Of Course It's a Cycle!

Which brings us to the fear part of our program. During 2022, we saw bitcoin dip as much as 70% from all-time highs. This was as bad as it was in 2014 before it then soared 1,200%. It was about as bad as it was in 2018 — before it then rocketed 1,800%. Dips represent the time where deployed capital has an opportunity to enjoy significant upside gain. How much?

Well, many experts still predict $100,000 bitcoin (or more). According to them, it's not an *if*, it's a *when*. We argue that select crypto assets representing solid technology projects will outpace that. Importantly, cycles have been pretty consistent, and we see nothing that points to this cycle changing. We even see greater support for a strong recovery as we have giant banks, government, credit cards, and businesses of all types all jumping into the crypto fray. Yes, the macro environment must get cleaned up — and it will. Yes, we're going to have businesses rise and fall. But this is why investments in this industry are measured in years, not months.

The events of 2022 remind us that crypto is a longer-term play, and we expect such cycles to repeat again. Don't play this game if you need a return in two months. Don't get in if you want a return in nine months. However, if you believe in the technology and understand these cycles, then you know that down cycles represent the best time to get in and, if you are in, also a great time to double down.

Centralized Crypto Exchange Celsius Melts Down

One of the reasons crypto took a huge hit in 2022 is Celsius, a centralized company that allowed individuals to earn interest on deposited collateral and take collateralized loans against their crypto. They were a market giant. As a quick synopsis, Celsius Network LLC had over $8 billion lent out to clients and $12 billion in assets under management as of May 2022. However, in a surprising announcement, on June 12, the firm stopped all withdrawals from its platform, citing "extreme market conditions." In July Celsius filed for bankruptcy.

That's bad news. When people can't get their money, it's terrible news. (We saw the writing on the wall, and our fund had no exposure to Celsius when it halted funds. Unfortunately, not everyone had this foresight.) The company, it seems, was overleveraged, and didn't have the capital to honor its obligations.

The Department of Justice, state regulators, and advocates for unsecured creditors (customers who aren't getting their money back) have been accumulating damning evidence against Celsius. According to *PC Gamer* reporting and court documents, "To put it mildly, the regulators don't like what they see. The Vermont Department of Financial Regulation has now filed against the firm in New York, and the state regulator is 'especially concerned about losses suffered by retail investors; for example, middle-class, unaccredited investors who may have invested entire college funds or retirement accounts with Celsius.' Vermont state prosecutors support the DOJ's request for a legal Examiner to protect such interests." According to the bankruptcy court filing, "This shows a high level of financial mismanagement and suggests that at least at some point in time, yields to existing investors were probably being paid with the assets of new investors."

Celsius apparently experienced losses of $454,074,042 between May 2, 2022, and May 12, 2022. "This $450 million loss in 10 days meant depositor funds were not safe, but Mashinsky and Celsius continued to pretend they were financially healthy," *PC Gamer* reports. In other words, they were running a Ponzi scheme.[2]

We deplore Celsius's mismanagement and misleading statements. Indeed, continued spin by the now-former CEO and others that Celsius will make a comeback sure sounds like whistling by the graveyard. With the DOJ and regulators involved, there's a chance that Celsius will release some funds to its customers. We have dear friends who have money locked and we understand how this meltdown really impacts people. However, as more facts are uncovered, it is becoming clear that what happened with Celsius isn't so much about the nature of *crypto* market investing as it is about ambitious founders/executives misleading investors and regulators. This is a centralized business that failed. In the crypto investing sphere, as in other financial sectors, be careful of firms that make a marketing promise that proves impossible to sustain, such as "deposit your digital assets and receive interest as high as 18 percent."[3]

This is crypto's too-good-to-be-true cautionary tale; what's more, not every business operating in a new technological field succeeds. Businesses come and businesses go. Some succeed, and some fail. This does not inherently mean that blockchain and crypto lending institutions are bad, any more than AltaVista's failure meant that search engines are bad. What is important to note at this point is that, while Celsius imploded, DeFi contracts kept chugging right along. It turns out that Celsius's implosion is actually a case for crypto.

Professor Krugman Is (Still) Wrong

We have tracked the columns of *New York Times* columnist Paul Krugman, who has made several passionate attacks on crypto. He's a famous economist and won the Nobel Prize in Economics. He's also best known for being the guy who said, "the Internet's Effect on the World Economy Would Be 'No Greater Than the Fax Machine's'" in 1998. We're just going to let that statement sit for a moment to sink in. We assert that his views on crypto, equally passionate, are also equally wrong.

In a January 10, 2022, op-ed, he wrote, "I've been in many meetings in which crypto skeptics ask, as respectfully as they can, for simple examples of things you can do better or more cheaply with cryptocurrency than via other forms of payment. I still haven't heard a clear example that didn't involve illegal activity – which may, to be fair, be easier to hide if you use crypto."

In July 2022, Professor Krugman filed the inevitable gloating installment of his crusade in which he attempts to spike the ball after crypto's downturn, repeating variations of the failed arguments in the January piece. One of those is that crypto doesn't have uses in the "real" economy, even as he cites examples (Venmo) of how crypto is used in household name financial tools:

> My answer is that while the crypto industry has never managed to come up with products that are much use in the real economy, it has been spectacularly successful at marketing itself, creating an image of being both cutting edge and respectable. It has done so, in particular, by cultivating prominent people and institutions.

Suppose, for example, that you use a digital payments app like Venmo, which has amply demonstrated its usefulness for real-world transactions (you can even use it to buy produce at sidewalk fruit stands). Well, if you go to Venmo's home page, you encounter an invitation to use the app to "begin your crypto journey"; in the app itself, a "Crypto" tab appears right after "Home" and "Cards."

First, there is the unintentional irony of Professor Krugman's point. The characteristics of Venmo he praises are true and will be true of crypto with no intermediary taking a fee. Second, he doesn't cite any research or knowledge that would indicate that Venmo (and by extension all the "prominent people and institutions") thinks crypto sucks and promotes it solely for the money.

This is also a lazy argument. Is he saying that, since he's been in meetings where no one could come up with a cryptocurrency use case that wasn't criminal, there isn't one? This is ludicrous. It's clear that Professor Krugman's not attending the right meetings. Here are three things you can do better with bitcoin and other cryptocurrencies:

1. Send money online 24/7 without waiting for or paying a middleman like a bank or payment processor. According to Coinbase, sending bitcoin is typically 60 times more cost-effective and up to 48 times faster than an international wire transfer.
2. Gain access to banking, investing, savings, loans, and other financial services no matter where you live. All you need is a smartphone.
3. Store value in a place that is not subject to the vicissitudes of local currencies and governmental monetary policy.

Professor Krugman makes a common logical mistake, that of *modus ponens* — affirming the consequent. For example, if I say, "Jim likes pizza; Susie doesn't like pizza; therefore, Susie doesn't like Jim," I would have made the same logical fallacy. While I can't prove my argument by invalidating Krugman's, I can prove that Krugman's argument is invalid. Just because Bitcoin can be used for harmful or illegal activity doesn't mean it is illegal or bad. It's just a tool. So are guns, knives, and hundred-dollar bills. They are used for unlawful activity all the time, but you don't hear people running around saying a hundred-dollar bill is bad or illegal, do you?

We also find Krugman's political analysis unfounded. He sees the seeds of right-wing extremism. He asserts in his January 31 opinion, ". . . Bitcoin plays into a fantasy of self-sufficient individualism, of protecting your family with your personal AR-15, treating your Covid with an anti-parasite drug or urine [usatoday.com] and managing your financial affairs with privately created money, untainted by institutions like governments or banks."

That's like saying that seditious extremists used private messaging services like Signal and Telegram to attack the U.S. capital, so therefore, private messaging apps are dangerous or bad. Signal and Telegram both allow users to encrypt communications to protect the data from being analyzed by third parties, including law enforcement. Does this technology help criminals? Sure. Does it also serve people with noncriminal intent? Yes. Like bitcoin – a hammer or a hundred-dollar bill – it's simply a tool. There is no agenda.

In July, Krugman slammed crypto's appeal as being due to "a combination of technobabble and libertarian derp," which must be news to Paul Tudor Jones, Starbucks, BlackRock, McKinsey, Goldman Sachs, and other globally significant investors and institutions that have invested heavily in blockchain and crypto.

In a January 27th opinion, Krugman conjures another boogie man: subprime mortgages. In this essay he asserts that, like people who signed up for subprime mortgages, individual crypto investors are being lured into a risky financial scheme they don't understand. "It turned out, however, that many borrowers didn't understand what they were getting into. Ned Gramlich, a Federal Reserve official who famously warned in vain about the growing financial dangers, asked [kansascityfed.org], 'Why are the riskiest loan products sold to the least sophisticated borrowers?'" He then declared, "The question answers itself."[4]

We don't think the question "answers itself." While we agree that there are plenty of fraudulent crypto schemes, and the market is extremely volatile, there's no logical comparison between a mortgage instrument designed to induce people to take on loans they can't afford and a new technology that could be used for an endless array of purposes. *Seriously* – what else can you use a subprime mortgage for?

Krugman proved his opinions quite wrong during the Age of Information and it looks like he's continuing that error in true form into the Age of Autonomy®. At least he is consistent.

As we've said, we advise the average individual investor (and opinion writer) to take some time to learn about the breakthrough of blockchain technology and with it, crypto assets, before jumping in, financially or rhetorically. There is an abundance of resources to get you started, this book being one, and, thanks to the unique nature of cryptocurrency (and certainly in bear markets), the price of entry is low. Unlike buying stock in Tesla, you can buy a small percentage of a bitcoin for $25, or even $1, for that matter. Start slow, stay curious, and educate yourself. There is a fascinating new world to discover for those willing to do their homework. Will you use your new crypto assets to mount a crime spree or launch a nonprofit? Well, like all things in life, that's entirely up to you.

Our Silver Lining Playbook

The Fed's hawkish policy on rates is a fact of life for investors in 2022, the time of this book's writing. The Fed announced the doubling of efforts of quantitative tightening (QT) starting in September 2022. They are raising the sales of Treasury bonds from $45 billion to $90 billion per month, thereby reducing the balance sheet at twice the initial rate to reduce the monetary supply and pulverize inflation into oblivion.

Markets don't like tightening and dislike twice the tightening twice as much. When you combine this with a strengthening dollar that is nearing all-time highs and battering other economies, it's clear that the Fed wrecking ball will tamp down growth. Our silver lining is that this is a (comparatively) short-term issue. Rates may continue to rise for a while, but we're already seeing signs of a lower CPI. Should this trend continue, we think the current tightening of the tightening may indeed be short-lived.

For years bitcoin has been touted as a hedge against inflation, but right now bitcoin (and the rest of the crypto markets) seems pretty tied to the Fed's actions. That's actually okay because, distinguished as such, this correlation can be used to one's advantage. Bitcoin is a hedge against monetary inflation, *not* consumer price inflation. Against monetary inflation, it does its job just fine. When we start to see more money printing from the Fed, we expect bitcoin will go up once again like it's done the past four times. For those who like value and understand that any crypto investment is a technology investment that will take a little time to mature, we argue that there may be no better time to buy than right now. For the contrarians, even if these markets don't go any lower, that would make this the bottom.

If you'd like another silver lining, consider the world's largest money manager – the one, the only, the titan, BlackRock. BlackRock, a firm that manages almost $5.7 trillion, announced a historic deal with Coinbase to allow their clients to trade via the Coinbase platform. This can only be the beginning of the next big step for the institutional players, and the validation here is obvious. Importantly, institutional money now being able to access these markets with a green light from their counterparties (banks, managers) is one of the harbingers of growth for which we have been waiting. Once the naysayers, the banks are now beating the drum. It is a glorious sound.

The Amazing Merge

Another big silver lining in 2022 is what the crypto world took to calling "The Merge," involving the king of smart contract platforms, Ethereum. Ethereum has market share and is the dominant chain, but it's (generally) slow, expensive, and doesn't scale well. Ethereum currently processes about 13 transactions a second, which is a woefully inadequate number considering that there are over one million transactions a day demanding attention on the chain. The Merge intends to solve this problem by setting the stage for future enhancements by moving to a new consensus mechanism.

Consensus is the process of all the nodes on a blockchain agreeing that a transaction is valid. Bitcoin and currently Ethereum use a proof-of-work (PoW) consensus mechanism, which, as we discussed in the previous chapter, means that there is a network of machines (miners) that have to spend a lot of computational processing power (energy) to confirm transactions.

Ethereum's proposed new consensus mechanism is called proof-of-stake (PoS), which, again simplified, has each computer running on the network (validators) pledging a certain amount of Ethereum (staking), which gives them the right to participate in the confirmation of transactions. This new methodology will be vastly more energy efficient. Some speculate that it will reduce the carbon footprint by as much as 95%. This efficiency opens the door for the next steps. It will *not* immediately impact the transaction fees and speed, but this new consensus mechanism will set the stage for sharding, which is processing transactions off-chain in a faster manner, as well as other enhancements.

The Merge is one of the seminal events in the world of blockchain technology and should fulfill its promises to reduce power consumption, set the stage for a faster and less expensive Ethereum and, importantly, create a more deflationary token. Some even think that, with its success, the Ethereum market cap will exceed that of Bitcoin.

This is yet another event that positions the technological footprint of blockchain to grow in the coming years. In the late 1990s, there was a massive battle for search engine dominance and, as we all know, Google won. This doesn't mean that there aren't other engines out there, but the fact is for the vast majority of humans, when looking for something on the web, we "Google" it. There were engines out before Google, such as AltaVista and Lycos, and, as noted, AltaVista went from market-dominating Internet darling to black sheep of the search world in a very short period of time.

Many other platforms exist that currently have this PoS consensus mechanism. They don't have the market share that Ethereum does, but better products tend to win over time, so this is a crucial juncture for Ethereum.

Watch Ethereum's price as The Merge evolves in global crypto marketplaces (see Figure 7.2).

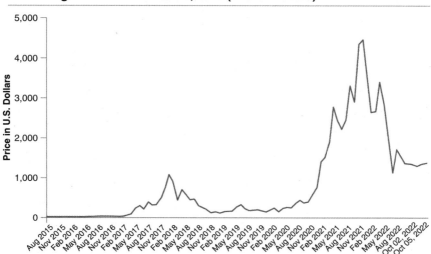

Figure 7.2 Ethereum Price per Day
Source: CoinGecko © Statista 2022.
Additional information: Worldwide; January 2019 to October 5, 2022; monthly figures are as of the end of that particular month; opening price.

For those of you looking at investing in blockchain technology (yes, I'm looking at you), this is a seminal event because it sets the stage for the landscape for years. Ethereum is set to rule the world as the premier Level 1 blockchain technology if they can successfully continue to upgrade their technology. This will allow them to not only keep market share but also address the cost/scalability dragon. The Merge was the next step to that. This puts them on the path of being like a Google to the search engine world.

The bear market hurt lots of investors and exposed some charlatans. We, and most every crypto pundit, want the bums out of our business. Focus on the technology; that's the driver of wealth and growth. What Professor Krugman and others haven't seen in the colder days of the bear market are events such as The Merge that demonstrate the resiliency and innovation of blockchain and Bitcoin.

8

Myth – Crypto Is Bad for the Environment

Like many of our colleagues in the crypto investing world, we feel strongly that our sector has the potential to lead in mitigating climate change. I understand that may sound like an oxymoron, but it's not. We absolutely believe blockchain can be a major positive factor. That's why it's frustrating to read headlines like "Bitcoin is a disaster for the planet." Slow down, cowboy. We need to agree on some basic facts before we start hardening our positions and making business and policy decisions that will determine the future of our economy and planet.

Before we point out the underreported benefits of the crypto sector for climate change, energy conservation, and emerging adaptations for energy sustainability, we won't soft-soap the facts. We're not going to underestimate the scope of the issue or the concerns about crypto assets' impact on energy use – they are real and we acknowledge that. That's where some advocates mess up. The crypto sector represents a massive transformation of the global economy and, yes, some hard issues must be addressed, which we can do within the industry and within the scientific and policy community. Bitcoin uses a lot of energy. There, we said it. Now that the not-so-genie is out of the bottle, let's explore some additional implications.

Bitcoin Energy Consumption

In order to accomplish this, we'll turn to a comprehensive and exceedingly well-crafted new federal report, "Climate and Energy Implications of Crypto-Assets in the United States." This was just released in September 2022 and written and published by the Office of Science and Technology Policy (OSTP), drawing on a wide number of interagency nonpartisan experts.[1] Some key findings:

- From 2018 to 2022, annualized electricity usage from global crypto assets multiplied, with estimates of electricity usage doubling to quadrupling. As of August 2022, published estimates of the total global electricity usage for crypto assets are between 120 and 240 billion kilowatt-hours per year, a range that exceeds the total annual electricity usage of many individual countries, such as Argentina or Australia. This is equivalent to 0.4% to 0.9% of global yearly electricity usage and is comparable to the annual electricity usage of all conventional data centers worldwide (see Figure 8.1).

- The United States is estimated to host about a third of global crypto-asset operations, which currently consume about 0.9% to 1.7% of total U.S. electricity usage. This range of electricity

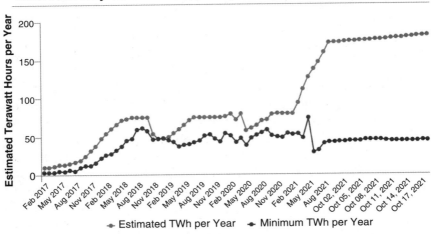

Figure 8.1 Bitcoin Energy Consumption Worldwide, 2017–2021
Source: BitcoinEnergyConsumption.com © Statista 2021.
Additional information: Worldwide; Digiconomist; February 2017–October 19, 2021.

usage is similar to all home computers or residential lighting in the United States. Crypto-asset mining is also highly mobile. The United States currently hosts the world's largest Bitcoin mining industry, totaling more than 38% of global Bitcoin activity, up from 3.5% in 2020. Despite the potential for rapid growth, future electricity demand from crypto-asset operations is uncertain, demonstrating the need for better data to understand and monitor electricity usage from crypto assets.

- The energy efficiency of mining equipment has been increasing, but electricity usage continues to rise. Other less energy-intensive crypto-asset ledger technologies exist, with different attributes and uses.

- Global electricity generation for the crypto assets with the largest market capitalizations resulted in 140 ± 30 million metric tons of carbon dioxide per year (Mt CO_2/y) or about 0.3% of global annual greenhouse gas emissions. Crypto-asset activity in the United States is estimated to result in approximately 25 to 50 Mt CO_2/y, which is 0.4% to 0.8% of total U.S. greenhouse gas emissions. This range of emissions is similar to emissions from diesel fuel used in railroads in the United States.

- Besides purchased grid electricity, crypto-asset mining operations can also cause local noise and water impacts, electronic waste, air and other pollution from any direct usage of fossil-fired electricity, and additional air, water, and waste impacts associated with all grid electricity usage. These local impacts can exacerbate environmental justice issues for neighboring communities, which are often already burdened with other pollutants, heat, traffic, or noise.

This is pretty damning stuff on its own. Having said that, let's put it in context. Yes, Bitcoin mining eats up a lot of electricity – this isn't news. According to the Cambridge Bitcoin Electricity Consumption Index, worldwide bitcoin mining uses about 105 terawatt hours of electricity per year – comparable to the consumption of the entire nation of Finland. But even that is a fraction of the energy required to run the world's traditional banking infrastructure. A 2021 report from Galaxy Digital found that the Bitcoin network consumes less than half the energy consumed by the banking or gold industries. No one barks about the energy the gold industry uses, but it's double that of Bitcoin. *Double.*

Drilling down a bit more, electricity use is not the same as measuring carbon emissions. So far, there's not a precise way to measure the source of energy bitcoin miners use – was it generated by coal plants? Or was it clean energy, like hydroelectric dams? Perhaps it was some combination of the two? The simple fact is that bitcoin miners can be located anywhere, which puts them in a good position to use so-called stranded renewables (sources of energy that otherwise go untapped). These are often the cheapest energy source out there, and some bitcoin miners are flocking to places where renewable power is abundant.

A fundamental aspect of electricity is that you can't use it unless you are located at the source of production or if there's an infrastructure in place (wires, grids, etc.) to transport it to where there's demand. That creates a dilemma for many remote wind, solar, and thermal energy operations. Depending on the weather, they produce too little or too much power to use locally, and the excess often goes to waste. Enter bitcoin miners – they can be located anywhere. And because so-called stranded renewables are usually the cheapest source of energy out there, miners are flocking to places where renewable power is abundant. It's become a new business model. Companies like Seetee exist to establish mining operations that transfer stranded electricity without stable demand locally into economic assets, like bitcoin, that can be used anywhere.

Until 2021–2022, hydropower in China and Scandinavia played a big part in keeping Bitcoin's energy consumption carbon-neutral, mainly due to the abundance of hydropower in the area. The percentage of bitcoin mining powered by renewables is anywhere from 20% to 70%, according to the Cambridge Bitcoin Electricity Consumption Index.

According to the *New York Times*, a 2022 study published in Joule by researchers from Vrije Universiteit Amsterdam, the Technical University of Munich, ETH Zurich, and the Massachusetts Institute of Technology found the Bitcoin network's use of renewable energy dropped from an average of 42% in 2020 to 25% in August 2021. China's action on hydropower-driven mining operations was the primary catalyst of this decrease. "China's crackdown on cryptocurrencies upended the world of Bitcoin last year, triggering a mass exodus of 'miners' – who use power-hungry computers to mine, or create, new bitcoins – to new locations around the world,"[2] reported Hiroko Tabuchi. But where China has pushed down, other opportunities are popping up.

In June 2021, the president of El Salvador announced that the country's state-run geothermal energy utility would begin using power derived from volcanoes for bitcoin mining. In other words, bitcoin mining will allow the country to translate local resources into global currency. The implications are mind-boggling.

The operation was underway and rolling by October 2021 at the Berlin Geothermal plant, two hours' drive east of the capital. The specialized mining machines on the site are using 1.5 megawatts of the 102 megawatts the plant produces, according to the AP news service; El Salvador's other geothermal plant in Ahuachapán produces another 95 megawatts. Together the plants provide power to 1.5 millions of El Salvador's 6.5 million citizens.

Blockchain Technologies and Climate Mitigation

In evaluating blockchain's social and environmental implications, numerous scholars agree that blockchain and distributed ledger technologies have potential benefits that would offset some of the short-term ecological impact.

As found by the OSTP report "Climate and Energy Implications of Crypto-Assets in the United States," blockchain "may have a role to play in enhancing market infrastructure for a range of environmental markets like carbon credit markets. Use cases are still emerging, and like all emerging technologies, there are potential positive and negative use cases yet to be imagined. Responsible development of this technology would encourage innovation in distributed ledger applications while reducing energy intensity and minimizing environmental damages." This is an interesting, if uncommon, opinion, but it points to the fact that there may well be more here than meets the eye, and blockchain technologies may well be part of the solution if weighed properly.

Susan Jones of The Aerospace Project agrees that crypto mining could be a catalyst for renewable energy projects and could move its energy needs into space:

> Crypto mining companies are often located near power sources to feed their power-hungry computers. As a result, crypto mining can be a catalyst or market driver for new renewable energy projects. For instance, Digital Power Optimization, in New York, now runs 400 mining computers from spare electricity produced by a hydroelectric dam in Hatfield, Wisconsin. There are many remote geographic areas where the energy demand market is not large enough to support a utility scale renewable energy site.[3]

There's incentive on the miners' side as well for, as miners, the lower the energy cost, the higher their profit margin, incentivizing the entire community to switch to cleaner energy where prices are cheaper. A bonus to that is its ripple effect. As miners turn to clean energy, utility companies will want to expand their capacity for renewable energy. This gives miners the option to buy more energy to fuel their process while benefiting and encouraging utility companies to pour more effort into expanding their green resources.

One salient example is flare gas. Flare gas is natural gas that is burned off at an oil rig, primarily because there is no cost-efficient distribution network for the resource. This is a boon for miners that, as noted, can be set up almost anywhere. A bitcoin mining rig that would use flare gas as an energy source would not only be more efficient; it would provide a double benefit in consuming what would be an otherwise wasted resource.

Bitcoin and its technology can provide some profound benefits to the global energy markets. It's well known that necessity is the mother of invention. As bitcoin specifically, and crypto in general, garner more and more adoption and demand, it is entirely reasonable to predict that ever greener solutions will be explored, identified, and implemented. Even Elon Musk, once a detractor and now a member of the Bitcoin Mining Counsel, is pushing for the move to renewable energy. The simple fact is, this is a problem that we want to solve, and we are well on the way to solving it.

All this being said, at the end of the day the most important factor in operating a mining operation is the input cost of energy. It is the more efficient operations that will win the right to mint new bitcoin and because of this, inefficient operators get forced out into bankruptcy and it's the efficient miners who win over time. Because of this, the miners who have near-free energy to power their operations will be the winners. Therefore, the winners will be ones who deploy renewable energy or sources of free energy.

In addition, it is relevant to note that all cryptocurrencies and platforms are not the same. They differ in many ways, including a consensus mechanism – the technology used on a blockchain to settle transactions and secure the network. As we've discussed, Bitcoin runs on a proof-of-work (PoW) consensus mechanism that requires using many powerful computers (bitcoin miners) running around the clock. People are understandably concerned that the energy costs may be too high, but they're missing an important part of the picture. There's a new generation of apps that uses a proof-of-stake (PoS) consensus mechanism. The Ethereum merge changed the blockchain to PoS, which does not require an energy-intensive mining task. Other, newer, blockchains like Polkadot and Polygon use a PoS consensus mechanism as well. Now, Ethereum has made this switch and continues to position itself as a force to be reckoned with. As a crypto enthusiast, we would encourage you to apply critical thinking and look at the entire landscape, not just the click-bait or generally perceived reality.

9

Myth – Crypto Empowers Crime

"Crypto is only used for illegal activity" is something people love to say at cocktail parties and boardrooms. As we debunked Professor Krugman in Chapter 7 regarding this issue, we are here to set this myth aside. Just like a camera or a hammer, crypto is a tool, and a tool serves the agenda of the one who wields it. If you look at the numbers, it's clear that most crypto is not used for criminal activity. According to a 2021 report from Chainalysis, criminal activity represented 2.1% of all cryptocurrency transaction volume in 2019. In 2020, the criminal share of all cryptocurrency activity fell to just 0.34%. There is far more crime involved in the use of dollars; it's just not new or sexy. We would argue that a hundred-dollar bill is more dangerous simply because it is used so much more often.

In the Chainalysis report on the year 2021, the trend continued. "Across all cryptocurrencies, total transaction volume grew to $15.8 trillion in 2021, up 567% from 2020's totals. Given that roaring adoption, it's no surprise that more cybercriminals are using cryptocurrency. But the fact that the increase of illegal activity was only 79% – nearly an order of magnitude lower than overall adoption – might be the biggest surprise of all."[1] Chainalysis found that with the growth of legitimate crypto far outpacing the growth of criminal usage, illicit activity's share of cryptocurrency transaction volume has never been lower. As cryptocurrency growth and use continues, we can expect there to be some portion that is related to crime and illicit activity. That's just how the world is. But what is not often realized is that crypto adoption is growing at a faster rate than illicit activity, which means that *the relatively small proportion of illegal activity continues to decline relative to the market size.*

Of course, the headlines are sensational. That same set of facts was republished in a *Fortune* article, but with the sensational headline "Crypto Crime Just Hit an All-Time High of $14 Billion." That may be true, but it is misleading, and it fuels opinions for those who don't take the time to digest the full content. *Forbes* pursued the topic in like form with the article "Cryptocurrency Fuels Growth of Crime." It's *Forbes*, so it must be true, right? Upon actually reading the article we find something a little different:

> Cryptocurrency utilization is exploding, most of it unrelated to criminal activity. It is certainly true that crypto-related crime has grown; one respected vendor reports it nearly doubled from 2020 to 2021, reaching an all-time high of $14 billion. That same vendor reports even more dramatic growth of overall cryptocurrency transactions, which was more than five times in the same period. As the vendor says: "Transactions involving illicit addresses represented just 0.15% of cryptocurrency transaction volume in 2021 despite the raw value of illicit transaction volume reaching its highest level ever."[2]

We see this summarized, over time, in Figure 9.1.

It's worth noting that this data is from Chainalysis' excellent report on crypto and crime, which we encourage readers to dive into if they want to go deeper.

This information is supported by research done by the RAND Corporation, which noted in a recent study on the perceived attractiveness of cryptocurrencies for money-laundering purposes that 99% of cryptocurrency transactions are performed through centralized exchanges, like Coinbase, which can be subject to regulation like traditional banks or exchanges.

So where does all the concern come from? Like many areas of crime, crypto crime shot up during the pandemic and there have been several high-profile crypto crimes – exchanges getting hacked, kidnappers demanding to be paid in crypto, the fraud cases discussed earlier. These disturbing stories distort the overall public understanding of crypto.

Illicit Share of All Cryptocurrency Transaction Volume, 2017 – 2021

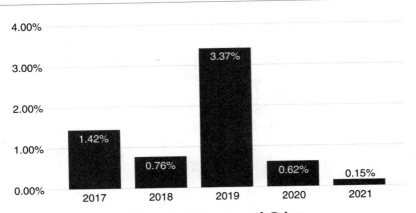

Figure 9.1 Crypto and Crime
Source: Chainalysis.

We want to pause for a moment here and be clear: it's not acceptable that crypto has been used in organized criminal and violent activities – not acceptable to us, law enforcement worldwide, or investors of any stripe. We're encouraged by the international cooperation among law enforcement agencies in successfully foiling the efforts of numerous crypto criminal gangs. We're not saying crime does not exist. We are saying it's not at the sensational level at which it is promoted.

As an emerging technology that was outside the banking system, early Bitcoin and fly-by-night token offerings certainly drew the kind of people who exploit early-stage technology to do misdeeds, just like the first banks and stagecoaches on the American frontier drew robbers.

In addition, although criminals are the same people who prefer hundred-dollar bills to hoard and hide their feloniously acquired cash, the Fed hasn't banned Benjamins and we all still use paper currency. Kidnappers are paid in cash, but still we do not ban it for other uses. By the same token, legitimate uses of crypto shouldn't be banned, either.

The Internet Is a Criminal Battlefield

In many respects, however, illegal usage of cryptocurrency and DeFi assets is paltry compared to that of the Internet, which changed the way we think, communicate, and exist in the world, but is also a tool for crime. Europol is the European Union's elite cyber-crime-fighting agency, and their Internet Organized Crime Threat Assessment (IOCTA) is the platinum standard for tracking cyber-crime trends. The IOCTA reported that in 2020 Europe saw the proliferation of crime-as-a-service cyberattacks, more ransomware attacks with "extra layers of extortion," and expanding use of "gray infrastructure enhancing criminals' operational security" (that is, "legal" services located in countries with a history of not cooperating with international law enforcement). These services are used by criminals and advertised in criminal forums. Examples of gray infrastructure services include unhackable servers, rogue cryptocurrency exchanges, and VPNs that provide safe havens. And it's not just these gray areas or sophisticated organizations. Anyone can google how to build a bomb and voilà, information appears. Do criminals use that information? Of course. Does that mean it's the only thing the Internet is used for? Of course not. The cost of worldwide Internet-enabled and -driven crime is in the trillions of dollars per year.

In contrast, crime is becoming a smaller and smaller part of the cryptocurrency ecosystem. Law enforcement in the United States and worldwide has deepened its bench and grown smarter about the transparent nature of blockchain as a crime-fighting tool, often hiring IT code breakers and crypto hackers to turn the tables on criminal organizations. We think it's important to keep this perspective. If crime is a measure of whether we should have a technology, then, well, we'd really not have any technology. If we throw the baby out with the bathwater, we all lose.

Tracing the Untraceable

In 2021, the Justice Department displayed its growing sophistication regarding the cyber world when it busted the criminals who hacked the Colonial Pipeline Company and recovered most of the ransom paid by the oil products company. In a blow to the "only criminals use crypto because it's untraceable" narrative, the FBI recovered almost 63.7 of the 75 bitcoin paid in ransom by tracking it. Yes, it was tracked. Despite everyone's attempt to say Bitcoin is anonymous, as we have discovered, it is really pseudonymous. Transactions are masked and the transactor's identity is generally not visible. Ultimately, however, if you onboard and offboard at any exchange or any system that requires a know your customer (KYC) process, your data can be tracked to you. Everything has a starting point and everything has an endpoint. Crypto is about empowering individuals to have freedom and flexibility without central control. This does not mean that it's immune to observation, laws, and common sense, as our ransomware attackers found. This was also discovered, much to their chagrin, by "Razzelkhan" and "Dutch," a couple who seemingly thought they would be able to move billions in bitcoin without anyone noticing. Let's explore just how this unfolded in both of these cases.

Ransomeware? Ransomthere!

The Russian hacker gang DarkSide ran the operation, attacking Colonial's computer network and embedding ransomware, resulting in the freezing of Colonial's pipeline on the East Coast. DarkSide harvested private and sensitive information, threatened to release it, adding blackmail to the list of its offenses, and demanded 75 bitcoins in their scheme. Colonial Pipeline executives decided to pay the ransom of 75 bitcoins while immediately notifying the FBI.

Agents traced DarkSide's bitcoin dealings by reviewing transactions on Bitcoin's blockchain, its public ledger. During the review, agents identified 63.7 bitcoins in a digital wallet linked to one of the members of DarkSide. To access the digital wallet, the FBI obtained a private key to recover the funds, although the FBI did not disclose its sources or the methods it used to obtain the private key to the digital wallet.

The FBI's seizure was the first time federal law enforcement recovered a ransomware payment since the U.S. Department of Justice created the Ransomware and Digital Extortion Task Force in April 2020 to target ransomware attacks and actors and recover ill-gotten gains.

"Following the money remains one of the most basic, yet powerful tools we have," said DOJ deputy attorney General Lisa O. Monaco. "Ransom payments are the fuel that propels the digital extortion engine, and [this] demonstrates that the United States will use all available tools to make these attacks more costly and less profitable for criminal enterprises. We will continue to target the entire ransomware ecosystem to disrupt and deter these attacks."

The *New York Times* followed:

> . . . for the growing community of cryptocurrency enthusiasts and investors, the fact that federal investigators had tracked the ransom as it moved through at least 23 different electronic accounts belonging to DarkSide, the hacking collective, before accessing one account showed that law enforcement was growing along with the industry.
>
> That's because the same properties that make cryptocurrencies attractive to cybercriminals — the ability to transfer money instantaneously without a bank's permission — can be leveraged by law enforcement to track and seize criminals' funds at the speed of the internet."[3]

Not Hiding in Plain Sight

DarkSide's ransomware was evocative of the shadowy criminal organization, but crimes are not always so obviously . . . dark. Sometimes they are just people capitalizing on greed and sometimes they are just downright weird. We have a couple who meets both of those criteria in one of the greatest grabs turned blunder in history.

Meet Heather "Razzlekhan" Morgan, the self-styled rapper and "Crocodile of Wall Street," and her "mentalist" investor, Russian husband Ilya "Dutch" Lichtenstein, alleged money launderers of the highest order, although on the surface they seemed anything but.

Morgan and Lichtenstein in 2016 deployed social media to promote themselves as financial hipsters while hatching a scheme to launder $4.5 billion in bitcoin stolen from the exchange Bitfinex. Razzlekhan is known for almost unwatchable rap (google at your own risk) with lyrics that painfully sort of rhyme but are about as appealing as a partially open banana that has been sitting in the sun for two weeks. As noted in Bloomberg, "It seems unlikely that someone who tried to rhyme 'Razzlekhan's the name' with 'that hot grandma you really wanna bang' could in fact be a master thief. Then again, this is the crypto world, where a lack of experience or competence hasn't always been a barrier." Perhaps a better clue was in the also tepid but revealing lyric "Spearphish your password / All your funds transferred." Bad taste, however, isn't a crime, so how did the couple get linked to one of the biggest crypto hacks in history?

It starts with an exchange. In 2016 the cryptocurrency exchange Bitfinex was hacked, and 100,000 bitcoins were stolen. The criminals were very good and lurked in the exchange for weeks until getting access to private keys that would allow them to transfer the bitcoin to external wallets. They then cleaned up their tracks and "poof" were gone. Sort of. The funds remained in plain sight in the wallets because, as we've discussed, blockchains are transparent. Eventually, the money moved and federal agents, including IRS investigators, conducted crypto-forensic analysis to trace the stolen funds:

- Through an unhosted crypto wallet containing over 2,000 Bitcoin addresses
- To accounts at the darknet market AlphaBay
- To seven interconnected virtual currency exchange accounts
- To various unhosted Bitcoin wallets
- To accounts the couple owned at six other virtual currency exchanges
- The last link, a $500 gift card to Walmart (yes, Walmart)

The Walmart card was sent to a Russian-registered email address that investigators were able to link to Lichtenstein. So, in a bizzaro turn of events the alleged launderers were using money linked to the Bitfinex hack to buy daily sundries, and $3.6 billion of the $4.5 billion in stolen bitcoin was recovered with the desire to use $500.

This type of investigation is not simple. It required a huge amount of forensic work. As noted earlier in this chapter, everything has a starting point and an ending point. Eighty percent of the bitcoin that was stolen has been recovered. This brings us to a contrarian argument – bitcoin, with its transparency, is more of a deterrent to would-be criminals. Cash, it would seem, is indeed king.

Everyone Evolves

The previous examples clearly demonstrate that cryptocurrencies are not anonymous. Every separate transaction is logged onto the blockchain, a ledger of all transactions distributed to all users in the network. Most blockchains are publicly available, making transactions traceable. This gives the authorities around the world access to substantially more information than a case involving cash. While privacy coins and several services and techniques make tracing more difficult, they by no means stop the good guys from finding out who is hiding behind the crime.

Importantly, the overall number and value of cryptocurrency transactions related to criminal activities still represent only a small portion of the illicit economy compared to cash and other transactions. The volatility of cryptocurrencies hampers widespread adoption by bad guys. Criminal networks continue to rely on traditional fiat money and transactions to a large degree, because cash isn't trackable through the Internet.

It's true that criminals have become more sophisticated in their use of cryptocurrencies. Illicit funds increasingly travel through a byzantine set of links involving financial entities, many of which are novel and thus not yet part of standardized, regulated financial and payment markets and, just as technology grows, the sophistication of criminals grows as well. Like a game of whack-a-mole, we think that there will always be new perpetrators, schemes, and "dark web" sites designed to move money illicitly.

We have honestly wondered, given the time, effort, and energy some of these schemes take, why the perpetrators don't just go legit. It sure seems like it would be easier. Regardless, criminals will continue to use and develop obfuscation methods and other countermeasures to exploit technology. They evolve. At the same time, everyone seems to forget that there are some pretty smart people in law enforcement as well, and they have access to the same tools the criminals do. They also evolve. So, while criminals are using the blockchain tool for their own purposes, law enforcement is doing the same thing. The point is that the tool itself is not the problem; it's the use of it. Ironically, we see that for those conducting illicit activity it may well be the silver bullet itself. In this case the "anonymous" bitcoin network is the bullet that ends up cracking the case open and ruining their nefarious plans.

10

Guarding Against Fraud

Surely it is a sign of the times when Kim Kardashian pumps an investment opportunity for EthereumMax to her hundreds of millions of followers on Instagram. Guess who came knocking? The SEC, of course. EthereumMax was built on the Ethereum blockchain but was otherwise unrelated to Ethereum. Because promoters were noting that buyers of the tokens could expect "reasonable returns," it was deemed a security, per SEC guidelines. SEC guidelines also include an anti-touting law, which says you can't promote a security (or anything that looks or smells or acts like a security) without disclosing that you were paid to do so. Ultimately, this resulted in a $1.26 million settlement with the celebrity for not disclosing the $250,000 she had received to promote the crypto token. Kardashian's paid boosting isn't quite a scam, but her reputation and cachet allowed her to drive followers to a product that, shall we say, didn't meet up to our standards. Importantly, this demonstrates the creeping spread of mass misinformation about crypto assets, and how easy it is to get drawn into something that seems credible but simply may not be.

While the actual criminal use of crypto is minimal, we'd be remiss if we didn't directly address the fact that there are plenty of scams out there designed to take advantage of you, the investor. These could be bogus protocols, illicit wallet addresses, suspect endorsements or even full websites that look just like legitimate blockchain projects. All of these are designed to confuse you and take your money, giving nothing in return but that sinking feeling in your stomach. My dad always said "Fool me once, shame on you, fool me twice, shame on me." Our intention in this chapter is to raise your awareness so that you don't get fooled at all.

Unfortunately crypto scams are real — just like Internet scams are real. The simple fact is that scams proliferate in new marketplaces where consumers don't fully understand the technology. They come in many forms. In a "rug pull" swindle, for example, a new coin, token, or platform appears overnight, garners lots of press, attracts investors, and then disappears. In a "pump and dump" scam, bad actors invest in a coin they know is worthless and pump up interest (sometimes using unwitting celebrities) to lure investors. They push the price up, and then sell all at once. The price collapses, leaving unsuspecting investors with worthless coins.

Scammers go after crypto wallets, email addresses, and phones — many have lost crypto assets this way. There's a lot to learn from the more infamous crypto frauds like OneCoin, an international Ponzi scheme that's estimated to have scammed people of $25 billion, and Quadriga, a Canadian exchange whose founder is suspected of absconding with almost $200 million in investors' funds and then faking his own death.

Yes, you need to be careful. Yet the mere presence of fraud does not invalidate the crypto market, any more than one crooked member of Congress invalidates the government. One or more bad actors in a company does not invalidate the company itself. Take, for example, JPMorgan, which was fined almost $1 billion in connection with schemes to defraud precious metals and U.S. Treasuries markets.[1] Fraud happens everywhere. Blockchain technology itself has never been broken, at least for Bitcoin.

We want you to be smart and prepared to succeed as an investor in crypto (or stocks, bonds, real estate, or any other asset), but we also want you to be prudent. Fraud is as old as humanity and will continue, and when an emerging mega-trend such as crypto rolls out to the world, thieves and fools rush in. Because it's not all sunshine and rainbows, we are going to close out this section by raising your awareness of some of the scenarios you might encounter, so that you are well rounded, can see the danger signs, and avoid some of the common pitfalls of this new world.

The SEC: Watchdogs on the Hunt

In May 2022, the SEC added 20 additional positions to the unit responsible for protecting investors in crypto markets and from cyber-related threats. The newly renamed Crypto Assets and Cyber Unit (formerly known as the Cyber Unit) in the Division of Enforcement grew to 50 dedicated positions.

"The U.S. has the greatest capital markets because investors have faith in them, and as more investors access the crypto markets, it is increasingly important to dedicate more resources to protecting them," said SEC chair Gary Gensler. "The Division of Enforcement's Crypto Assets and Cyber Unit has successfully brought dozens of cases against those seeking to take advantage of investors in crypto markets. By nearly doubling the size of this key unit, the SEC will be better equipped to police wrongdoing in the crypto markets while continuing to identify disclosure and controls issues with respect to cybersecurity."[2]

Gurbir S. Grewal, director of the SEC's Division of Enforcement, added that crypto markets "exploded in recent years, with retail investors withstanding the worst of abuses in this space. Meanwhile, cyber-related threats continue to pose existential risks to our financial markets and participants. The bolstered Crypto Assets and Cyber Unit will be at the forefront of protecting investors and ensuring fair and orderly markets in the face of these critical challenges."[3]

The additional positions include supervisors, investigative staff attorneys, trial counsels, and fraud analysts. At an SEC Speaks conference, Grewal said that the best way to describe the SEC's approach is "intentionality." By this he means assertively seeking cooperation from traders, trading platforms, and issuers, issuing clear guidance, and providing extensive explanations of its enforcement actions. In part, the SEC is responding to widespread criticism that it is enforcing crypto assets as securities without having apparent authority or settled rules. As we observed earlier, Congress wants to pass laws dealing with this issue, and is likely to do so soon.

Many in the crypto community rankle against the SEC's aggressive posture – or crackdown, in the eyes of many – and we're watching the watchdogs to ensure that the rules, to the extent we know them, are fair and fairly enforced. To date, the SEC's significant cases focus on bad actors who explicitly harmed investors. And the SEC nails scammers across all security classes, of course, not just crypto. Among the actions pursued by the SEC in 2022 are the following:

- The Hydrogen Technology Corporation, its former CEO, Michael Ross Kane, and Tyler Ostern, the CEO of Moonwalkers Trading Limited, a self-described "market making" firm, perpetrated a scheme to manipulate the trading volume and price of crypto securities.

- Chicago Crypto Capital LLC, its owner, Brian Amoah, and former salespeople Darcas Oliver Young and Elbert "Al" Elliott allegedly defrauded investors during their unregistered offering of crypto asset securities.

- John Joseph Roets and three entities he controls, Dragonchain, Inc., Dragonchain Foundation, and the Dragon Company, raised $16.5 million without registering their crypto-asset securities offerings.

- Eleven individuals were charged for creating and promoting Forsage, a fraudulent crypto pyramid and Ponzi scheme that raised more than $300 million from millions of retail investors worldwide, including in the United States. Those charged include the four founders of Forsage.

- Block Bits Capital, LLC; Block Bits Capital GP I, LLC; and their co-founders, Japheth Dillman and David Mata, conducted a fraudulent unregistered securities offering.

- MCC International Corp. fraudulently sold investment plans called mining packages to thousands of investors.

- Siblings John and JonAtina (Tina) Barksdale were charged with defrauding thousands of retail investors out of more than $124 million through two unregistered fraudulent offerings of securities involving a digital token called "Ormeus Coin."

- Paul A. Garcia of Severance, Colorado, allegedly defrauded investors by stealing approximately one quarter of investors' funds raised for Gold Hawgs Development Corp., a failed cryptocurrency venture.

The Commodity Futures Trading Commission (CFTC) also expanded enforcement hiring and actions in 2022. In one July 14 announcement, the CFTC entered a consent order against Jimmy Gale Watson of Dallas, Texas, for a manipulative and deceptive digital asset "pump-and-dump" scheme. "The CFTC will continue actively to use its enforcement authority in the digital asset space to combat fraud and manipulation," said CFTC acting director of enforcement Gretchen Lowe at the time.

With both agencies jockeying for jurisdiction, there is merit to observations that they stepped up enforcement "arrests" before their fiscal year ended at the end of September (just as government agencies have done for centuries). Considering the size of the crypto sector, 130 or so enforcement actions in five years involve and impact only a fraction of the crypto securities and commodities available to investors; however, this does not mean that any project that you invest in could be subject to investigation, even large-scale projects.

Let's look at Ripple, a technology company that created XRP. Ripple created a system of payment settlement and remittance and XRP has been the darling of many. Seven years after its founding, however, the SEC filed actions against it for being an unregistered security (do you see a pattern here?). This sent the price plummeting and its overall long-term success is in question. The founders disagreed and a legal battle ensued. Time will tell where this ends up; it may well be either a fine and a slap on the wrist or the project getting shut down. The point is that the SEC is not to be trifled with, so our advice is, don't trifle with them. Remember the Howey Test, and if you see a project that could be categorized as a security, buyer beware. There are plenty of great projects that don't fall into this category.

Risk Management and Red Flags

Here's the rule: If it sounds too good to be true, it probably is. Use common sense, ask for references and evidence of performance, and don't believe what you see on the Internet without further verification.

The SEC's Office of Investor Education and Advocacy and the CFTC's Office of Customer Education and Outreach have repeatedly warned investors to beware of websites "purporting to operate advisory and trading businesses related to digital assets. These websites often contain 'red flags' of fraud, including claims of high guaranteed returns and promises that the investments carry little or even no risk. ... In some cases, the fraudsters claim to invest customers' funds in proprietary crypto trading systems or in 'mining' farms, promising high guaranteed returns (for example, 20–50%) with little or no risk." *Folks, if you want little or no risk, invest in municipal bonds and Treasuries. Claims of risk-free returns of this nature are total bull.*

With that being said, in addition to keeping the Howey test in mind, here are our 10 red flags to watch for, with thanks to the SEC, CFTC, and other federal agencies:

1. **Investors are asked to pay additional costs** (such as taxes) to withdraw fake "profits" earned from the investment. We call this an advance fee fraud swindle, where you are asked to pay a bogus fee in advance of receiving proceeds, money, stock, or warrants.[4]

2. **Offerings are presented in complicated jargon and language that is difficult to understand.** Beware claims of complex innovative technologies that aren't something you can find on Google. Bad guys will claim that their technology is highly secret. Be suspicious of hard-to-understand pitches that accompany promises of whopping returns. Spelling, grammar, and typographical errors that confuse the description are clues.

3. **Unlicensed sellers.** Many investment schemes involve unlicensed individuals or unregistered firms. Check license and registration statuses on Investor.gov.

4. **Unsolicited offers.** Buyer beware when you get a cold pitch or unsolicited offer – meaning you didn't ask for it and don't know the sender – about an investment opportunity. Fraudsters may use fake names and misleading photos and provide U.S. phone numbers even though they may be operating abroad. You may also know this as "phishing," where you are sent an email or other communication asking you to click a link. Never click any links unless you have requested them or are expecting them.

5. **FOMO alert.** Trust no one who wants your money right away, ever. Creating a false sense of urgency is an old trick to trigger your fear of missing out. Take your time researching an investment prospect before forking over your dollars. It will be there in another day or two if it's legit. Before making any investment, study the information provided to you, and verify the truth of every statement you

are told about the investment. For more information about how to research an investment, read SEC Office of Investor Education and Advocacy's publication *Ask Questions*.

6. **Sex, lies, and social media.** Many terrific journalists, money managers, and asset owners, including we two authors, post good high-quality content on Twitter and the rest of social media. Most investors follow their favorite influencers, investors, and analysts. While social media can benefit investors, it also creates opportunities for fraud. Social media allows charlatans to contact many people quickly, cheaply, and without much effort – and it is easy for fraudsters to post information on social media that looks real and credible.

Swindlers may circulate misleading information anonymously or while pretending to be someone else. They may issue fabricated credentials, create fake profiles, or pretend to be associated with a legitimate source. It's easy to hide behind an anonymous social media account while laying the groundwork for fraud. Whether it's Kim Kardashian or your favorite NFL player, do not give testimonials or celebrity endorsements a micron of credibility when making an investment decision. Phonies sometimes pay actors to pose as normal-people-turned-millionaires to tout an investment on social media.

The SEC: ". . . fraudsters may set up an account name, profile, or handle designed to mimic a particular individual or firm. They may go so far as to create a webpage that uses the actual firm's logo, links to the firm's actual website, or references the name of an actual person who works for the firm. Fraudsters also may direct investors to an imposter website by posting comments in the social media account of brokers, investment advisers, or other sources of market information. When you receive investment information through social media, verify the identity of the underlying source. Look for slight variations or typos in the sender's account name, profile, email address, screen name, or handle, or other signs that the sender may be an imposter."[5]

Con artists have also found victims by hacking their social media profile and sending fraudulent investment opportunities to their contacts. Be wary if someone – even someone you trust – sends a social media message recommending an investment and be sure to check with them offline to make sure that person actually sent the message.

7. **Swipe never – dating app scams.** In yet another utterly unsurprising chapter in the book of human nature, the ubiquity of dating apps and the fragility of millions of good people using them to seek authentic love and companionship have unleashed an endless torrent of fraud and crime worldwide. One reason is that con artists can assume the identity of someone living in another country and cement an illusory bond through intense texting and phone calls. The creep can then manipulate the victim to "loan" them money or reveal bank or brokerage account information, tax forms, credit card information, passport, driver's licenses, birthdates, and so forth. In some cases, people are bilked out of their life savings.

   "These keyboard Casanovas reportedly dazzle people with their supposed wealth and sophistication. Before long, they casually offer tips on getting started with crypto investing and help with making investments. People who take them up on the offer report that what they really got was a tutorial on sending crypto to a scammer. The median individual reported crypto loss to romance scammers is an astounding $10,000," reported the FTC.[6]

   Many romance ripoffs persuade victims to send money allegedly to invest or trade cryptocurrency. After the fraudster establishes an online relationship with the victim, they claim to know about lucrative cryptocurrency investments or trading opportunities. "The fraudster directs the victim to a fraudulent website or app," the FBI explains. "After the victim invests and sees a purported profit, the website or app allows the victim to withdraw a small amount of money, further gaining the victim's trust. The fraudster then instructs the victim to invest larger amounts of money and conveys a sense of urgency. When the victim tries to withdraw funds again, the victim is instructed to pay additional funds, claiming that taxes or fees need to be paid or a minimum account balance must be met."

8. **Good old penny stock/token fraud.** We remember the 1990s when penny stock peddlers would blast out faxes to the known universe promoting can't-miss deals. The faxes would end up strewn on the floor or lying on the counter. It boggles the mind that this must have worked for a time. Just as microcap and penny

stocks are more susceptible to market manipulation, so it is with low-cost, out-of-nowhere, initial token offerings and other assets. Exercise extreme caution.

9. **Avoid crypto-only payments.** If a seemingly credible person or retail establishment claims they cannot accept any currency other than bitcoin, ether, or other (and only) crypto assets, it's likely a scam. Bitcoin and other altcoins are a burgeoning asset class, so experts say credible institutions aren't going to accept crypto and not also accept U.S. dollars through normal means like wire transfers, checks, credit and debit card payments, and cash.

10. **Affinity fraud.** In the most consequential Ponzi scheme of all time, Bernie Madoff used affinity fraud to bilk affluent Jewish New York investors out of billions. Madoff wasn't the only one; affinity fraud is relatively common. The feds have gone after affinity fraud, which targets members of groups with common ties based on ethnicity, nationality, religion, sexual orientation, military service, or age, for decades. Many communities use social media to stay connected and share information. Swindlers may be (or pretend to be) part of the group they are trying to mislead and may solicit potential victims on social media through posts or direct contact. Affinity crime often starts with enlisting a group leader, who spreads the word about the scheme on social media. Those leaders may not realize that the "investment" is actually a fraud, which means that they, too, may be victims. This happens with crypto schemes.

While the following case doesn't involve crypto, it is an instructive example from the files of the FBI. The bust went down in 2021.

> When members of the Pennsylvania Amish and Mennonite communities were offered the opportunity to invest with someone they knew and trusted, many jumped at the chance. Philip Elvin Riehl, an accountant in Berks County, Pennsylvania, claimed he would invest their money in local businesses, offering a solid return.

But Riehl was not licensed to invest people's money: "He did minimal research on the companies he was loaning money to. For example, he loaned much of the money he received to a failing creamery that went out of business, leaving investors with nothing. He also forgave loans if borrowers left their faith, making it impossible to collect the money," the FBI reported. Special Agent Michael Mocadlo investigated this case out of the FBI's Philadelphia field office. About 400 Amish and Mennonite families in Pennsylvania lost a combined $59 million.

Because of their religious beliefs, many in these communities often do not pay into Social Security, so some members seek out their own opportunities to fund their retirement. Because many of the victims invested for the long term, they often didn't ask for their money for years. So, they saw statements that showed their money was doing fine, when it had actually been invested in failing businesses and was gone.[7]

Don't Do Stupid Stuff

President Obama and his team adopted this mantra in looking at foreign policy decisions. It is a helpful reminder for all investors when it comes to evaluating investments. Regulators and other watchdogs correctly remind us that crypto investments are not insured like bank deposits, or (supposedly) safeguarded from fraudulent losses through the SIPC (Securities Investor Protection Corporation), which protects against the loss of cash and securities – such as stocks and bonds – held by a customer at a financially troubled SIPC-member brokerage firm. There is critical context to keep in mind. Crypto investments aren't shielded by the FDIC, which limits its insurance to savings and checking accounts at banks, true, but neither are real estate, stocks, bonds, derivatives, futures, commodities, or the entire universe of investments not held at banks. The SIPC has very limited reserves and powers to refund fraud-driven losses, and then only at SIPC-member brokers. It is a self-regulated organization, meaning that the recovery guardrails it puts in place must be funded by the industry and supported by the industry. Brokers and Congress have long failed to adequately fund the SIPC and defanged its enforcement roles.

Most fraudulent schemes need cash at ever-increasing volumes to keep the con going, so, as with any pitch or scheme, manufactured urgency is a very bad sign. Everybody wants your money in life, but crypto crooks want it desperately.

Crypto assets are like any higher-risk investment. Invest what you can afford to lose. Research your investment targets and get performance data. Remember that if it looks too good to be true, it probably is, so stay alert. And, in addition to being aware of fraudulent offers, follow a commonsense approach to managing your assets. Mind your wallet and where you attach it and never ever share your private keys. Incorporate risk-management tools into your crypto portfolio so you can sleep at night and enjoy managing your money.

PART III
THE BREAKTHROUGH

In Part Three, we focus on the innovation of all the technology that is at the heart of making the future possible. It's technological innovation that allows us to do things we couldn't do before. Moving value across borders and doing so without human intervention in a peer-to-peer fashion wasn't possible prior to blockchain technology. New forms of money can now be created. The converging of IoT, AI, and robotics with blockchain using digital assets allows a new future to be possible. As companies compete, it's technology that gives an edge against competitors.

There's a concept we love from Andreas Antonopolous called "infrastructure inversion." Look it up on YouTube, because it'll be worth your time. The idea encapsulates a period of time in a new technological revolution when the new innovation is being played with and utilized by the early adopters, then new infrastructure gets laid out, and then you can do anything from the past easier/faster/cheaper plus a whole lot more. The new infrastructure that is laid out on top of the old infrastructure creates conflict initially. In the beginning of the adoption of new technology, it is implemented on the existing technology that it's disrupting and at first glance it looks useless.

Andreas starts his video out with an example from the oil and automobile technological revolution.[1] He starts out by explaining the complainers of the "new tech": What are these automobiles? Those noisy machines are going to kill us all. You can't feed them and how do you travel over 100 miles? Why would anyone want to use those crazy contraptions when we have perfectly good horses? Their tires get stuck in the mud and they're death traps, killing people who don't see them coming. What are these rich people doing with these toys? Horses with carriages are much better. You see, that's what happens when innovation is initially employed; it's met with resistance at first.

Now, 20 years into the new technological revolution, its innovation looks obvious in hindsight. When roads and interstates and gas stations become prevalent, the use of cars seems obvious. However, in those early years, it's hard to explain to the masses. We hope this part of the book helps explain why and how the current innovations are going to revolutionize everything we think about commerce, transacting, and requiring trust to do so.

During the Internet Age, if companies didn't figure out a digital communication strategy, they were left in the dust. Just ask Blockbuster. It's the same this time around. As companies and organizations are able to implement more autonomous operations, they create a competitive edge. In this part of the book, we aim to illustrate all the technology and to give an understanding of what got solved from a problem standpoint and what's now possible.

11

A Primer on Technological Innovation

Technological innovation drives long-term economic cycles, and if you can see the opportunity at the beginning of the cycle, you will do well to invest early. This chapter will show how innovation is one of the most impactful ways to invest and to realize capital appreciation, especially when an investor has conviction, and is in the early stages of a technology adoption cycle.

When we talk about "crypto," it's easy to focus on cryptocurrencies and crypto assets, which is the financial construct that gets bought and sold. For example, when we focus on bitcoin, a lot of the time we focus on the "little b" bitcoin, not the "big B" Bitcoin. We focus on the currency, not the blockchain and technology. But that's where the innovation is. We're all here because of the technological innovation of the blockchain.

I'm involved with a men's group called METal International. The group started in LA, but when COVID hit, it went online. In LA, we'd meet every Saturday at one of those old theaters that are sprinkled through LA in Westwood and Hollywood. You go into these big, old, restored theaters from the golden age of film and you can feel the history from the building.

METal stands for media, entertainment, and technology, so the group is comprised of entrepreneurs and execs from all over those sectors. There are famous actors, entrepreneurs who run venture-backed startups, and people from all through the media industry. Makes sense for a group founded in LA. It's great because you can meet and interact with like-minded people. A lot of times, it can get lonely if you're the CEO of your own company and you don't have anyone to talk to who really knows what it's like. It can get lonely at the top.

When the group moved to an online setting, all the meetings were done through Zoom. That part, as almost everyone can relate to, was a little weird at first. However, the group expanded because anyone from around the world could join. Two of the most attended groups are the investors' group and the Crypto Roundtable, both on Thursday nights. I help lead the Crypto Roundtable, although it was started before I joined and was run by three others. But they invited me to join the leadership and it's been great to be able to contribute and make a difference for others in the realm of crypto investment. When we're in a crypto bull market, the group can get up to 80 or 90 people. When we're in a bear market, however, the group can trickle down to 20 or 30. That's how it always is, right? When things are going great, everyone wants to be involved. That's FOMO in action, and the irony is that big money is made when deploying in down markets.

We also have a Telegram group. A lot of the time, the threads and discussions can be focused on what token is going to have a big run, or the latest small-cap token that's just about to have a token-generating event (TGE). That's when a token launches for public trading for the first time. When we're in a bull market, everyone wants to talk about these coins and tokens. Most of the conversation can be around these types of discussions. During the Thursday night Zoom call, we also almost always have a section where we talk about technical analysis of price charts and various aspects of trading. These talks are almost identical to the types of discussions an investment group may have about stock investing. The group is focused on talking about the financial capital, the asset, and its investment prospects. No one really cares why a token is succeeding; they just want to know which one is.

As with many crypto enthusiasts, our group needs to increase our focus on the technology and the technological innovation. Often there's a focus on "can I make money?" without any clear understanding of why this technology is relevant. That's what we want to underscore here, and

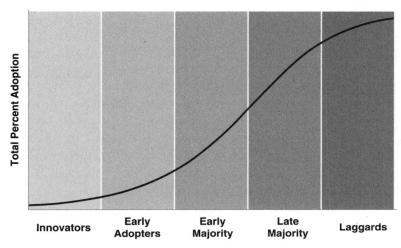

Figure 11.1 The Adoption Curve, the S–Curve
Source: © Stratechi.

we want everyone to be able to answer the question "What does crypto and blockchain innovation allow us to do that we couldn't do before?" This is critical, because it's that innovation that's driving the early aspects of this new long-wave economic cycle. It's that innovation that's in its early phase of tech adoption. In March 2021, there was an article that claimed that 17% of Americans have a crypto investing account or a wallet. This was about the same number of people who had email accounts in 1997. As you can surmise, both sets of innovation data were illustrating technology adoption. One was of this new crypto/blockchain cycle, and one was from the Internet, the Age of Information. Both show roughly where the tipping point is with any adoption cycle. The tipping point is when there's no going back – a technological innovation is going to be adopted by the masses. At 17%, that's roughly where the cycle goes from the early adopters to the middle adopters. This is a critical milestone in any technological revolution (see Figure 11.1).

The Convergence of AI, IoT and Robotics

These technologies are powerful in and of themselves, but it's the convergence of these technologies that create the real value. AI itself has provided powerful search capability for a company like Google. Google has gone on a startup buying tear, spending billions each year to gobble up IoT and robotics companies. Why? Because the market is coming down to just a handful of companies that are owning the commerce of the future. They are competing with Apple and Uber in autonomous driving and delivery. Amazon, too. The convergence of AI, IoT, robotics, and now blockchain technology will provide a company with their greatest competitive advantage. As we see this unfold, and as we talked about in our earlier book, *The Age of Autonomy®*, it's these four technologies and their convergence that will create the most value and the greatest competitive edge in the decades to come.

Artificial Intelligence

Artificial intelligence (AI) is a past specialty of mine. I spent my university days getting a degree in computer science with a focus on AI. This was in the late 1990s. Back then, we were trying to solve significant problems with artificial neural networks (deep learning). These included natural language processing; vision systems/image processing; autonomous motion (autonomous robots); and expert systems (pattern matching), among other areas. We made some progress back then, but we really couldn't address the problem set comprehensively, the main reason being that we needed to wait for the hardware and the processing to greatly improve.

That finally happened around 2010 or so. There were big improvements in central processing units (CPUs), the processing heart of a computer, and we also moved off a lot of graphics processing to separate graphics processing units (GPUs). The hardware had finally caught up to the software, and in the 2010s we really started to see AI take off. We saw expert systems and pattern-matching win games of *Go*, beating the best humans. We saw autonomous robotics come into the mainstream along with autonomous driving. There were AI innovations everywhere, and today, AI is the critical component for both corporations and nations alike to take the lead and beat the competition.

In the next technological revolution, it will be the converging of AI and blockchain that creates the competitive advantage. Companies and organizations will build AI systems to process and convert data into knowledge. Then, that knowledge can be integrated with crypto assets via smart contracts and generate economic activity without human intervention.

Blockchains are intersecting with AI in several key areas. Today, many of the trades that happen on crypto and stock exchanges are run by trading algorithms (bots). These are AI software applications that decide when and how to trade stocks, commodities, and digital assets. Soon, trading will become a subroutine inside a bigger process.

Imagine a farm that uses software to autonomously run its operations – from buying seeds to irrigating crops. Blockchains coupled with AI will allow the entire management of operations to become a completely autonomous system. When that happens, it will become common for trading bots to handle the buying and selling. That trend will gain momentum as assets become digital and more of them are managed autonomously. There will even be marketplaces that buy and sell bots, and autonomous systems will buy and upgrade their own bots!

The Internet of Things and Sensors

The Internet of Things (IoT) is generating massive amounts of data that will be the source of training AI systems and feeding data into those expert systems for a broader application. I mentioned in my first book, *The Knowledge Doubling Curve*, the idea originated with famed inventor Buckminster Fuller, who estimated in 1900 that knowledge doubled every 100 years. By 1945, knowledge would double roughly every 25 years. Then, initially forecasted and later confirmed by IBM, that knowledge would be doubling every 12 hours by 2020. Imagine that! Then imagine a world where competition determines whether a company survives or dies. Can humans, without computer processing and AI, compete with companies with sensor and AI-based solutions that process massive amounts of data into knowledge? We don't think so. That concept will be extended to the new economy with digital assets and blockchains.

As we discussed in Part One, blockchains can intersect with IoT sensors, which will facilitate a return to owning, controlling, and monetizing (if you want) your personal data. Start with the data you generate at home – the sensors in your fridge, for example. Perhaps your eating habits are worth money to some company. For the right price, maybe you're willing to sell your data if it's properly anonymized.

Or think about that autonomous farm. It will have sensors that measure how much seed was planted, how much water was used, and how much crop yield occurred. The intersection of IoT sensors and blockchain gives that farm operation data they can use internally or sell. The data itself are digital assets – and blockchains provide a secure place to store and deploy these assets – with no intermediary.

Robotics

Robotics and autonomous vehicles have made huge strides in the past decade. How many times have you seen Google self-driving vehicles around town? Further, they have almost mastered long-haul trucking with autonomous driving to such a degree that it's estimated that we could see trucks on the road as early as 2024.

Similar strides have been made in robotics. Most warehouses are equipped with autonomous robots that do most of the work. Robots are used throughout manufacturing and other sectors. Robots may or may not integrate directly with blockchains, but it will be AI systems and economic activity that is managed and processed by blockchains that will drive decision-making and other aspects that will affect what work robots do, and those decisions will be made in real time in the field.

Vision, Image Processing, and Autonomous Motion

Over the past 30 years, we've made serious progress into what's possible with vision systems, image processing, and the ability of vehicles and robots to move without human intervention. That comes in the form of facial recognition systems being able to classify and process images for AI systems to "know" what's in an image and then be able to act. It comes in the form of 18-wheelers to begin a trip in California and make it to the East Coast autonomously.

We've experienced that the few companies who've mastered artificial intelligence are able to capitalize and monetize all of commerce. Amazon started out as a book-selling company, but since 2000, they are now basically the sole company to sell products over the Internet (or at least they own the top spot in the sector). They used AI, IoT, and robotics to outcompete, and they won. Google started out as a search engine, but now they're in everything, including autonomous vehicles. They will compete with Uber on many aspects of autonomous delivery once autonomous vehicles are commonplace. They've bought more AI startups than anyone. Apple has a similar story, as do

Microsoft, Uber, Hulu, and Netflix. These few tech companies are near monopolies and own or control their market. It's these companies that were able to master image processing, vision systems, and autonomous motion — it was the application of AI, along with robotics and IoT, that gave them a moat, a competitive advantage that's now near unstoppable. Each has a blockchain strategy that will take them through the Age of Autonomy.® It will be interesting to watch whether some power can be taken back by the individual as Web 3.0 and other technologies mature and come to market.

From Automation to Autonomy

AI is taking automation even further. Businesses use AI to improve systems ranging from health care records to navigation. Robots perform rote physical tasks. IoT sensors are embedded in everything from refrigerators to warehouse pallets.

Automation is mind boggling on its own. But there's another leap to make: from automation to autonomy. By linking AI, IoT, and robotics to blockchain technology, you can create fully autonomous systems. That's right: systems that can govern, manage, and run themselves year-round, all day every day. Blockchains make it possible to process, store, and transfer economic value without human intervention. We call this technological revolution the Age of Autonomy®.

We predict that in the not-too-distant future, every industry, community, and government will use autonomous systems to produce work and to generate, transfer, and store value. These systems will combine AI and IoT sensors with blockchains.

Robots can perform tasks autonomously. IoT sensors measure, generate, and communicate massive amounts of data. AI provides judgment, expertise, and evaluation to transform that data into knowledge.

The Crucial Connector

This all comes together when considering digital assets. Digital assets managed on blockchains will allow organizations to govern and enforce the transfer and storage of value from the work produced, with the ability to turn that knowledge into economic action, autonomously. More specifically, when we talk about the convergence of blockchain with other key technologies and innovations, we're talking about the implementation of smart contracts on smart contract blockchains. Layer 1 blockchains like Ethereum ($ETH), Solana ($SOL), and Algorand ($ALGO) are smart contract platforms that allow users to build and implement smart contracts, and it is these very smart contracts that provide the mechanism to build robust functionality. Importantly, these contracts allow these convergent systems to conduct capital transactions in a peer-to-peer manner without any human intervention. In the new decentralized, digital economy, IoT produces data, AI systems will turn that data into actionable "knowledge," robotics can express that knowledge in the physical world, and blockchain provides the missing piece, via smart contracts that will then drive economic transactions and activity.

Putting It All Together

A cluster of innovations are converging to deliver possibilities that were previously not possible. It's not just the innovations themselves that are valuable. They combine in novel ways that bring on a new technological revolution.

As I discussed in my first book, technological revolutions drive the long-wave economic cycle. Investing early in adoption brings about the outsized performance gains we're looking for as investors. It's hard to be a part of a small group of early adopters against the screaming mob of nonbelievers. Conviction requires taking and maintaining that position in the minority. And it's that conviction in these innovations that will bring you, the innovative investor, to move, move early, and stay for the ride – even in the face of volatility, risk, and adversity.

12

The Byzantine Generals Problem

The Byzantine Generals Problem is one of history's top 10 computer science problems, and this chapter will go into detail about what the problem is and how blockchain technology solves it. Most people don't understand that this is the root, so we feel that if you have your arms around this, you have taken a giant leap in your understanding of why blockchains are relevant.

The problem asks how any network can come to consensus without a trusted third party or central authority. For the past 50 years, there was no way to get to consensus without having that trusted third party. Bitcoin and blockchain solve this problem in such an innovative way that new things are now possible in many areas, including money and currency. We'll keep it light and fun.

Some Other Top Computer Science Problems

There's been a list of top computer science problems going back to the early days of the computer. Many of the problems on that list have been there for decades. We have waited to solve the Byzantine Generals Problem for over four decades, so when a solution did come in 2009, it was surprising how little fanfare greeted the proposal.

Other top computer science problems that are still on the list include things like:

- An optimal solution for a binary tree search algorithm—how to find the solution the fastest within a sorted data structure
- Computational complexity—how to classify and optimize computational problems according to their resource usage
- Optimal algorithm for matrix multiplication—how to determine if there is a proven fastest solution to matrix multiplication, which has to do with multidimensional arrays (lists) of numbers
- Natural language processing algorithm—how to determine if there is an optimal algorithm for stemming, syllabification, phrase chunking, and discerning pronoun ambiguity in a natural language like English
- Evasiveness conjecture—how to determine questions like "Is there an edge between vertex y and vertex z?" This would answer the question if every single number would have to be compared or if there might be a shortcut of some kind. This is a group of related conjectures. A solution to this problem could have wide application, from the ultimate voice recognition software to creating the best resource allocation optimization algorithms, saving any logistics companies billions, to breaking the current encryption that secures all Internet commerce. Encryption is at the backbone of so many applications. This could improve all software applications, and the solution to this problem is worth trillions of dollars.

Many of these computer science problems have to do with finding an answer in an optimal way and being able to prove that it is the optimal solution. The biggest outstanding computer science problem today is "real one-way functions." These mathematical functions can process every single input very easily, but obtaining the input back from a random set of output values is very difficult. We have theories about one-way functions, but we have yet to prove them. The way cryptography and hash functions are used in blockchain technology is theorized to be an application of one-way functions, but we can't prove it. An answer to each of these top computer science problems is worth trillions of dollars, which shows just how hard of a problem they are to solve.

We understand that, for most readers, this is about as dry as chewing on saltines, but we want to underscore that this is not trivial stuff. This is not funny money or magic digital art. This is a breakthrough that had computer scientists all over the world popping bottles of Dom Perignon.

What Is BGP and Why Is It So Important?

The problem that got solved with the invention of Bitcoin and block-chain technology is called the Byzantine Generals Problem (BGP). BGP is a game-theory problem that explains the complexity of organizing an attack using decentralized parties that must agree (gain consensus) without having one trusted leader to organize the whole thing. This is also compounded by all inside mistrust. In a network where no participant can verify the identity of other participants, how can the group collectively agree on a solution?

The explanation goes like this. Say you have a bunch of generals from one army trying to besiege the enemy city of Byzantium. They are all staged around the city but are not under any kind of central coordination. The army must coordinate an attack so that they all strike simultaneously, so the generals must reach an agreement (consensus). If all the armies attack simultaneously, they will win the battle. But if they don't and attack at different times, they will lose. Defenders can send false messages. They do not have secure communications, so messages could be intercepted, or the enemy could employ counterintelligence to sabotage their coordinated attack. How can the generals coordinate their attack?

Solving this problem is important because prior to solving this, all circumstances similar to this required a trusted central party to solve the problem. A centralized solution then comes with the problem that there is now a single point of failure. In the example of the coordinated battle, if the central leader is killed, no coordination is possible. In the example of money and commerce, the whole system dies if the trusted third party, be it a bank, a government, or a company, is compromised.

How Bitcoin Solved BGP

As a monetary system, Bitcoin needed a way to manage ownership and prevent double spends. If all nodes in the Bitcoin network could agree on which transactions occurred and in what order, they could verify each transaction, the ownership of each bitcoin, and establish a functioning, trustless money without a centralized authority. In our BGP example, the nodes are like the generals, operating as peers but without a central control.

By implementing PoW consensus, Bitcoin solved the Byzantine Generals Problem by implementing an objective ruleset for the blockchain. In order to add a set of ordered transactions, called blocks, to the blockchain, a node of the network must publish proof that they have invested considerable work into creating the block by computing a new hash. This work imposes large costs and thus incentivizes them to publish honest information.

Because the rules are objective, there can be no disagreement or deception with the information published to the public ledger. The ruleset governing which transactions are valid is also objective, as is the system for determining who can earn block rewards (mint new bitcoin). Additionally, once a block has been added to the blockchain, it is permanent, making Bitcoin's historical transactions immutable.

Bitcoin, a Peer-to-Peer Electronic Cash System

The solution to the BGP came in the form of an interest in Bitcoin, a new system of money, which proposed a solution that was later called a blockchain. Solving this problem allowed Bitcoin to be invented! Bitcoin became the first (and best known) application of this new blockchain system. The system has two parts: the first is the transactions that are broadcast to all nodes in the decentralized network of servers that validate the data. The second is the chain of blocks created by packaging up all the ordered transactions. As noted in Chapter 1, miners work diligently to find a new hash, which occurs about every 10 minutes or so. The first miner to successfully do so gets to propose the correct order of transactions, collectively called a block (the set of ordered transactions that accurately reflect which addresses hold the entire amount of circulated bitcoin). Newly minted blocks connect to the previously mined blocks and the order of all the blocks is collectively called a blockchain. The winning node gets the mining reward, which is an amount of new bitcoin to be added to the circulating supply of all bitcoin mined. What's novel about this application is how cryptography was applied to create a system.

Other Applications of P2P Consensus

There are many applications for peer-to-peer (P2P) consensus, such as communications, transaction settlement, spam/email, digital signatures, and confirming (gaining consensus) that a message came from a particular sender. Each of these had similar solutions in the past that used a centralized solution, and each had a similar set of problems in that centralization then has a single point of failure. A decentralized architecture provides a solution to that problem.

With Elon Musk's purchase of Twitter, he's been clear that one of his major goals is to reduce/eliminate the harm that bots and anonymous accounts do to the "digital town square" – the service Twitter ultimately provides. There's a great TikTok summarizing his thoughts from a banking conference that I'd recommend everyone watch. His goal is to upgrade the Twitter algorithm so that the real verified users of Twitter have a higher priority in being seen than the anonymous bot accounts, which have caused so much harm, from hateful speech to elections.

Blockchain technology can play a role here. The architecture of Twitter wouldn't be to use a blockchain for every tweet – that would be extremely inefficient. Where a blockchain could be used, though, is to gain consensus on confirming who is really who they say they are instead of trusting Twitter to suss it out for the community. Twitter could use peer-to-peer messages and consensus to confirm that people are who they say they are, thereby removing the requirement to trust Twitter to do it. This application of blockchain technology would make Twitter a true Web 3.0 application and could transform what's possible for our digital town square. Let's see what Elon does with Twitter over the coming years and see if he draws the same conclusions. I hope so.

There are many applications of P2P consensus that could take web applications from Web 2.0 to Web 3.0, where people are in control of their own data and switch flip who controls and profits from that data. Blockchain technology and solving the BGP allows for a whole new world to be created where the users control and profit from their data and not just Big Tech, like Microsoft, Google, Hulu, and Uber. It'll be exciting to see what gets built in the coming decades.

BBC Show *Fake or Fortune* Illustrates the Problem

One of my favorite ways to spend my time is to watch documentaries and series on Amazon. I've watched all the mainstream series so many times I have to dig. One hot summer evening here in Austin, I stumbled upon a series from the BBC called *Fake or Fortune*. I'm really into art, especially contemporary art, but this show covers fine art from the masters like Degas, Picasso, Rembrandt, and Monet. The series follows people who have purchased art on the belief that they have a real original work from a master, and then the show's duo, Phillip and Fiona, set out to help prove whether the artwork is, in fact, a fake or a fortune. They team up to investigate these sleeper paintings that could be forgeries or genuine original masterpieces that no one knew existed. The team uses cutting-edge technology, forensics, and their experience to see if they can help people determine whether their artwork is a fake or a fortune, just as the name of the series implies.

The first episode starts with "The art world, filled with glamour, wealth, intrigue" and shows an auction with an auctioneer spouting prices of "$100,000, $200,000 ... sold for $95,000,000." It explains that there's a darker side of the art world filled with high stakes and gambles. This episode follows a man who believed he had found a real Claude Monet picture. The painting is framed with the thick gold leaf framing you would expect to encase a landscape scene from the Impressionist period for which Monet is known. The man had purchased his painting almost two decades earlier and is looking to prove that it's a genuine Monet.

There's something a little different about how one goes about determining whether a Monet is considered a Monet. There is a book published by a powerful billionaire art dealer family, the Wildensteins, called the *Monet Catalog Raisonne*. This five-volume tome is what all the major auction houses use to determine whether a painting is considered a genuine Monet or not. The patriarch, Daniel Wildenstein, first published the catalog in 1974. After he died in 2001, his son, Guy, took over for the family, and he heads the Monet Committee, which publishes the catalog and determines which works of art make it into the catalog. Guy, almost single-handedly, inherited the power to determine whether a Monet is considered genuine through his position on the Monet Committee and being the publisher of the catalog.

Eighty-two-year-old David Joel is the owner of *Bords de la Seine à Argenteuil*, the work in question, and he's been trying to get the painting into the catalog for 18 years. He's written the Committee many times. Initially, it was the father Daniel who rejected the painting, saying that it was not a real Monet. The Wildensteins say they need two pieces of evidence: documentary evidence that the painting existed in Monet's lifetime and the provenance to track the painting's ownership through art dealer records that would prove the work was sold through one of Monet's dealers at the time. The provenance of the painting needs to track the entire history of ownership. If David can provide these two pieces of evidence, they say the painting will make it into the catalog. So, with his wife, David continues to mount evidence that his painting is an actual Monet.

The series takes the viewer through many adventures from England to Paris to Cairo, Egypt. Phillip, the art expert of the show duo, starts by comparing the signature of Claude Monet. Using experts and special HD camera technology, they compare the signature on David's picture to other Monet paintings that have been validated. The signature does match! The show takes us to Paris where they first look at a stamp on the back of the painting, which says "La Touche." La Touche was an art supplier to many Impressionists back in the day. The duo can prove that La Touche supplied Monet with his art supplies and specific chemicals to make the colors Monet used in his works. They can show that Monet and La Touche were actual friends, proving the painting existed during Monet's lifetime. And it continues.

The show takes us to an art salesroom in Norwich, England, where David bought the painting for about £40,000, a substantial amount of money, but nothing compared to what it would be worth if it were to be entered into the catalog as a genuine Monet. The painting would easily be worth over a million pounds. After the La Touche connection is made, we go to Paris to the Musée Marmottan, which houses the largest collection of Monets in the world. The team uses a Lumiere HD Camera with 240 m pixels, some 100 times more detailed than an average HD camera. The camera can see more about the paint and the work to make this picture. Under the lighting, the camera shows that the brush strokes match Monet's. There we also discover the package stamp on the back of the painting, indicating a dealer stamp with a number. This number is an inventory number of a dealer and, with that in hand, the team travels to Cairo to gather even more evidence. The duo, Phillip and Fiona, find more than they could imagine. The dealer stamp matches up with the leading Monet art dealer of the time, which clearly shows that the painting went directly from Monet to his main art dealer at the time and provides the provenance David needs to prove that his picture is the real McCoy. The episode goes on to show the viewers a list of leading Monet scholars, like the Royal Collection Trust and connoisseurs who believe the painting is genuine.

So, the show ends with the team enlisting professor John House, whom we were introduced to earlier, to take the painting in front of the Monet Committee and, with all the new evidence in hand, get a new determination from the Committee. Recall that two items were requested: documented evidence that the painting existed in Monet's time and proof that the piece was sold by one of Monet's dealers. Our protagonist provided both, yet, even with that and the mountain of evidence, Guy Wildenstein refuses to go against his father's original decision and does not reverse the Committee's stance. It is an epic blow to David and all of the viewers that this injustice is not rectified. It all comes down to this one person, and because of politics or something that has nothing to do with whether this painting is real or not, the painting does not make it into the catalog and therefore will not be considered a real Monet. Welcome to the impact of a system that is centralized – in this case, around one person.

While this isn't a big deal in consideration of everything that's going on in the world, it is an excellent analogy to all the problems that come with having one person or a small group determine a decision. A jury of 12 can be bribed. It's not only conceivable that one person can be coopted (which is generally enough), it's a small enough group that it's conceivable that a majority could be compromised. When consensus requires thousands or hundreds of thousands of participants, it becomes nearly impossible for a corrupt person or group, an unreasonable few, or a powerful self-serving person or persons to blow up a good process. That's the power of blockchain and peer-to-peer consensus. Mature blockchains use hundreds of thousands of nodes in their decentralized network that all need to agree in order to input a valid list of transactions. The resolution to the BGP will lead to innovations we cannot even conceive of at this point in time. It affects applications of digital signatures, art provenance, and title history provenance for real estate or art or luxury brands. It applies to supply chain management and food to ensure that the record of ownership is accurate and true. It applies to medical records and a digital money system. Separating ownership and possession and implementing a public ledger whose entries are immutable create vast possibilities for a digital world that previously just was not possible. The ramifications of solving BGP will become ever more apparent in the years to come. We can do things now we couldn't do before. This, then, is what we call the blockchain breakthrough. This is why we care about any of this at all.

13

Peer-to-Peer Models

As the previous chapter has proven, the economic dynamics of blockchain are embedded in the economics of decentralized peer-to-peer models and architecture. We have more to learn about peer-to-peer issues to inform our understanding of investing for the long run. Consider this our master class in peer-to-peer.

In a peer-to-peer transaction, people create cooperative value directly with one another in a business or personal interaction, contributing to shared production with one another with little to no intermediation by third parties. The Internet and blockchain are force multipliers in increasing the ability of people to engage in peer-to-peer economic activity. For example, Airbnb rentals depend on a complex cooperative system of Internet-based consumer and owner reviews. This virtuous feedback cycle fosters the trust needed for the renter to fork over cash for a rental with no third-party certification and, conversely, for the owner to open their home or apartment to strangers. It's the community that fosters the trust; however, the centralized corporation (Airbnb) is the facilitator of this two-sided marketplace. We think it's pretty clear that these two sides could work without a central arbiter, but up until the blockchain breakthrough this was just not possible.

Designing your sneakers on the Nike platform isn't peer-to-peer; it's a co-creation between a behemoth corporation and a consumer. Venmo transactions are not true peer-to-peer, because Venmo is owned and supported by one firm, PayPal. An e-book is a digital purchase, but usually from one supplier.

We agree with the views of many that peer-to-peer beats traditional businesses in economies of scale, transaction costs, customer engagement, and resilience, and therefore is a secular mega-trend worthy of investor attention. MIT's Geoffrey Parker, Marshall Van Alstyne, and Sangeet Choudhary call this *The Platform Revolution* in their brilliant book of the same title, where they make the case-closed argument for the advantages of peer-to-peer in terms of two-sided marketplaces like Airbnb or Uber. They demonstrate how platform businesses (two-sided marketplaces) beat out pipeline (traditional) businesses because platform businesses can build a defensible moat against the competition.

The MIT authors show that platforms typically employ just a tiny fraction of the people the incumbents employ, as the ecosystem partners provide labor and capacity. By contrast, a pipeline business operates a step-by-step arrangement for creating and transferring value, with producers at one end and consumers at the other as in a traditional linear value chain. In a *Harvard Business Review* article, the authors write that "platform businesses bring together producers and consumers in high-value exchanges. Their chief assets are information and interactions, which together are also the source of the value they create and their competitive advantage." According to the authors, businesses — newcomers and traditional firms reinventing themselves — must understand the new rules, and executives must make intelligent choices about access and governance.

Platform businesses can beat traditional companies by harnessing resources they do not own and scaling at a pace traditional firms cannot match. This has proven itself — and we argue that now, platform businesses can exist even more efficiently in a peer-to-peer mode. We're living in a truly progressive age.

Computer Networking

Peer-to-peer evolved into a business model, but started as an innovation in computer science, where a network consists of a group of devices that collectively store and share files. Each participant or node acts as an individual peer. Typically, all nodes have equal power and perform the same tasks. In financial technology (fintech), of course, peer-to-peer refers to the exchange of cryptocurrencies or digital assets via a distributed network. A peer-to-peer system operates through a network of users with no central administrator or server. Each node holds a copy of the files, which are accessible to all nodes and also contribute to networked operating capacity. Each node can download files from other nodes or upload files to them. This differentiates peer-to-peer networks from traditional client–server systems, in which client devices download files from a centralized server.

Networks use software that mediates data sharing so users can query other devices on the network to find and download files. Once a user has downloaded a given file, they can act as a source of that file.

We've seen now how peer-to-peer networks create the decentralized architecture empowering innovations; decentralized architecture does not have a single point of failure, whereas centralized architecture does. This makes peer-to-peer models more resilient than centralized ones.

Recent developments in microgrids – individual or small energy grids – demonstrate this very well. If a flood or wildfire takes out a big power plant, everybody locally loses power. However, community-based networked solar panels make it possible for communities to source power through microgrids. If communities tap a microgrid powered by solar panels on their roofs, they can share power during an outage.

We've seen peer-to-peer applications in the past, such as music sharing and file sharing. Cutting out the middleman and rent-seekers opens a world of new possibilities since a trusted third party is no longer required for economic transactions. This is changing the world and how we will go about economic activity in the future.

We can consider peer-to-peer services in four archetypes, according to a team of Swedish and Danish researchers who presented their findings at a conference in Milan, Italy:[1]

- **File-sharing platforms**, such as BitTorrent, facilitate the sharing of digital media content such as music, software, or books.
- **Trading platforms**, such as eBay, enable trading of physical goods. These platforms frequently facilitate asynchronous interaction (e.g., bidding via agents) between peer consumers and peer providers.
- **Goods-sharing platforms** based on rental concepts (with eBay and similar sites, one person buys from another) involve relatively expensive physical objects such as scarce parking spaces (Parkatmy-House), accommodations (Couchsurfing, Airbnb), and car rental sharing (Turo, and to some extent, ZipCar).

- **Service-sharing** entails the peer provider and peer consumer collaborating on a mutually beneficial service or experience. Think of TaskRabbit or ThumbTack, the platform for hiring an amateur handyperson peer-to-peer to assemble furniture or exercise equipment, fix a drain spout, install windows, what have you. The Nordic researchers dig into cooperative ridesharing, essentially a digital platform and algorithm for carpooling. A notable example is BlaBlaCar, a French online marketplace for carpooling. Its website and mobile apps connect drivers and passengers willing to travel together between cities and share the cost of the journey. In peer-to-peer style, the company owns no vehicles; it is a broker and receives a commission from every booking.[2]

Due to its architecture, a peer-to-peer network can offer its users many advantages, including easy file sharing, reduced costs, adaptability, reliability, high performance, and efficiency. Let's look at these benefits one by one.

Easy File Sharing

File sharing to the peer-to-peer economy is what slot machines are to casinos: the simplest, fastest application of the ecosystem in which they are allowed. The world first learned about this through the MP3 song-sharing software Napster, which torched conventional music industry models in two notorious short years, from 1999 to 2001. Napster's moment recalls the words of Edna St. Vincent Millay, recited in the film *A River Runs Through It*: "My candle burns at both ends; It will not last the night; But ah, my foes, and oh, my friends – It gives a lovely light!"

Founded by Shawn Fanning and Sean Parker, Napster took the next step after Usenet (founded in 1979) gained popularity as an early Internet discussion platform that allowed the sharing of files. (Usenet would experience the growing pains of early tech as it became swamped with ads, spam, and porn, but it nevertheless served as an excellent preliminary use case and pilot for things to come.) Napster did two things well: it allowed people to share their MP3 music files, thereby cutting out the music industry (and the artists), and provided an easy-to-understand interface.

Napster had 80 million registered users at its peak.[3] Parents wondered where their kids were getting all this music, the record industry scrambled to a war footing, and debates raged over the reality that artists were not being paid. What's more, Napster was breaking the soul of campus IT administrators.

"Private network administrators, however, look upon Napster as a malignant organism devouring bandwidth by the kilobyte and sucking the life out of finite network facilities," reported Pauline Fusco for *ISP Planet* in the year 2000. "Some system administrators said Napster accounted for 40 to 61% of their networks' overall traffic. Yet others found that as little as 5% of their bandwidth was usurped by MP3 file transport. Approximately a dozen university facilities in the U.S. and U.K. have blocked access to the service; students are naturally fighting the ban."

With millions of songs traded through peer-to-peer, the music industry and musicians faced an existential pivot; they needed to kill Napster and start streaming services of their own. So, of course, they sued. As is often the case with the first soldiers over the barbed wire, Napster's owners and customers took the bullets. "That case – *A&M Records, Inc. v. Napster, Inc.* – wended its way through the courts throughout 2000 and early 2001 before being decided in favor of the RIAA on February 12, 2001," recounted History.com. "The decision by the United States Court of Appeals for the Ninth Circuit rejected Napster's claims of fair use, as well as its call for the court to institute a payment system that would have compensated the record labels while allowing Napster to stay in business." On March 5, 2001, District Court Judge Marilyn Patel issued a preliminary injunction requiring Napster to remove any songs named by the plaintiffs in their list of copyrighted material contained on Napster. After these events, the company would attempt to stay afloat, but it shut down its service just three months later.[4]

In these later days of computer processing power, which was a distant dream in 2000, file sharing is easy, fast, and limitless. An advanced peer-to-peer network can share files quickly over large distances. Files can be accessed anytime. Whenever a user wants to download a particular file, the downloading action from multiple locations can take place simultaneously without any hassle. File-sharing peer-to-peer networks range across the universe of known content. They include file hosts such as Dropbox, Mediafire, and Google Drive, which offer the efficiency of sharing documents with no slogging through emails and versions. Peer-to-peer video-sharing sites are led by the household name YouTube (the world's second most visited URL address), Dailymotion, and PeerTube. Several sites skirt or break copyrighted law through film sharing, such as Putlocker and 123Movies.

The German firm StriveCast uses peer-to-peer architecture to solve the problems of dropped signals, jumpy feeds, and poor lighting in corporate video communications. The firm deploys a network of video experts and resources to provide video distribution and video analytics software to companies that heavily rely on online video's smooth and reliable performance. StriveCast serves 150,000 customers daily with a smaller workforce than a football team.

BitTorrent sites deploy a communication protocol that enables users to distribute and share data and electronic files over the Internet in a peer-to-peer manner. The BitTorrent software allows users to send or receive files, while a BitTorrent client is a computer program that implements the BitTorrent protocol. BitTorrent trackers provide a list of files for transfer and permit the client to find peer users, known as "seeds," who may transfer the files. It's worth noting that many of these sites violate copyright laws and are eventually closed; however, they demonstrate the demand for unqualified interaction.

Reduced Costs

A peer-to-peer network doesn't require a server, a network operating system, or a full-time system administrator. Multitudes of users are willing to pay the micro-fractional costs of owning and operating their computers to share in the benefits of the Internet, including peer-to-peer networks. We encourage you to keep an investor's eye on platform-powered businesses which, as we've seen, are disruptive to industry. Cryptocurrency disrupts global financial markets. Uber has driven down the value of New York taxi medallions. Airbnb has challenged the hotel conglomerate. As pointed out by the authors of *Platform Revolution*, platforms eat pipelines.

One big reason is *the costs to scale are radically lower.*

For example, the Internet largely replaced newspapers as the leading source of news for many. News organizations don't have to pay for paper, printing, distribution, and countless other expenses when they publish online. Only the biggest media brands could afford to subsidize their printed editions. Many regional newspapers merged or went out of business. An efficient method of dispersing the news "ate" a less efficient pipeline. The Internet provides infrastructure and coordinates communication.

Social media sites provide a decentralized architecture for citizens to share news and their views of it. We know from recent experience that these online echo chambers aren't necessarily good for civic discourse and cohesion. But there's no putting the Twitter genie back in the bottle, so the challenge must be reforms that are supported by users to improve discourse on the big channels. Twitter, for example, prompts readers to "read the article first" when the headline is tweeted out.

Just as the Internet changed the news industry, it is the lubricant of decentralized platform businesses and peer-to-peer software. Platforms make use of these characteristics for transactions all over the planet. The Internet cuts costs, making peer platforms more efficient than pipelines so they can scale rapidly. They profit from the network effect, which gives them the economic edge over pipelines. They can grow faster than traditional businesses.[5]

Blockchain technology similarly enables a user to transfer crypto-currency across the globe without needing any middleman or intermediary. Therefore, users do not pay the implicit costs for a financial institution to have buildings, facilities, and workforces to maintain those facilities. In the blockchain, each user adds to security and verification; the network helps maintain a complete replica of the records, ensuring data accuracy.

Adaptability

Peer-to-peer networks further extend to include new clients quickly. This benefit makes these networks more flexible than client-server networks. Scalability is cheaper and faster, as we've seen with German startup StriveCast, which serves 150,000 customers daily with a small staff but a robust network of computing power.

Likewise with crisis management. The global pandemic crisis of COVID-19 was devastating and unprecedented in the loss of life, illness, and impact on families, communities, society, and the global economy. The sacrifice and service of healthcare professionals, first responders, and frontline workers deserve to be honored and remembered in history. No one can diminish their courage or the cost of lives and loss.

In the face of this crisis, peer-to-peer companies such as Lyft and Uber, with their decentralized legions of solopreneur drivers, adapted fast to the circumstances and responded to serve their communities. They lacked the hierarchical structure of companies such as FedEx and UPS that went into overdrive, deploying armies of trucks and drivers for two years and more at a 24/7 pace while coordinating closely with the federal government.

Lyft and Uber pivoted with the agility of a super-hive mind. Among the measures taken during the worst of the pandemic:

> The companies installed safety standards, deployed their driver networks, and launched innovative programs. Lyft launched food delivery programs in ten cities. Drivers picked up meals from distribution centers and delivered them to individuals in need, including seniors and low-income families whose children usually rely on free or reduced-fare lunch but were currently out of school.

Simultaneously, Uber made 10 million free rides and deliveries to healthcare workers, seniors, and people in need. During the pandemic Uber Freight carried over one billion pounds of emergency relief equipment and helped distribute PPE to drivers. In addition, Uber Eats waived the delivery fee for more than 100,000 restaurants across the United States and Canada, facilitating noncontact delivery, while also launching "Work Hub," a system to connect drivers to other work opportunities while ride requests were lower. Uber also partnered with the National Restaurant Association to create the Restaurant Employee Relief Fund, which will give grants to restaurant industry employees impacted by COVID-19.

The LyftUp Critical Workforce Program was launched to provide first responders, healthcare, transit, and certain nonprofit workers with free bike and scooter rides as they serve the public on the frontlines. In New York City, Lyft partnered with Citi and Mastercard to fund free annual Citi Bike® memberships for 27,000 critical workers to help them get to work safely during the pandemic. Further, Lyft offered monthly bikeshare memberships to essential workers at no charge in the San Francisco Bay Area, Boston, Chicago, Columbus, Washington, DC, Minneapolis, and Portland. Free 30-minute scooter rides were also available for critical workers in Austin, Denver, Los Angeles, Washington, DC, San Diego, and Santa Monica. Lyft also engineered several options for getting essential workers where they needed to be. In July 2020, Lyft launched LyftPass, a customizable ride-sharing program for employers that provided a way for organizations to pay for the Lyft rides of anyone, from essential workers to guests. In 2020, Lyft helped over 200,000 employees obtain employer-sponsored rides.

This is the power of a platform-based system.

Reliability

Unlike a client–server network, which can crash if the central server malfunctions, a peer-to-peer network will remain functional even if a server crashes. If a single computer goes down, the others continue as usual. This also prevents bottlenecking since traffic is distributed across multiple computers. Point being, it is extremely tough to bring these networks down. Even if one of the sections is about to shut down, other pairs continue to operate and communicate. Some peer-to-peer human-technology networks even thrive under stress and chaos because their decentralized aspect allows them to respond and operate apart from massive institutional infrastructure.

In his book *Antifragile*, Nassim Taleb coined that same term: "Some things benefit from shocks; they thrive and grow when exposed to volatility, randomness, disorder, and stressors and love adventure, risk, and uncertainty. Yet, in spite of the ubiquity of the phenomenon, there is no word for the exact opposite of fragile. Let us call it antifragile. Antifragility is beyond resilience or robustness. The resilient resists shocks and stays the same; the antifragile gets better.... Fragility implies more to lose than to gain, equals more downside than upside, equals unfavorable asymmetry. Antifragility implies more to gain than to lose, equals more upside than downside, equals favorable asymmetry."

Peer-to-peer systems are antifragile, a quality we often discuss as being true of blockchain. On Twitter, for example, the content is exchanged between peers. Users can participate in discussions with other members of the platform and share information. In democratic and populist uprisings against an authoritarian state, such as in Iran, Twitter became an antifragile communications system.

While crypto got clawed by the bear in 2022, we expect it to rebound, and one reason is that it is antifragile. When fiat currency is stressed, decentralized currency thrives. When contracts break, when parties default, those who physically control their assets will be the winners. Crypto assets are bearer instruments and those who possess them control them. Remember the adage "Possession is 9/10ths of the law." Crypto assets are the epitome of antifragility.

Even a diversified portfolio with stocks, bonds, commodities, real estate, gold, private equity, and venture capital cannot help in a sovereign debt crisis. You need assets that do not require trust to transact. You need peer-to-peer networks. You need blockchain.

14

Trusting Trustless Transactions

When we use the word *trust* in crypto investing, we're talking about the often-unconscious assumptions that underlie our economic activity. Technology continues to challenge and revise those assumptions, and crypto is no different. Consider how AI and the Internet of Things continue to shift the duties of the auto mechanic in diagnosing and fixing newer cars. While we still need mechanics, we no longer need to trust them as much to check our car's fluids or diagnose auto systems because sensors do that. Economically and socially, the role of the local mechanic we trusted with our family car is slowly shifting. At some point, perhaps soon, states will have to scrap the current certification process for driving instructors as cars with self-driving features become more common. There is a world that has just begun to open up to us.

So the auto parts and auto repair landscape shifts, as does as the auto industry at a macroeconomic level, because the nature of trust has evolved. If you would invest in the sustainable energy or electric vehicle industry sectors, we urge you to also consider how crypto is taking money in a similar direction.

The consciousness of consumer trust is always shifting. You trust the bank to honor its agreements with you. You trust that the store's bank and payment systems will operate as expected. And so on. This is why brands are so valuable: they are marks of trust. We see it even among the most sophisticated financial and corporate entities, when they've asked people to "trust our public statements, trust our brand, trust our history," but they have often failed to live up to that trust, and have not allowed the transparency needed for us all to be able to verify their trustworthiness.

Stock trading app Robinhood faced dozens of lawsuits after it froze trading on a handful of booming "meme stocks" the app itself had facilitated. These included GameStop ($GME) as well as AMC ($AMC), Black-Berry ($BB), Bed Bath & Beyond ($BBBY), and Nokia ($NOK). Lawsuits alleged that Robinhood users lost millions of dollars because they could not buy or sell stock during the freeze and that the company chose to "manipulate the market" to help other financial institutions. Robinhood settled a class action lawsuit in May 2022.

Zelle, the instant payment system owned by seven U.S. banks, experienced rising fraud rates, revealed little about itself, didn't reimburse customers, and misled Congress. Similarly, revered brand Volkswagen (VW) rigged emissions technology to meet emissions standards only during testing, in a way that could not be achieved in the real world, then covered it up. This resulted in cars that met emissions standards in the laboratory or testing station but emitted nitrogen oxides at levels up to 40 times the standard during normal driving. This "defeat device" broke federal law, and the EPA exposed the fraud. VW's malfeasance devastated consumer trust and cast a cloud over the entire auto industry.

We're not saying that crypto is immune to fraud. Far from it, as, clearly, there is fraud in the crypto industry as well, but the point here is that the examples just mentioned are supposedly "superstar," credible brands that never offered transparency into their processes and technology. These megabrands violated our trust.

"Trust-based systems are baked into our society," wrote Cynthia Martin of Bankless DAO. "But they're fallible. . . . For anyone living in the developing world or a country with an unstable currency, trusting their finances and their lives to the whims of government officials and corrupt politicians has proved faulty again and again."

Lest this sound like a manifesto, we will simply reiterate the point. Any time one can operate peer-to-peer without requiring the validation of an overlord (even a benevolent one like Volkswagen), we're simply much better off.

The Trust-Minimized Advantage

Trust, but verify, goes the Ronald Reagan line, which is about transparency. Blockchains possess the fundamental quality of being transparent. That means that everyone knows what everyone else is doing. There is no opacity or obfuscation.

In the crypto economy, trust is less important, because you don't need a third party to facilitate and settle transactions. When you deposit money into your cryptocurrency wallet, you're assured that the blockchain keeps track of everything. Interested in a work of art? On the blockchain, you can see its provenance (history of ownership and origin). No third parties needed. No need for trust. Instead, everything is authenticated cryptographically.

Trust is an essential part of any transaction. In traditional systems, a central entity validates that a transaction has happened. In the blockchain world, you might hear the word *trustless*. Blockchains are often described as trustless, but this is really a misnomer and, at first glance, gives the impression that there is no trust at all. It really means that business can be conducted on the network without requiring the "trust" or validation of a central entity to keep things running smoothly. It is also about our cultural expectations and mores, as noted earlier.

We prefer the term *trust-minimized*. Trust minimization is the concept that we can conduct business and do a transaction without needing to trust in a single third party who may have motives and biases different from ours. It's these motives and biases that we want to minimize, which prevents deceit, fraud, and abuse. This would stem the tsunami of misinformation crippling our private sector and civil society.

In the blockchain world, we have minimized the need to trust any specific organization or institution because there is no specific central entity. Instead, we rely on the overall community to validate transactions. Obviously, we still need to trust the miner who validates the block; however, we can do so when we consider that thousands of other miners validate their work, and, because all the code of the network is open source, all parties can see exactly how the network is running at all times and exactly how transactions are processed. Bad actors get flushed out, community prevails, and we can do business with minimal reliance on any single party. The need for trust is indeed minimized.

Open-source software is a powerful model and metaphor for per-missionless trust, where transparency is radical and universal. We've only begun to explore the power of this transformation.

Open-Source Software

I know this is getting a little deep but hang with us. We want you to really wrap your head around this because these distinctions will change everything. Public blockchains are open source, meaning anyone can read them. Anyone can also copy them to create their own network via a fork. This huge breakthrough flies in the face of everything we've been taught about proprietary software, that is, that it must be kept secret, must be controlled, and, if it is copied, legal and business consequences must follow.

Open-source code turned the software costs and benefits conversation on its ear. It minimizes shenanigans and opacity in the software but also impels all miners (the ones who are running the network) to work together for the success of all. Anyone can audit the software. Any third party can look at the network at any time and determine whether it's operating as expected. In the world of proprietary software and consumer tech more generally, third parties have no idea how a system is performing its tasks and whether to trust those tasks. As a result, trust is broken, such as in the cases of Microsoft's virus protection software, Apple's battery technology, or Zelle's fraud protection.

Open-source software is the purest expression of a benign open market. Let the best product win and let the consumers decide without regulators putting their thumb on the scale.

More importantly, open-source software reduces risk since it requires all actors in the system to work for the benefit of all in the network and only allows survival if value is produced. "People can cooperate with more peace of mind and security when a system is in place that allows users to have a range of motivations and morals, while the contract still executes the transaction," writes Cynthia Martin.

Software doesn't have bias or change its position. It does what it's been programmed to do, and there is an elegance to that which we rarely find when dealing with entities in power. Before the twenty-first century, it was impossible to imagine a world without trusted systems. But with blockchain technology, that is all changing.

15

No Permission Required

The Permission Monster

The old saying goes that it's better to ask forgiveness than permission. The supposition here is that sometimes permission (for whatever it is that you are wanting to do) won't be granted and *most* things, even if they weren't going to be technically allowed, are forgivable. (Note, we are not talking about breaking the law. Don't break the law.) The concept of acting now and asking for forgiveness later has been used by schoolkids and business magnates, professors and politicians, dear friends and not-so-dear colleagues. It points to something common, however: that there is an authority who must allow whatever action you are taking.

Never was this truer than in the world of finance, where your bank is the ultimate authority on whether or not you can access your money. Your bank is a gatekeeper of funds – and that's for those who can get a bank account. Many cannot even get permission to open a bank account.

As noted in Chapter 4, as of 2021 24% of the world does *not* have a bank account (see Figure 15.1). That's approximately 1.9 *billion* humans; if we take out minors, that's 1.4 *billion* adults.[1]

The reasons for this are wide and varied but ultimately boil down to a lack of funds to meet bank minimums or fees, denying access and availability of financial institutions, especially in emerging markets. The common element here is that banks require you to meet certain requirements to use them. In some cases – whether it is your credit, past history,

24% of the World Does Not Have a Bank Account

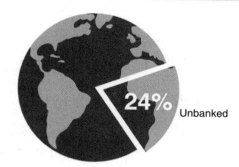

Figure 15.1 Unbanked World Population

availability of funds, or just reporting errors on public (and private) data-bases – people can be denied access even if they *do* have funds. That's permission required.

This problem is exacerbated as almost all unbanked people are in emerging markets, with India having the most unbanked in the world, followed by China, Pakistan, Indonesia, and Nigeria. Not to make this even more inflammatory, but the facts also reveal that the majority of the unbanked are women.[2] Finally, lest one think that this is still an emerging market–only problem, approximately 4.5% of all U.S. adults are currently unbanked.[3] Permission required.

Now, an essential corollary to this is that we need to consider that banks aren't interested in *everyone* having access to financial services. They are businesses run as businesses in order to make a profit and, if you can't help them do that, or if you are considered too high a risk, then, voilà, no bank for you. Permission required.

The Permission Monster can even step in when you are trying to use your *own* money. Lest you think that this is not a problem in the Western world, it happens here all the time. As a case in point, I have a colleague who was looking to invest in a business and the bank simply refused to wire his money at his direction. He had valid ID, proof of funds, and a working bank account at a global institution (that shall remain name-less), but they just wouldn't send the wire, for reasons known only to the bank. Ultimately, he withdrew all of his funds – which was a significant amount – walked across the street, and opened up an account with the bank's competitor, who then gladly wired the funds. What a pain for my friend, though. Permission required.

Please note that I'm talking about bank basics here – a place to store, access, and transfer money. The permission problem grows *exponentially* when one considers loans and credit, as anyone who has ever been declined a loan knows, or simply to have a way to have one's money work for them. Permission required.

The Permissionless Solution

What if you could conduct a transaction and you didn't need to get Big Brother's blessing? What if you could make a trade or purchase simply because you and someone else wanted to, without asking a bank, a vendor, or the government (or your parents, for that matter)? Well, that's *exactly* what you can do with the blockchain breakthrough. We're going to call this the Permissionless Solution.

Blockchains are built to be permissionless, meaning that they are open to everyone. Anyone can create a wallet, which, as noted in Chapter 2, is simply a place on a phone or computer that has access to crypto assets. Anyone can store funds there. Anyone can then send them to anyone else. No one has to grant permission. Period. This breakthrough cannot be oversold.

Let's say Bob, who lives in America, wants to send Sally, who lives in Africa, $1,000. If we look at the traditional banking example, there are a few hoops to jump through, and the process would look something like this: First, Bob needs to apply for a bank account. Apply. Once the myriad paperwork is filed, someone allows Bob to use a bank by granting him a bank account (permission). Once the bank grants Bob an account, Bob needs to ensure that Sally has a bank account (permission). Then, through interbank transfer, generally wire and *with the bank's consent*, Bob can send money from his account to Sally's. We want to underscore the bank's permission point here. I have seen plenty of places where banks refused transactions for reasons that are – absurd. Mostly because they didn't want to. Finally, for the privilege of using your own money, the bank will generally charge one or even both of you a fee.

One of the breakthroughs that blockchain technology provides is the ability to get things done without any of these hoops. Technically, these permissionless transactions occur on public blockchains. That's a mouthful of words, so let's break it down. A public blockchain is a blockchain that anyone can use. It's available to you, me, our parents, our kids, the janitor, the president, and anyone else. Bitcoin is an example of a public blockchain. It is also permissionless, which means that anyone can use it. There is no approval to be granted. It's the opposite of big banks. All Bob needs to do is to create a wallet using any of hundreds of wallet apps. In general, as long as you have a phone or a computer with access to the Internet, you can get a free wallet. Crypto wallets are many and we're making no recommendations here, but they include soft wallets like Exodus and Electrum or hard wallets like Ledger and Trezor. Fortunately, most humans on the planet have a cell phone, including the unbanked.[4] It costs no money to keep money in your Bitcoin wallet. There are no bank fees. You don't need approval to do anything with your money. And a whole new world of financial solutions are available. This changes everything.

Back to Bob. In our permissionless example, Bob has a wallet. Sally has a wallet. Bob sends Sally some bitcoin (BTC). It shows up in minutes and costs pennies. Notably, there were no gatekeepers. No fees. No approvals. No *wonder* it's taken the big banks a while to warm up to this – they lose control! Note that most crypto wallets are not just limited to BTC; they can also store NFTs (digital goods), governance tokens, utility tokens – any crypto asset. For this chapter, we're just going to focus on money, but this universe expands quickly.

The Game, Changed

Imagine, if you will, then, that you were unbanked. You had no way to easily store, save, and transfer money. How would life be different? Consider first that buying food would be a challenge. Buying clothes would be a challenge. Buying . . . anything . . . would be a challenge. A good portion of your day would be devoted to addressing basic human needs – and this is without even considering that more and more, we're moving to a worldwide society that favors cashless transactions. Without a place to safely store and accumulate money, it's virtually impossible not only to transact but to handle life's necessities. Your life would ostensibly be about . . . surviving life. This is how it is for approximately one-quarter of the world.

There is an argument that the unbanked are generally poor and therefore don't have enough money to put into a bank account, but we argue that this is a case of the expense of poverty creating a vicious circle. Let's take a look at an example close to home. Say Mike earns minimum wage but has no bank account. The current federal minimum wage is $7.25 per hour, so working full-time Mike would earn a gross income of $15,080 per year, which we think we can all agree is not livable, so let's double that to a basic minimum of $15 per hr. At that wage, Mike is now earning $31,200, or $1,200 every two weeks, as a *gross* number. After deductions, in Texas that comes to about $992 net (note that Texas is a state with no state income tax!). But how does Mike get access to his money? Well, with no bank account, that leaves cash. Check-cashing services are most happy to provide a service and give you cash, but this privilege can cost anywhere from 1% to 12%. For purposes of our example, let's take a lower-end number of 3%. This means that of that $992, Mike would have a check-cashing payment of $29.72 per check, or almost $30 in fees per month. That's insane.

In this case, banks make it almost impossible for those who do not have a means to save because they are nickel-and-dimed (literally) with fees. No wonder Mike remains unbanked – it's expensive! Now, what happens if Mike wants to send money abroad? There's just no cost-effective way to do it. Wires cost money, cashier's checks cost money, and services like Western Union certainly cost money; even if a transaction is not fee-based, there are hidden costs baked into currency exchange rates. Sending cash in the mail is a fool's errand, so there are no good solutions. The bottom line is that operating without a bank account is simply expensive.

Now, let's change the game. Let's suppose Mike could receive payment directly into a crypto wallet with no fees regardless of the source, whether the deposit is from his work, his family, a friend, or whatever. In the case of work, it makes a *huge* difference, bringing an additional 3% in realized funds into his account. Now that the funds are in his control, he can safely store, save, and transmit funds at virtually no cost to anyone in the world who has a crypto wallet.

This now also opens the world to permissionless financial services. These are services that are not available to Mike if he is unbanked. Now we bring in DeFi protocols, introduced in Chapter 4, where you generally don't need permission to utilize a blockchain DeFi contract. You simply need a crypto wallet.

This changes the game. Mike can put the 3% he would have spent in fees into a DeFi protocol and *make money on his money*. If Mike opted for a DeFi contract that earned him 5%, the net difference to him at the end of the year is $832. At the end of five years it is $4,474. That's money the banks would have gobbled up in fees. Saving requires some discipline, but at least there is the opportunity available that simply was not available before.

Now let's take this global. With citizens worldwide now able to save a little more, to help their families a little bit more, to keep the money they earn, we can impact economies across the world. We can decrease poverty and make the world a better place for everyone. According to the Borgen Project:

> Issues like hunger, illness, and poor sanitation are all causes and effects of poverty. That is to say, that not having food means being poor, but being poor also means being unable to afford food or clean water. The effects of poverty are often interrelated so that one problem rarely occurs alone. Bad sanitation makes one susceptible to diseases, and hunger and lack of clean water makes one even more vulnerable to diseases. Impoverished countries and communities often suffer from discrimination and end up caught in a cycle of poverty.[5]

Helping people not only keep their money but providing the ability for them to grow their money is powerful. We're not naïve here; we know that such a change is not going to happen overnight, but empowering people with money universally is something that is possible with blockchain-based permissionless systems.

We saw this with the impact of cell phones and microloans, which are small loans (in some cases as little as $50–$100) made available to even the unbanked. Both are transformational tools for 24% of the world's population without access to banks. Cell phones allow the availability of information that was, to many, inaccessible. In addition to simply providing the ability to communicate, they allow access to global news, educational content, political information, economic tools, social networks, and so much more.[6] With landlines generally almost impossible to get in many emerging markets such as Africa, the cell phone has allowed those traditionally excluded from society to engage. It has allowed them to have access to information that others simply take for granted. This has had a profound effect on learning and opportunity. Cell phones have provided the initial entry into the world of mobile payments with applications such as M-Pesa (an African application that allows users to store and transfer money via their phones), which we would consider a proof of concept if you will for permissionless wallets.[7]

Cell phones also provide access to a variety of data, such as usage habits, which have been used in emerging markets to determine creditworthiness and lead to microloans. Microloans have significantly changed the shape of emerging markets by providing basic, working capital to individuals and small businesses. In the West, where just about everyone has a credit card, we take this for granted, where the ability to charge now and pay later for groceries, rent, supplies, and so on is a way of life. Getting credit is equivalent to traveling to the Moon in emerging markets where it's difficult to get a bank account. A few have done it, but it's pretty rare indeed. Enter microloans, which can ease the burden of everyday life and financial hardship. According to a research study conducted in Bangladesh, microfinance accounted for a 40% reduction of poverty. In addition, farmers across the African countries are adopting microlending to buy crops. People in rural areas are taking loans from microlenders to set their own business and raise their standard of living, which propels the growth of the market.[8] Mobile phones and microloans are technological advancements that have changed emerging markets.

Permissionless blockchains serve as a transformative tool for people to access and leverage money, including people who haven't traditionally had that access. This is a game changer for those individuals and the communities and economies they live in. These tools not only will drive positive social and economic impact in emerging markets, but will help anyone looking to have a powerful relationship to their money because, frankly, it is theirs. Last I checked, you shouldn't need to get permission to use your own things. Game changed.

16

Digital Scarcity

As a science fiction geek, life changed when *Star Wars* was released. Like many kids, I soon had a complete set of action figures representing my favorite characters from my favorite movie, which took place long ago in a galaxy far, far away. The full set, including Luke, Leia, Obi-Wan, Darth Vader – I mean all – were my toybox's treasure. As time passed, some were lost, some were destroyed in a house fire, and some were kept for years and then just given away. Little did I think that 45 short years later, these figures could be worth hundreds, thousands, or, in some cases, hundreds of thousands of dollars. An auction in 2019 demonstrated a Ben (Obi-Wan) Kenobi figure that sold for $64,900 and a Darth Vader action figure that sold for $62,823.20.[1] Of course, not all figures command these prices. A quick Etsy search shows that I can find a 1979 Boba Fett figure for as little as $75, while the same figure in mint condition in its original packaging can be found on eBay for $575. However, this is quite different from the vintage "Boba Fett J-Slot shooting prototype," which sold for $204,435[2] in 2022. The difference? Scarcity.

Every collector pretty much had the basic Boba Fett figure, so, while we don't know exactly how many were made, we can reasonably assume there are millions in circulation. If you want one, it's not too hard to get. Of the J-Slot shooting prototype, however, only 30 were ever made, which points to the $204,435 price. That, my friends, is the power of scarcity.

The simple fact that has stood the test of time is that if there aren't many of something, and many people want that something, then that will tend to drive up prices. Scarcity creates something special. Something rare. Something that not everyone can have and, therefore, something that is quite desirable. Scarce items can be of limited quantity or can be as exclusive as one-of-a-kind. Think *Mona Lisa*. The Hope Diamond. *Starry Night*. You get the point. These are one-of-a-kind items that are impossible to replicate and, to the right people, are priceless.

Provable Scarcity

Let's break down this concept of scarcity a little more formally. Let's define something scarce as having two specific characteristics. *The first characteristic is that it must be rare AND hard to acquire.* If there are a lot of copies of something, if it is plentiful, then it's just not scarce. Let's look at gold, for example. Gold is rare. There's a limited amount on the planet. Importantly, it's also very hard to get. If you could just go to your backyard, dig a hole, and find a deposit of gold, it wouldn't quite have the same value, would it? The corollary to this is that something isn't scarce just because you say it's rare and hard to get. It's scarce when it is *provably scarce*. This means that you can prove that an item, whatever item that may be, is indeed rare and hard to get. Artists do this all the time with limited editions, issuing say, a run of 100 signed prints of a particular image. That establishes rarity. In addition, if these prints are only sold at an auction, or through very specific dealers, or have so much demand that they sell out as soon as they hit the market, they in turn also become hard to get. This is demonstrable.

The other component to scarcity is that there must be *acceptance* that the item has value. The fact is that my hand-painted pet rock could be one of a kind – but if nobody wants it, if it's not generally accepted as a thing of value, then it ultimately has no monetary worth. Likewise, there may be a limited run of photographs that my neighbor made (great neighbor, great photographer), but if no one wants her work, if there is no acceptance, then there is no real value. Items that are produced in limited numbers, that can be proven to be rare *and* hard to get *and* are something people want – those, we can call *provably scarce*. It's human nature to want things we can't have and, as such, provably scarce items have the greatest chance of value appreciation.

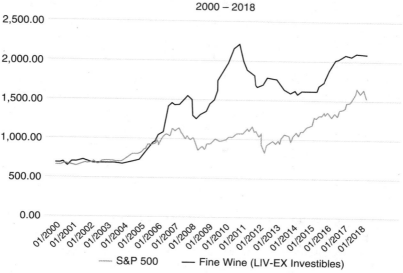

2000 – 2018

— S&P 500   — Fine Wine (LIV-EX Investibles)

Figure 16.1 Fine Wine versus S&P 500
Source: Adapted from LIV-EX.COM and Bloomberg.

We see this concept of provable scarcity in watches, cars, art, even wine! In fact, it may surprise you to learn that rare and desired wine, on the whole, has appreciated at a rate of 13.8% per year (see Figure 16.1). This is more than the rate of return of the S&P 500, which has a history of returning 10.6% per year.[3]

As if that's not enough, according to the ArtPrice 100 index, rare art has outpaced the S&P 500 by 250% from the year 2000 to 2020 and was up 36% in 2021 alone.[4] This is the power of scarcity, and an example of how provable scarcity (rare wine) over time has more value than production capital (investing in stocks).

Digital Scarcity: The New Frontier

It's easy to determine scarcity in the physical world. What about the digital world? This has been another thing entirely, as digital items are generally very easy to replicate. In many ways, this was one of the advantages that the Internet provided, the ability to share information with anybody, anywhere, at virtually no cost. Email revolutionized communication, and it was easy to send a message or a digital picture to a friend, a colleague, a neighbor, or, by publishing it on social media, share it with the world. In most cases take a right-click of a mouse and you have a digital copy that can be shared.

What this sharing did not address, however, was this concept of a unique digital object. You see, digital objects exist today. Think of them as something that's represented electronically. Think of a file on a computer – these can easily be copied and transmitted. They can be documents, data, or graphics, but in general there is nothing to demonstrate their uniqueness. In addition, digital objects can include items from a video game, for example, or the number of dollars that your bank says is in your account.

This is the breakthrough of blockchain, as now we can have *provably scarce* digital items. Provably scarce digital items are items that cannot be properly copied in their entirety and/or are not controlled by a central entity like a bank or a video game. They are objects that reside in a cryptographically secure wallet that only you control and, at the same time, are provably scarce. This was not possible before blockchains. This is important for many reasons.

The Case for Money

So now, let's look at bitcoin. It follows the principles of "sound money"; however, the most important of these principles is provable scarcity. Bitcoin, as discussed earlier, has a supply limited to 21 million bitcoin, approximately 19 million of which are in circulation.

This is a fundamental principle of sound money: sound money must be scarce. In this case, bitcoin is provably scarce due to its fixed reserve pool (see Figure 16.2). The reserve pool of bitcoin has been limited by design, as is part of the actual software programming. We know this is the case because the software is transparent, everyone can see it, and all miners must adhere to it in order to be miners. Slowly, tokens from this pool are released onto the network. Tokens are rare and hard to get (miners compete for allocation of supply) and, over time, we've seen a rise in demand as bitcoin has become more and more accepted while, at the same time, the available supply has been shrinking. Provable scarcity. Imagine, if you will, that bitcoin had an unlimited supply available. It would then cease to hold any value because there would be no provable scarcity. Notably, bitcoin is an example of a *fungible* scarce object.

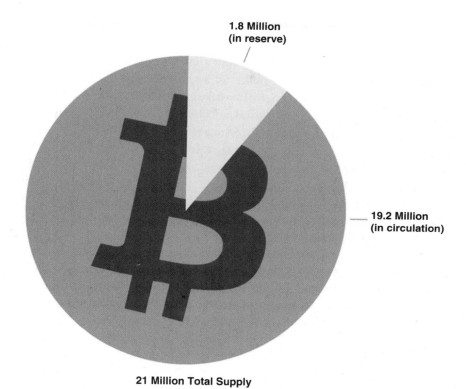

1.8 Million (in reserve)

19.2 Million (in circulation)

21 Million Total Supply

Figure 16.2 Bitcoin Circulation versus Supply

We discussed briefly earlier: fungibility is a property of nonunique-ness. Anything fungible can be swapped with any other like fungible item and it has the same value. This could be a bitcoin, a can of cola from a store, or even a U.S. dollar. A dollar is a dollar, a can of cola is a can of cola, and, likewise, a bitcoin is a bitcoin. They are, ostensibly, the same. Not particularly unique in and of themselves when compared to each other. Specifically, no bitcoin is more or less rare than any other bitcoin and no bitcoin is more or less unique than any other bitcoin. Fungible items can be provably scarce, such as bitcoin, or not provably scarce, such as cola (it's pretty easy to get a can of cola almost anywhere in the world) or toilet paper (except in the middle of a pandemic). A bitcoin can't be copied with a mouse click, and blocks, once written, can't be changed.

The Case for Goods

So that's money. However, as we have demonstrated, blockchains are not just for money. They are really all kinds of digital items. An item can be money, such as bitcoin, utility tokens like ether, the token of the Ethereum network, or even digital goods that can represent any kind of property, be it art, a house, a tree, a record, anything. Just as digital money on the blockchain can have value due to provable scarcity, goods on the blockchain can now have value because they can also be provably scarce. In 2018 the St. Regis Aspen Resort famously issued tokens to represent fractional ownership of their property. They issued 18,000,000 tokens at $1 each, which represented a par value of the property. As the value of the property goes up and down (as all real estate does), the concept is that the fractional value of each token will go up and down. Importantly, these tokens are provably scarce. There was a limited number issued and they are distinct, therefore they can maintain their value. Real-world representations such as this are just the beginning, however.

Scarcity in the Metaverse

The metaverse opens up a whole new world (literally!). It's a digital-only world inside of which we can participate. It's easy to demonstrate owner-ship and provable scarcity in the physical world, and that gives things value, and now we can move that into the metaverse. This is the evolution of the use of non-fungible tokens (NFTs).

We see that in art, real estate, even sneakers (which are cult col-lectibles), with the most valuable pair in the world having originally retailed for $60 and now on sale for $90,000 at the time of this book's printing.[5] Well, we can have that same phenomenon now in the metaverse. Imagine, if you will, that you put on your VR headset and are now walking in a virtual world. You're going to meet some friends, one of whom lives in Paris and another in Australia, for a virtual game of cards. What will you wear? The biggest brands in the world – Nike, Adidas, even Louis Vuitton, are betting that you're going to want to go into your virtual closet, put on your virtual sneakers, sling your virtual Louis Vuitton bag over your shoulder, and know that each item is provably scarce. That's right. Your kids are doing this now in video games — they are *buying* digital goods that have provable scarcity, and the big brands believe that before long everyone will do the same *just like they do in the real world*. This may sound crazy, but the point is that we now have the possibility of supply and demand of goods.

NFTs – Provable Uniqueness

At this point we need to touch on NFTs, non-fungible tokens. Fungible means easily replaced by another item of the same kind — interchangeable, as it were. So then, a non-fungible token is a token (a digital object) that cannot be swapped with any other object, because it is unique.

NFTs get to be NFTs because of provable scarcity. In fact, they are in a very special subset in that they are *provably* unique. An NFT may *not* be exchanged for another NFT like a bitcoin or a can of cola, because each NFT is a unique, one-of-a-kind representation of a digital good. This is why our scenario works. Your avatar can only put on its digital Nike sneakers because it controls the NFT for that pair of sneakers. Likewise with the Louis Vuitton bag. This creates a whole new dimension of digital ownership, for, unlike right-clicking on the Internet, that pair of sneakers can't be copied and used by anyone else. Now, you could let someone borrow your digital sneakers by sending them the token, but they then control that item and, just like in real life, if they don't give it back, you don't have access to it.

So, to sum all this up, provable scarcity is at the heart of supply and demand, and blockchain allows us to translate this concept into the digital world. Understanding this is fundamental to understanding why properly defined tokens can have value. If a token is desired, and provably scarce, it can retain or grow in value. If it is not, well then, it simply won't.

17

A New Decentralized, Autonomous Economy

With digital money, digital assets, and public decentralized digital infrastructure, a key set of benefits arise that vastly improve the nature of commerce. More market participants, reduced friction, increased transparency, reduced risk, and increased capabilities create new possibilities for the global economy as we know it. New production capital invented during the Age of Autonomy® brings forth a new set of tools and infrastructure for an entirely novel system for how we go about commerce and business – a system that looks nothing like the system we have today. And it's just around the corner. This new economic system addresses the large issues we're faced with today and extends to create capabilities not previously thought possible.

Now, when we say autonomous economy, we don't mean that the entire economy is one big robot with no people participating in the production of products and services. More people will be involved and more human interaction will occur, not less. It's the way we will contribute that is transforming. New tools are being innovated and brought to market just like new tools were used in the last technological revolution, the Age of Information, with the Internet: email, the web, software as a service (SaaS), the massive increase in intellectual property (IP), domain names, smartphones, wireless networking, 4G telecommunications networks, intranets. New tools, in the form of new products and services as well as new production capital, paved the way for the paradigm shift we experienced over the past four decades. The way people worked utterly transformed with the Internet and everything that came with it. So too will the new autonomous economy bring about such a transformation.

In this chapter, we will talk about the new decentralized digital economy. In this economy, new money can have sound money principles. Bitcoin is the application of sound money principles in digital format, like gold is the application of sound money principles in an analog format. Money is required, but not sufficient in a new decentralized digital economy: more financial services are possible, and an entire production and economy are possible with the advent of blockchain technology.

Sound Money, Required but Not Sufficient

In the new decentralized, autonomous economy, sound money is required but not sufficient. To the Bitcoin Maximalist, I say consider this: sound money, invented and applied by Bitcoin, is an extremely important innovation in and of itself. It will have strong and wide-reaching effects. Being able to implement an economy on top of sound money principles will help the global economy get away from the damaging effects of having the world reserve currency being fiat currency. Billions more people will be able to participate in the new economy because they will be able to transact on the new public financial infrastructure provided by Bitcoin and a few other Layer 1 blockchains. They will have access to simple financial services like having an account (a wallet) and being able to store value and send value anywhere around the world. That's powerful. They can also earn interest on their capital, if they so choose, by lending it out and creating an interest rate, which generates cash flow from their capital (i.e., their stored value). Anyone with a phone and Internet connection can create a wallet and start to transact. For the billions of people who don't have access to basic financial services, this will have an enormous impact for themselves and the world at large.

However, it doesn't end there. Sound money is required, but not sufficient. An entire decentralized financial system can be built with the power of smart contracts. We can build trust-minimized, permissionless, decentralized public financial infrastructure that provides all the basic financial services. From fractionalization of ownership, through creating, distributing, and holding digital assets (i.e., tokens), insurance, exchange services, derivatives, and all the basic services that banking, insurance companies, asset management companies, and venture capital companies provide today. With sound money, debt, and ownership interest in the form of holding digital assets, you've now got a full financial system that required no permission and no third party, which means — no counterparty risk.

Financial Capital versus Production Capital

In my first book, I build a lot on Carlota Perez's work with her book, *Technological Revolutions and Financial Capital*. In her book, she details a framework for what occurs in all technological revolutions, and she outlines five long-wave economic cycles that have occurred in the past 200 years. She also distinguishes the difference between financial capital and production capital. Financial capital is primary paper assets, like stocks, bonds, and money, that allow agents to store and grow wealth and generate passive investment income. Production capital is new assets that allow an agent to produce goods and perform services. Most times, each new long-wave economic cycle (and technological revolution) creates new forms of production capital.

During the Industrial Revolution, new production capital might be factories and raw materials. During the Age of Information, it might be domain names (.coms), intellectual property (IP), and SaaS websites. During the Age of Autonomy®, I expect new production capital to come in the form of decentralized autonomous organizations/corporations, autonomous protocols, open-source crypto projects, and on-chain governance infrastructure.

Production Capital Supporting the Autonomous Economy

There are many ways production capital will occur in the autonomous economy, and this topic could truly be a book all on its own. As a teaser, we want to explore just a few of these to provide an understanding of how these new structures will begin to transform the ways we interact.

DAOs and DACs: A New Structure for Organization

Associated to blockchains, decentralized autonomous organizations (DAOs) and decentralized autonomous corporations (DACs) are a new method for groups for people to organize around ideas, investments, work, or goals. DAOs and DACs are just a set of wallets and smart contracts themselves running on a platform Layer 1 blockchain. DAOs allow people to come together for a specific reason, whether that's as an investment club, to manage a particular crypto project, or as a group of people with shared goals. Same with DACs, although DACs have an associated legal entity, a corporation residing in a specific jurisdiction, for tax purposes and legal protection.

During various past long-wave economic cycles, human capital was organized differently, whether it was during the Industrial Revolution when people came out of the fields and into manufacturing plants or during the Internet Age when people worked for venture-backed start-ups or their own single-person S corporation or LLC. New structures for how labor will organize typically come with the new period and the Age of Autonomy® is no different.

As of the writing of this book in late 2022, two types of DAOs are in operation. Some DAOs manage a blockchain or crypto project (e.g., MakerDAO), and there are DAOs that act like a venture capital firm (e.g., DuckDAO). We have also seen single-use DAOs, the best example of which is Constitution DAO, an organization formed to purchase an original copy of the United States Constitution. This is an example of how peers could come together as a group and, with an average contribution of $217, collaborate to raise $47 million. Although the group failed to win at the auction, it was a successful example of peer-to-peer collaboration in this new structure.

For the most part, that's the extent of the use of DAOs. But in the not-too-distant future, I think we'll see DAOs used for Age of Autonomy® enterprises to manage and participate with production capital. We'll cover that in the last chapter of this book.

Smart Contracts and Autonomous Protocols

Smart contracts provide the robust capability to programmatically interact with wallets, tokens, DAOs, other smart contracts, protocols, services, AI, and just about everything you want to build in the Autonomous Economy. Autonomous contracts form a particular type of smart contract that focuses on autonomous management and execution. For example, in the world of DeFi, there is a DeFi service called Curve (token, $CRV). One of its features is to poll various other liquidity pools and yield providers and always provide the highest interest rate for a particular stablecoin. This protocol executes and manages itself (i.e., it is autonomous) to provide the best yield within the Curve ecosystem. It is a function that can be called by any other DeFi service or smart contract.

Autonomous Governance

We discussed governance tokens and their relevance to DeFi, but we see them as much, much bigger, really a cornerstone of the Autonomous Age. Governance tokens are a specific type of digital asset. In my first book, I go into some detail about outlining the various crypto asset classes. Governance tokens create their own type of crypto asset class because they have a unique set of properties. In some ways, governance tokens are akin to equity, as they both provide *a right*. Equity is an enterprise's right to cash flows after all expenses are paid. Governance tokens provide a right, but a different right – a holder of a governance token has the right to vote within the associated on-chain governance platform. Most on-chain governance systems are currently *one token, one vote*. However, that may change as governance systems get more sophisticated. We posit that as a particular crypto project ecosystem and network grow and appreciate, so too do the rights to govern it. Only the governance token asset comes with a right.

Many new crypto projects use governance tokens as a part of their token economy. Owners use tokens to incentivize particular behaviors and actions that contribute to the service's economy – the internal activities that occur and contribute within that blockchain.

On-chain governance is a set of services provided through web pages and smart contracts that allow holders of the Curve governance token to initiate proposals and vote on which of those should be adopted. In the Curve example, users must first lock up their tokens in a voting escrow vault (you can see this at https://dao.curve.fi/locker). A user then connects their wallet and interacts with the system. For Curve, users can review and act on specific proposals after they lock

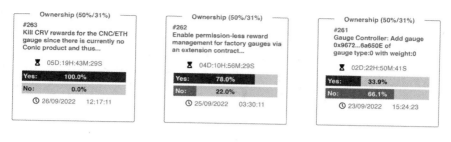

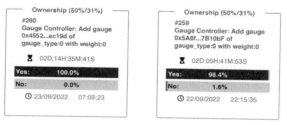

Figure 17.1 Governance Page for Curve Financial – Voting on Proposals

up their tokens for voting. You can see an example of current proposals in Figure 17.1. We're not going to go into detail about each proposal, which isn't well detailed in this diagram, but the point is to illustrate that each specific proposal has votes that are calculated (yes/no) and lead to whether the proposal is accepted or rejected by the community of governance token holders.

Proposals are how a blockchain service gets upgraded, altered, and maintained. Users may propose a new feature or function. They can also suggest different economic settings for how the system operates. Some DeFi projects allow certain thresholds to be voted on that impact the financial economics of the DeFi service. It's also possible that users may vote on how the income gets distributed. On-chain governance provides transparency just like the open-source nature of the blockchain projects themselves. If you want to see the exact code that the Bitcoin miners run, you can see that on GitHub, where most crypto projects maintain their open-source software. Transparency at every level removes opacity and uncertainty. Removing uncertainty removes risk, and eliminating risk adds value. Having on-chain governance creates a systematic methodology to how a blockchain operates, and that, in and of itself, creates value. In the Autonomous Economy, on-chain governance provides a critical method for how users and DAOs interact within their specific community and their particular ecosystem.

The Autonomous Economy Realized

The global economy operates synchronously. That is, transactions are happening in real time, and generally people are waiting for a transaction to be processed. Once complete, they go on their merry way but, until then, they are on hold. (You can see this any time you go to the grocery store.)

In spite of this we're also starting to see more and more automation trickle in to how we make purchases. These are asynchronous in nature. A couple of examples might be turning on bill-pay to automatically pay a bill or setting up recurring purchases on Amazon. These things happen at the time they are supposed to happen, and they aren't waiting for anything else in order to process the transaction.

New Tools Create New Possibilities

As we progress with new economic tools and infrastructure, the economy is simultaneously moving toward an autonomous economy. That is, we have agents acting on our behalf, making real-time decisions, then transacting based on those decisions. Autonomous operations are automation 2.0 – making decisions in the field and operating toward a goal or set of goals. An example of autonomous operation that's right around the corner is autonomous driving. The vehicle is observing its environment, making real-time decisions, and then acting, in this case driving, toward the goal of making it to a set destination. The Autonomous Economy is the transacting of business by an agent on our behalf with minimal human intervention.

As public financial infrastructure gets built out and more widely adopted, via blockchains and digital assets, more economic activity can occur with less human intervention required. IoT sensors generate massive amounts of data. AI turns that data into knowledge. Robots operate autonomously to achieve set goals in the physical world. Then blockchains, with digital assets, can turn knowledge into economic activity without human intervention. *Autonomy is the ultimate competitive advantage*, as it allows for more economies of scale. The autonomous economy is what's possible when the Age of Autonomy® delivers on its designed vision.

The nature of autonomous design makes possible several improvements to what exists today. One is the 24/7, always-on nature of software. No longer do we care if a store is open 9 a.m.–5 p.m., Monday through Friday, with limited hours on the weekends. Or not open on

Sundays, like many stores here in the South. Economic activity can occur with much less friction – being less costly to operate and with fewer rent-seeking go-betweens. No longer are you waiting in line for someone to check you out in a synchronous transaction process. Now, with asynchronous processing as a part of the design, people can initiate a transaction, go about the next thing, and then get notified once a transaction is complete. Transacting can be more secure, although risks can exist if systems aren't designed well. One example is privacy. If we aren't careful, surveillance could intrude on these new financial systems. This is where Web 3.0 comes in, so that everyone owns and controls their data and who has access to it.

New Types of Owners and Ownership

Transformation in the autonomous economy also brings forth new ownership capabilities. In September 2020, the first AI-based CEO was announced to head up Chinese metaverse game company NetDragon WebSoft, which is valued at nearly $10 billion. Ms. Tang Yu, an AI-based robot, will oversee operations for the company. Now, what if AI-driven robots and agents could own property? This is entirely possible now with the production capital built in the Age of Autonomy®.

New production capital, in the form of autonomous protocols, smart contracts, DAOs, governance tokens, and on-chain governance, now make it possible for an AI agent to own and control money and digital assets. The West's capital system is enforced through its legal system. As such, capital and property are associated with personhood. Here in the United States, the Fourteenth Amendment to the Constitution gave certain rights to people. Then, the 1886 case *Santa Clara County v. Southern Pacific Rail Road* concluded that corporations were "artificial persons," which granted them most of the same Constitutional rights as their "natural" persons brethren. It is not too hard to see this definition extend to a different type of "artificial persons," an artificially intelligent robot or agent.

DACs, DAOs, and AI agents will be able to own and control assets within the new economy. This brings about a revolution of what's possible. Famed crypto investor, author, and advocate Andreas Antonopolous talks about extending this possibility to also have smart resources and smart property. This concept embeds the programmatic capability of smart contracts inside ownership-represented NFTs to bring any software functionality to resources and property, both digital and physical.

18

Liquid Venture

We all seem to enjoy the benefits of new technology – from mobile phones to health trackers, video games to social media, the list goes on and on. Many of these programs and products are so ubiquitous that we can't seem to live without them, but it's important to note that, at some point, every technology that you use now was just an idea in someone's head, brought to fruition – generally, via a young, under-funded startup. Enter venture capital. Very simply, venture capital is money directly invested into private companies with the belief that they will grow and, as such, the investment will yield a return. Technology startups always need capital, and technology investing via venture capital is the main way most technology startups get funded. It's also one of the ways that, for investors, money multiplies. Silicon Valley loves a "unicorn": a company that grows to a billion-dollar valuation. Unicorn hunting by placing direct investments into early-stage startups or injecting capital into private companies as they grow has been a proven formula for decades. We've seen it with Amazon and Google, Twitter, and Facebook. We've romanticized these investments as seen in the series *Super Pumped*, which chronicles the rise of Uber. We've celebrated them and then lamented the rise and fall of entrepreneurs and companies like WeWork. We are entertained by the stories of moguls such as Bobby Axelrod on *Billions*. Let's face it – investment has become entertainment and we're enthralled with it. It's not always glamorous, however.

When we look at the success stories mentioned above, each of these companies had something in common: strong early investment and then continued investment by venture capital companies. That's the glamour group. Yet there is a harsh reality: for every success, there are far more failures. The *Wall Street Journal* has noted that three out of every four startups fail.[1]

In addition to this failure rate, it often takes 5 to 13 years for any venture investment to return capital. A very common metric for venture capital is the concept that for every 10 investments seven will fail, two will do okay, and one will win, with a win, in this case, defined as a return that's a multiple of the initial investment and provides enough profitable returns that it makes up for all the other investments. Of course, all investors are searching for the fabled unicorn, a private company with a value that exceeds $1 billion. Venture capital is rarefied air indeed, an environment inhabited by those with the wealth to withstand time and adversity in search of that legendary fabled creature. Importantly, venture capital is *the* way to get in early on a company and get an outsized return. If you want to invest in private tech, you do it through venture investing.

What if there was another way – a way to invest that was available to everyone and did not require millions of dollars or long-term holding periods? You guessed it. This is now possible because of the blockchain breakthrough.

A Cautionary Tale

To fully frame this paradigm shift, we need to look at a bit of history. Let's get in the wayback machine and go back to the year 1998. The Internet was growing and so, too, was this concept of search engines. A savvy venture investor may have picked this up and decided to make an investment in the search engine sector, speculating that such companies would be a major force in the Internet world (yes, there was a time before we googled everything).

One of the frontrunners in this developing world of search engines was AltaVista. They controlled the market, were the envy of all, and seemed the apparent homerun play. AltaVista was as sure a thing as a thing could get. Realizing this, our intrepid venture capitalist could invest in AltaVista. In such case, our investor would be betting on the success of that company and, ultimately, time would tell (set the oven to "bake" for 5–13 years) whether it would turn into a success or a failure.

Suddenly, however, a newcomer, Google, shows up and causes a big splash in the search engine world. Our investor may see this and want to invest in Google as well. That's all well and good, as long as the investor has more capital to deploy, because the funds dedicated to AltaVista are locked up; they are not liquid or retrievable. In this case, an additional investment could be made in Google, but the original investment in AltaVista would have to remain. By 1999, AltaVista was valued at around $2.7 billion, and an initial public offering (IPO) was in the cards. By 2001, however, its IPO was canceled, staff were laid off, and investors lost their investment.

By the way, if you're under 30, you probably have no idea about this story or AltaVista, so you'll have to google it. By doing so, you have again proved our point. Google won, AltaVista lost, and their respective investors won or lost accordingly.

Crypto Assets Revolutionize Investing

You see, before crypto assets, this was it. The *only* way one could invest in a technology company was by directly investing into a technology company, which, as noted earlier, generally requires deep pockets, long holding periods, and a ridiculous risk tolerance. Imagine, however, taking the AltaVista investment and moving it to Google. That would be amazing.

We can do that now via crypto asset investing. We can purchase *liquid* tokens that fractionally represent a blockchain, with the operative word being *liquid*. Because of this, we can trade them on public exchanges. Said slightly differently, we can invest directly in technologies we believe in by purchasing tokens associated with the blockchain, but we aren't forced to hold these tokens forever. Notably, one is getting to invest *early* in the lifecycle of a project, something that could only be done before via direct investment.

This gets very interesting when looking at investing in sectors. If one has conviction in a theme, say, smart contract platforms (or, in our example way back when, search engines), then the *theme* drives the investment strategy. You don't need to pick the winner out of the gate because, as the players evolve, the investment (our purchase of a token) can be shifted to be in the best performers of the theme since the investment is liquid.

This is what we do in our own fund, by the way – we ensure that we have well-chosen themes and that we're always in the best expression of that investment theme while also diversifying to minimize/manage risk.

A New Name, a New Game

We call this concept *liquid venture* and crypto assets, via the blockchain breakthrough, make it possible. It allows all the benefits of technology investments with many additional benefits. Tokens as digital representatives of blockchain offer wonderful liquidity. You can trade them directly or on an exchange. You can purchase tokens in large amounts or with fractions of a dollar. No longer are $1 million investments required – anyone can invest in a blockchain technology at virtually any dollar amount. In addition, it's (generally) easier for you to exit investments.

This liquidity is the difference maker. Imagine, for example, that instead of directly investing in AltaVista, one could purchase AltaVista Token. If AltaVista succeeded and gained more usage, we'd generally expect a properly set-up token to appreciate, to grow in value. Note that we're overgeneralizing here, but let's run with it for the moment. If, conversely, confidence in the AltaVista investment was lost, AltaVista Token could be sold and that investment placed elsewhere. We think that this concept is grossly underappreciated and has the potential of changing venture investing for good.

Other Advantages

So far, we've seen some great advantages. Investments are not "stuck" either in product or timeline, and investments can be made in almost any amount. There is one more advantage worth mentioning, one that we didn't have back in the Internet Age. We've used the search engine analogy quite a bit so let's revisit it. Back in the day, one could not invest in the Internet. An investor could invest in a company building on Internet protocols, but not the protocol itself. In the case of the Internet, the protocol is the Hypertext Transfer Protocol (HTTP), which serves up web pages and allows web applications to talk to each other. Investing in HTTP was not possible then – protocols were given away for free and entrepreneurs built programs on top of them. You could speculate on which company would build the best application (Amazon or Pets.com), but you would not be able to benefit financially by investing *in* the HTTP protocol. Imagine, though, that you could have and that when the Internet was being built you invested $5,000 and, in return, every time a page was viewed, your investment returned to you one one-millionth of one penny ($0.000001). In the early days, with little usage that might have seemed crazy. Today, with approximately five billion Internet users[2] and each user viewing an average of 138 pages a day (note that this number is based on the best data we could find and is a little dated; the number may be significantly more than that), your investment would be returning (5,000,000,000 × 138 × $0.000001) = $690 *per day*. That's $251,850 per year. That's a pretty good ROI for a $5,000 investment. Unfortunately, we couldn't invest in protocols this way back in the day.

Now we can. In blockchain, you can invest directly in the foundational protocols that will build the next generation of technologies by owning their token. A token is a fractional representation of that blockchain. Take, for example, smart contract platforms. We don't know which one will be dominant over time, but we can invest in the platform's token, manage that investment via our concept of liquid venture, and then we don't care whether the platform is Amazon or Pets.com. If someone has built an application and uses the smart contract platform, that platform has greater demand and (in theory and with proper tokenomics) should appreciate over time. This is now possible and is a breakthrough for investors.

Risks Still Exist

Now, before everyone reading this runs off and starts buying crypto willy-nilly (don't do that), let's discuss some of the downsides. Not every blockchain will succeed. Not every crypto asset is a good investment. In fact, of the universe of crypto assets, we would probably say that between scams and general failure rates, most aren't going to make it.

I'm not saying they are all pump-and-dump schemes, although there are plenty of those. Many more, however, will fall victim to the primary challenges of building any business. It's not as if because we have the blockchain breakthrough that the rules of building a successful business go out the window. Just as in the early days of the Internet, most companies fail, especially inside new technology paradigms. (Strangely, many people seem to forget this history.) In order to better understand, let's go back to our Internet example. The Internet has changed our lives; however, the number of companies that didn't make it is staggering. For every Amazon, there were countless copycats, like Buy.com, that most of those reading this will never have heard of. In addition, many entrepreneurs thought they could get rich because they had a great URL such as "Pets.com" but had no viable, differentiated business strategy. Companies like Pets.com, which was founded in 1998 and imploded in 2000, have become a cautionary tale. So, just because something *sounds* like a good idea doesn't mean it is. Even more so, many great ideas never get fulfilled due to competition, funding, poor implementation or execution, and so on. It's more than we'll go into here; however, note that we do have a guide for asset selection that we follow, discussed in Chapter 19.

Remember, we live in a volatile world. In the world of traditional venture, investors are not generally exposed to day-to-day or month-to-month volatility. Back to Uber, if the volatility of that company was actually charted, we propose that it would be far, far scarier than an Ethereum chart. Long-term growth investing, betting on a bull, which is what venture investing is, keeps an eye on the long game and knows that success comes from proper entry and then hanging on.

Get Rich Slow

Liquid venture is a fantastic tool to have in one's investing toolbelt but following this liquid venture approach is not a get-rich-quick scheme. The liquid venture approach is the opposite of the "pick a winner" strategy. In our fund, for example, we are rarely searching to find something that's at pennies with the hope it becomes dollars, although every day we get asked about this coin or that token, many of which we've never heard of. This is not market timing, momentum investing, or gambling on the most talked-about meme coin. Liquid venture strategies are not "one and done."

Instead, we're looking for well-thought-out themes with well-thought-out blockchains that will be meaningful over time. Liquid venture allows one to make calculated investments and then move the investment if a better player shows up in the space. Investing of any kind requires researching and understanding the themes that are most likely to be foundational (such as smart contract platforms) and careful evaluation of the blockchains that have the best chances of delivering on that theme. Execution is an art and science in and of itself; this is a more conservative style of investing. It's time-consuming. Over time, however, this concept of liquid venture allows an investor to greatly increase their chances of success while minimizing the risk of technology investing.

As Warren Buffett has famously stated, "I'd rather be certain of a good result than hopeful of a great one." From our purview, we now get the best of both worlds, and "we are not uncertain" that liquid venture is a very good thing.

PART IV
THE APPLICATION

Now that you understand the technology that's in place, it's time to take action. How can you take advantage of all these new innovations? Remember, investing in innovation can be the most profitable type of investing. If you can learn more and before the other guy/gal, you can be early in the adoption of the next great technology. Those who can understand the technology well enough to gain conviction have the best chance to invest to generate outsized returns.

But make no mistake about it, investing in innovation can be hard. You have to be able to hold your conviction while the average person is mocking you. Famed investor Mark Yusko has this pinned on his Twitter profile:

> The greatest wealth is created by being an early investor in #Innovation
> Making that investment requires believing in something before the majority of people understand it
> You will be mocked, ridiculed & criticized for your non-consensus action. It is absolutely worth it!

We think this is absolutely accurate.

19

Signals versus Noise

We've often said that you can't turn on a financial news station without hearing crypto mentioned incessantly. That, and with constant failures in the world of crypto companies (just like in the early days of the Internet), there is a lot of information out there. We assert that most of it is noise, and our goal now is to give you the tools to sort through the barrage of information to find the true gold. Our goal is to separate the signals from the noise.

All That Glitters Is Not Gold

We live in a world in which crypto has been seen to be the latest, greatest, and perhaps most accessible get-rich-quick scheme. It seems obvious, given the stories of teens who, in 2012, invested a few hundred dollars to buy bitcoin and are now driving Lamborghinis. It begs the question, which is sourced from a nonflattering combination of fear, greed, and envy, "Why can't I do that?"

We're happy for those who had the wisdom/hopefulness/foolishness to look ahead 10 years ago, take a risk, hold on for a decade, and suddenly reap the benefits of such a speculative investment. However, that period is over, so we need to look ahead. Is it possible to generate 1,000× gains on a crypto asset? Yes – but picking those is very, very hard to do. At the time of this writing, CoinMarketCap lists just slightly less than 9,500 crypto assets in the marketplace. That's a *lot* of assets, so let's see if we can narrow that down to a reasonable subset of viable investments.

First, let's weed out the copycats – the get-rich-quick schemes. It's impossible to know the exact number of these, but we can do some quick calculations. Dogecoin, for example, was created as a joke. Certainly, people have made money on it, but it has no real differentiation and no real use but, hey, money is money. Because of its popularity and acceptance, let's call it "real" for a moment. After a quick look again at CoinMarketCap, we find over 100 coins with the name Doge in it, each expecting to be the next big thing. These are schemes created as a copy of something that was originally created as a joke – and it goes further than that, as one of the more successful copies of Doge was Shiba Inu, another meme coin that basically copied Doge. It gets worse because, looking at CoinMarketCap again, we can see over 100 additional coins with the name Shiba in it. The simple fact is that there is almost no barrier to entry. Anyone can copy any other blockchain and make another "get rich" coin. So, even if we consider Dogecoin and Shiba Inu "legitimate," we have 200 copies for each of these coins, or a ratio of 1/100, legitimate/copies. The proper ratio of legitimate coins to copies is *probably* not 1/100, but it's certainly a lot. We can't identify all of these, but we're going to go out on a limb and call it something like 50%. This assumption brings us down to 4,750 legitimate blockchain projects represented by tokens. We highly doubt that there are almost 5,000 legitimate public blockchains right now but for the sake of argument, let's say there are. We know from our Chapter 18 discussion of liquid venture that 75% of all viable technology startups fail. If we apply this metric to our universe of 4,750, there are now 1,187 viable projects that will stand the test of time, or a little over 10% that will make it (see Figure 19.1).

The point is that we believe that the universe of viable assets is a minimal subset of the assets out there. So how do we choose which ones to invest in? It depends on what you are trying to do. Are you trying to pick something for a penny and hope it becomes a dollar? If so, we suggest you save some time, head over to the Vegas Strip, and start putting some money on roulette. You will have much better odds, in our opinion. If, on the other hand, you're looking to make investments in technology that will become foundational, then we do have some criteria to separate the signal (what is valid) from the noise (everything that you hear).

Universe of Assets

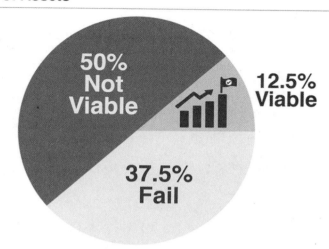

Figure 19.1 Viable Crypto Assets (Estimated)

Sound Assets

First let's look at the two most important criteria of sound money. One, which we discussed in Chapter 16, is scarcity; the other is acceptability. As a quick review, scarcity is important because if something is everywhere, or ubiquitous, and everybody has it, it will probably not have immense value. Like sand. Or rocks – rocks are not scarce. Gold, however, is. This is one of the reasons gold has value. Scarcity is not the only important property, because objects that have value must be accepted.

Acceptance points to the fact that people are using, or at least want to use, whatever that asset is. Gold is scarce and accepted. Radioactive waste is also scarce, yet people really don't want to deal with it (unless, of course, you have a radioactive waste company). Radioactive waste does *not* have acceptance as something of value. Now, if suddenly you could power your car with this waste and it would clean the environment, we might have a different understanding of acceptance. Since we don't, it allows us to illustrate that these two principles are key. We're noting this now because these principles apply not only to money but also to technologies. With that background, let's now look at the characteristics of viable projects.

What Makes a Crypto Asset Valuable

We suggest you consider seven core characteristics when selecting crypto assets as an investment; two noted above, scarcity and acceptance, and five others. The complete list then is:

1. USP
2. Moat
3. Team
4. Market capitalization
5. Acceptance
6. Scarcity
7. Regulatory risk

USP

USP stands for unique selling proposition. A USP is what distinguishes a product or project from all others in the marketplace. To succeed, differentiation is required. As an example, let's look at the USP of the first two popular electric cars. The Tesla S differentiated itself by being the first luxury electric car. The Toyota Prius, on the other hand, was the first affordable electric car of quality. Both differentiated from the marketplace by being electric, and they differentiated from each other based on price. Back to blockchain, just about everyone conflates crypto assets with cryptocurrency, but we find them to be distinct. Cryptocurrencies are tokens that are related to blockchains that are intended to be money. Crypto assets are tokens that relate to blockchains that are not intended to be money, for example, a smart contract platform.

Bitcoin is a blockchain that is being used as money, as an exchange of value, and that's pretty much it (it is a money use case). At this point, it is one of hundreds or maybe even thousands of crypto assets that don't do anything but act as an exchange of value. From our purview, Bitcoin solved the money use case. However, let's look at some of the copies. Litecoin is perhaps the most famous. It is a fork (copy) of the Bitcoin blockchain, and it modified some of the ways the Bitcoin blockchain worked and, yes, it has a faster confirmation time, but we don't see this as being sufficient differentiation. At the end of the day, it doesn't do anything that Bitcoin doesn't do.

Neither does Bitcoin Cash, BitcoinSV, Dash, Digibyte, Dogecoin, and so on. Sure, people have still made money on these coins, but we must consider whether they provide something new and different. If an offering lacks differentiation, it won't succeed. Will they stand the test of time? Some tout better speed or privacy, which might be important, but is it enough to make that coin stand out uniquely? In the case of apples-to-apples comparisons, on the surface, there isn't much of a USP for any of these.

Case in point, if I open up a coffee shop next to Starbucks and I serve essentially the same product but have a different logo — maybe an orange whale instead of a green mermaid — what will incentivize people to buy my coffee? Sure, some will because it's *not* Starbucks but, in general, Starbucks has solved the quality, consistent coffee problem and established such a marketplace that without differentiation, it's hard for new coffee shops to compete. Some now focus on pour-overs, have a more casual environment, better pricing, or specify the essence of their roasting of beans. Some are much higher end. These shops may succeed, but copycats that produce a similar product with similar quality and price simply won't compete.

With regard to nonmonetary assets, let's revisit smart contracts. Smart contract platforms include projects like Ethereum, Solana, Cardano, Algorand, and many others. The overall goal of a smart contract platform is to allow the building of blockchain applications. They are toolkits to launch other blockchain projects, which include, but are not limited to, NFTs, DeFi protocols, Metaverse platforms, and, in general, other blockchains. Ethereum was the first to popularize the concept of smart contracts, and that was their USP. Ethereum also became notorious for being expensive and not very scalable. While the Ethereum Foundation is admirably working to resolve these problems (and may indeed have done so by the time you read this), they opened up the door for other players to compete. Solana, a competitor, ostensibly does the same thing as Ethereum but proposed a new type of consensus mechanism. Where Ethereum initially used proof of work, then migrated to proof of stake, Solana considered the idea of a proof of history mechanism. Proof of history uses blockchain timestamps to determine consensus much faster and at a lower cost. Solana brought a unique selling proposition to the table. Tron, on the other hand, basically copied Ethereum and (upon launch) didn't bring anything unique to the table. We argue that Tron has no distinguishable USP of significant value.

Moat

We all know of medieval times when kings and queens would reside in towering castles to rule their kingdoms. These images of lavish stone fortresses almost always are envisioned with a drawbridge that allows people to cross over a body of water – a moat – that surrounded the castle. The purpose of a moat is quite simple: to make the castle difficult to attack. The arduous task of swimming through a body of water to get the right to scale a stone wall while castle guards shoot arrows down at you is enough to scare most attackers off. Those who did attempt to overrun the compound found that the cost of life was significant and that traversing a moat is not that easy.

That's pretty dramatic; however, the principle of a moat as a characteristic of a project remains the same. If a project can be easily attacked, it becomes more vulnerable, so we want to consider projects that are defensible and have a moat. In 2009 it could be argued that Bitcoin did not have much of a moat. Anyone could copy the chain and attempt to build a better Bitcoin; in fact, many did. Fast-forward, however, and Bitcoin now has a sizable moat, given by a 13-year history, a $1 trillion market cap at its peak (as of this writing), the largest mining community in the world, and growing acceptance as money. Now, the moat is formidable. Its nearest competitor, Litecoin, had, at its peak, a $21 billion market cap, and very little acceptance during the same periods. Where Bitcoin has had continued strong support from the technical community Litecoin has languished. Even the founder of Litecoin, Charlie Lee, sold all of his Litecoin in 2017 – not exactly a vote of confidence. With that, by the way, many coins are competing with Litecoin for the position of being the "second" blockchain money, but we have to note here that we believe stablecoins (crypto assets pegged to another asset, such as a U.S. dollar) will ultimately solve the problem of exchange of value, while Bitcoin will most likely become a store of value for the digital world. With these in place, we just don't see that there's much of a chance of a secondary coin being viable over the long term.

If we look at smart contract platforms, the moat here seems primarily to be the technology. Everyone is trying to build a better (scalable, faster, less expensive) smart contract platform. Some, such as Solana, brought proprietary technology to the table, which became a part of their moat, because this technology is more difficult 'to copy and maintain. In this case, we see that specific technologies can be a moat themselves. In any case, when considering assets, be sure that they are defensible – if they are easily replicated or attacked, that becomes a problem.

Team

With any new blockchain, new token, or any project of any kind, really, consider that the team is everything. As such, we encourage you to take the time to understand who the team is. Have they successfully executed technology projects before? Do they have significant backing from known venture firms? Do they have credible advisors with a proven history of success?

While the mysterious Satoshi Nakamoto remains anonymous, the code that runs the Bitcoin blockchain has been reviewed, vetted, and is publicly visible and available. This code, known as the Bitcoin core, is maintained by a group of developers, the lead of which is currently Wladimir Van Der Laan, who has been involved since 2011 and who took over the lead role from original core lead Gavin Andressen in 2014. In addition to Van Der Lan, many other core developers maintain the project, and, as there is no "company" behind Bitcoin, these developers are subsidized by grants by well-known institutions. For example, Van Der Laan's work is funded by MIT Media Lab's Digital Currency Initiative (MIT DCI). Other noted developers have been funded by Square, Blockstream, Gemini, Coinbase, and other major players. In this case, we have a team led by someone with a proven track record of delivering on the code, supported by one of the greatest academic institutions in the world, MIT. Similarly, Polkadot was founded and is anchored by Gavin Wood, a research scientist at Microsoft before becoming one of the founders of the Ethereum blockchain. When considering Polkadot as a project, the fact that it had a lead with a proven track record goes a long way.

Regarding the counterexample, rather than throw anyone under the bus, we'll say that there are many blockchains and many tokens that have been created with teams that are not identifiable, have no history of technological success, or, even worse, have checkered pasts. Know your team.

Market Capitalization

Market capitalization, the overall public value of a blockchain, offers another important metric. This doesn't necessarily demonstrate who the users of a given project are. However, it does show how the market views a blockchain. Market capitalization is calculated by multiplying the number of tokens in circulation by the price of each token. Ultimately, projects that gain acceptance or at least are viewed to have potential will have a higher value per token and, as such, a higher market capitalization. There is an obvious question: If the number of tokens in circulation values a blockchain, why doesn't every project just circulate hundreds of billions of tokens? The short answer is, as we learned from the conversation about scarcity, more of something does not necessarily make it worth more. In fact, too much of anything will almost always depress prices, so this is a self-correcting system in many ways. Projects that provide value and therefore demand that also have tokens of a proper supply will, by nature, have a higher market cap than projects that don't. Market capitalization measures this balance.

Market capitalization can be tricky, however, because there are many projects such as Dogecoin that, at one point, had a top-10 market capitalization. While this may seem promising, this coin lacks every other key attribute listed here and, importantly, has not always maintained a strong market cap. We would then extend this concept to consider market capitalization over time. Ethereum, for example, has had the largest market capitalization of any Layer 1 smart contract platform since its inception. Other similar protocols have come and gone. Some have briefly danced alongside Ethereum and then have been abandoned. As a guideline, if a token has less than $500,000 in market capitalization, we would, in general, be very wary before adding it to our portfolio.

Acceptance

Acceptance in the world of crypto assets – particularly technologies – boils down to a simple test: Is anyone using the platform? For many years, in the case of Bitcoin, no one was, and this was one of the main concerns of detractors. Now, however, you can use bitcoin at Microsoft, Whole Foods, Starbucks, and many other retailers. There is also a new trend where homebuyers can spend bitcoin to buy real property. In addition, you can also use bitcoin to pay taxes in some states, such as Colorado.[1] Every day there is more acceptance. Conversely, although one can use bitcoin, other alternative cryptocurrencies are generally not accepted at these retailers. This is important.

On the platform front, one only has to look at Ethereum to see that it has been the platform of choice for building blockchain projects since its inception. It has acceptance. Developers have constructed DeFi apps, NFTs, metaverse projects, decentralized exchanges, and many other assets on this blockchain. Recently, however, we've seen other chains start to gain traction, so this will be an exciting space to watch. Many DeFi projects moved to Solana in consideration of Ethereum's scalability concerns, and others, like Algorand, have recently cemented deals with FIFA. When examining any project, look to see who is using it.

Scarcity

As noted earlier, scarcity is an essential characteristic of sound money, and things that are scarce tend to have more value over time than things that are not. Consider what has happened with the U.S. economy over the past years. During the pandemic, the U.S. government printed approximately 40% of all dollars in circulation in a matter of a few years. That's a staggering number, and it's no surprise that, with inflation taking hold, we see that the average dollar is worth less than it was a year ago. In fact, as of this writing, it's worth about 9% less as measured by the July 2022 Consumer Price Index. Mo' money mo' problems, indeed. You would think that we would have learned, as we see from economies such as Zimbabwe, which realized almost unimaginable inflation, primarily due to overprinting money (see Figure 19.2).

How does this apply to crypto assets? Well, let's take bitcoin as an example. Bitcoin, as we've discussed, has a supply limited to 21 million coins. Period. With 19.2 million in circulation currently, the only way you can get a bitcoin is if someone wants to sell one at the price you are offering. Over time bitcoin has had significant price gains, and we believe this will continue in the future. Ethereum also takes this concept seriously as, originally, an unlimited supply was available. Realizing that this would not promote value appreciation in 2021, a code change was agreed upon by the Ethereum community and implemented in what

Inflation and Money Supply Rise in Tandem in Zimbabwe

The chart below gives the relation between the rise in inflation and money supply in Zimbabwe (1994–2009).

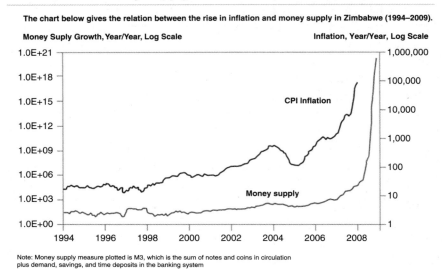

Note: Money supply measure plotted is M3, which is the sum of notes and coins in circulation
plus demand, savings, and time deposits in the banking system

Figure 19.2 Inflation and Money Supply in Zimbabwe
Source: Reserve Bank of Zimbabwe Monthly Economic Reviews.

was known as the London hard fork. Among other things, this code
change made Ethereum *disinflationary*, meaning that coins were being
taken out of circulation every time a block was made.

Conversely, let's consider Dogecoin. There are currently approximately 10,000 new doge put into circulation every minute. We challenge
you to name anything with a potential unlimited number of copies, with
more and more copies entering the market every day, that ultimately
increases in value. That's not how it works. Scarcity drives values in all
things, and digital assets, whether money, NFTs, or any other asset, are
no different.

Regulatory Risk

In Chapter 6 we discovered that regulators are trying to get their arms
around digital assets. It's a whole new world for them, and the SEC and
CFTC are duking it out for control. Rather than ban crypto, however,
they are really looking to ensure that it's implemented safely. The main
thing the government wants is to ensure that crypto assets, which are the

tokens related to a blockchain, are not sold like securities. As a quick callback to our regulatory chapter, securities are assets sold with an expectation of a return, and they are heavily regulated.

Let's say you take a functioning crypto asset like a token, and say, "okay, it's like bitcoin." Then you conclude it's a commodity, therefore you're good to go and you buy some of the token, expecting a return. We would argue that process matters, and it's hard to qualify one-offs or solitary initial coin offerings as commodities. They're not part of a bigger pool of goods that are largely the same. The whole point here is to understand when an asset has the potential to be categorized as a security because, if it does, then you run a risk of the project being challenged – which often means "death by regulation."

Let's say a digital asset comes into existence via an initial coin offering (ICO), where the offering is tokens in exchange for money upfront before a working network or product exists and where the investor expects to make a return. You're buying a stake in a new thing. It's speculation, and anything that falls into this category is most likely going to be classified as a security and will have to follow securities laws. This is exactly what you don't want to do as an investor, because you run the risk of the SEC challenging any project that looks and smells like a security. We urge you to not get caught up in the hype. Look instead at fundamentals and understand your risk.

Risk is a shopworn concept in finance, and we best understand risk as a continuum. It's important to assess where you are with your project or crypto asset, as an entrepreneur or as an investor, on this continuum. We use seven factors to evaluate regulatory risk for any particular crypto asset:

1. Is it a coin or a token?
2. If it's a coin, is it mineable?
3. If it's a coin, is it decentralized?
4. Is it functioning in production?
5. Was there an ICO?
6. Was it offered in the United States in a public or private sale?
7. If it is public in the United States, was there a know-your-customer (KYC)/anti–money laundering (AML) measure performed?

We can evaluate answers to these questions and see where we land in the continuum of regulatory risk. The least risky crypto asset is a coin being used in a functioning decentralized blockchain network. A coin by definition facilitates the operation of its blockchain and network. If the coin is mineable, so much the better because it's got different economics than if people bought it in an ICO (or other means) because, in such a case, miners received coins for work. This notion came out when the SEC announced that bitcoin was not a security. This was huge.

Conversely, if it's an ICO that was offered privately with a pre-mined and centralized token with no KYC/AML performed, there is a very good chance that the SEC could come calling. At the very least we recommend that you use these two endpoints in your continuum and evaluate everything else as they relate to these points.

In a 2018 hearing before the House Appropriations Committee, Congressman Chris Stewart asked SEC chairman Jay Clayton to clarify his view on how regulatory oversight of cryptocurrencies could be split between the SEC and CFTC. Clayton responded:

> It's a complicated area. Because, as you said, there are different types of crypto assets. Let me try and divide them into two areas. A pure medium of exchange, the one that's most often cited, is bitcoin. As a replacement for currency, that has been determined by most people to not be a security.
>
> Then there are tokens, which are used to finance projects. I've been on the record saying there are very few, there's none that I've seen, tokens that aren't securities. To the extent something is a security, we should regulate it as a security, and our securities regulations are disclosure-based, and people should follow those and provide the information that we require.

We don't agree that all tokens are securities, but we do acknowledge that a great many sure look like them upon examination. These are the ones to be wary of. Finally, if a coin is premined and centralized, it's the riskiest type of coin. There are good chances that it has a high regulatory risk of being classified as a security. If the project is decentralized, it will be much less risky because it can be argued it's not a common enterprise. Tokens, by definition, are created on existing blockchains. For tokens the first question is: Is its network functioning? If the token has a functioning network, protocol, utility, or product, then it's less risky and is not a security. This notion emerged when the SEC announced that Ethereum is not a security because it has the features of being an active operating and functioning business enterprise with products and protocols.

The next set of questions revolves around how the crypto asset came into existence. Was there an ICO (money paid to get tokens before it hit the public market)? If so, there's more risk. If it was airdropped or came into existence another way, there's less risk. If there was a public sale in the United States, it's riskier than a private sale. A public sale of a token that did not do a KYC/AML is riskier than one that did. If you have a token that did an ICO and it's not currently functioning and you did a public ICO in the United States with no AML/KYC, then you have the most regulatory risk and you will most likely have to deal with the SEC.

Ripple Labs is in the midst of this as, in December 2020, the SEC sued, claiming they had raised $1.3 billion by selling XRP through unregistered security transactions. Ripple Labs and the SEC are basically dueling it out right now, with the main question being "did they pass or fail the Howey Test?" This will probably be resolved by the time you read this and, if we had to predict, there will be some kind of a deal made. This is of course at the conclusion of a long and drawn-out three-year court case, during which the price of the token cratered as well as soared only to crater again. Importantly, no one knows how this will turn out, but, we argue, why take the risk? We specifically avoid investing in anything that remotely resembles a security. We recommend that you do the same.

In addition, we recommend that you stay abreast of regulations – we know that can be a lot and a daunting task, but this universe is evolving. Our hope is that we see slow but steady regulation like the Token Taxonomy Act (introduced in 2021 and still pending), which excludes digital tokens from the definition of a security under federal securities laws. As clarity such as this unfolds you will be able to make more sound investments but, until then, we always recommend a more measured approach. The last thing you want is for your amazing investment to be clamped down by Uncle Sam.

Putting It All Together

We suggest that all of these characteristics need to be taken into careful consideration. Not every asset that grows in value will necessarily have all seven of these boxes checked right at the outset, but we have seen over time that those that consistently seem to stand the test of time do embrace all of these characteristics. A ubiquitous phrase in the crypto world is "Do Your Homework!" Our intent in outlining the above is to provide a framework for you to do just that. Happy studying!

20

Interpreting Charts

With a rich but accessible understanding of history and context, we can now deliver step-by-step guidance on making crypto a productive element of any portfolio. This is enhanced because public blockchains provide a rich dataset from which investors can analyze information and make a more informed decision. With stocks, an investor may have company data to aid in investment decision making and then use technical price analysis to make more informed trading decisions. With crypto, an investor has crypto project information to analyze, similar to company data, but perhaps not as rich. However, they have fundamental analysis of blockchain data and technical analysis of price movement.

This blockchain data can be quite rich with information to glean because a lot of activity is tracked. Remember, blockchains are networks and provide a network good; therefore, they also have network effects. In essence, network effects focus on the theory of Metcalfe's law – that the value of the network is proportional to the square root of the users (see Figure 20.1). Think about it. If you have one user of the Facebook social network, the value is not zero, but it's close. Now, if you add another user, the value goes up nonlinearly. When you add hundreds of users, the value increases. When you add tens of millions of users, the network becomes defensible against competitors.

A good example is Facebook against Google+. When Google+ came out, it had a lot more features than Facebook. Technically, it was better, but it didn't beat out Facebook because all the users of Facebook

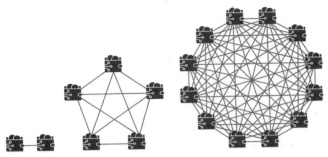

Figure 20.1 Metcalfe's Law

had already uploaded their photos and added their friends. They've shared content and put in work. They don't want to have to do that all over again. Facebook has a powerful "moat" against competitors — it's tough for a new social network that's similar to Facebook to beat it. That's valuable.

On-Chain Metrics

In this chapter, we'll give you a good way to understand blockchain on-chain metrics to analyze as fundamental analysis and how an investor can read charts just like a stock's for technical analysis of crypto assets.

Let's get back to the fundamental data that's available to crypto investors. This public data is called on-chain metrics. Several tools focus on these metrics; tools like Glassnode (see Figure 20.2) and CoinMetrics provide access to this blockchain data but in a chart format. This allows an investor to view historical trends and values for all types of metrics, with data focused on addresses, derivatives, distribution, exchanges, market indicators, and more.

Basic Trend Analysis

The two most important metrics to track are the number of wallets used daily and the amount transacted daily on a blockchain. For example, the Bitcoin blockchains Daily Number of Wallets and Daily Total Transactions give you a feel for how many people are using the network and transacting and how much money is moving through the system. These are the two most important metrics to track trends from

Figure 20.2 Glassnode On-Chain Metrics Home Page

a fundamental analysis perspective. An investor can determine a network's basic value with just these two data points. Value is distinct from price. So, when an investor thinks the value is lower than the price, they can sell, and, conversely, when value is higher than price, they can buy. We like using trend data instead of absolute data because these networks are new and there isn't an established market price for the value like there is with more mature asset classes. If an investor can see that the trend is going up or down, they can make informed investment decisions about how much they want invested in any token based on this fundamental data.

Advanced Analysis

Trend is just one of the things that we review. Analysis of blockchain metrics can get much more sophisticated. The rabbit hole can get deep pretty fast, but we wanted to be sure to outline some of the more important indicators to watch. We recommend that you review these, then revisit them as your knowledge and familiarity with this world increases. As it did for us, this information may need a few passes for it to stick, but stay with it!

Advanced analysis can focus on several core metrics and indicators like:

- *Volatility:* A measure calculated by finding out the square root of the variance of a daily (periodic) price.
- *Market capitalization:* A measure of market capitalization colloquially, although network value more specifically, which is calculated by multiplying the price and the total supply.
- *Daily trading volume:* A measure of the dollar value of an asset traded daily.
- *Realized capitalization:* An alternative calculation of market capitalization derived by multiplying the price of each coin last traded by the size of each trade.

Transaction Metrics

- *Transaction count:* A measure of the number of transactions per day on a blockchain.
- *Transaction value (USD):* A measure of the amount of U.S. dollar value that is transacted/transferred in a day.
- *Active/New addresses:* A measure of counting various actions per day.
- *UTXOs (Profit/Loss/Created/Spent):* A measure of unspent transaction output (UTXO) actions per day.

Production Metrics

- *Issuance (USD):* A measure of value in U.S. dollar terms of how much bitcoin was issued or mined for a period, typically a day.
- *Current (circulating) supply:* A measure of how many coins have been mined and are in use; distinct from total supply, which is how many coins can possibly be issued by the end of the scheduled supply.
- *Mean difficulty:* A measure of the average mean of how hard it is to find a hash below a given target.
- *Hash rate:* The measuring unit of the processing power of the crypto asset blockchain network.
- *Mining profitability:* A percentage calculation that determines income after expense consideration based on mining difficulty, exchange rate, power costs, and hash rate.

Ratios

- *NVT (network value to transactions) ratio:* A crypto asset valuation metric that takes the market capitalization (network value) of an asset and divides it by the transaction value, which is how much is being transacted, exchanged, or transferred each day, in USD.
- *NVT (network value to transactions) signal:* A valuation metric that improves on the NVT ratio by using the same NVT ratio and adding a smoothing mechanism of a moving average.
- *Mayer multiple:* The current price of bitcoin divided by its 200-day moving average (named after Trace Mayer).
- *Metcalfe's ratio:* Like the NVT ratio, except that it relates to Metcalfe's law; calculates price divided by $n \log n$ of the number of UTXOs; can be a relative valuation ratio.

Social Metrics

- *Tweets per day:* A measure of the number of tweets per day that contain crypto-related hashtags.
- *GTrends (Google Trends):* A measure of the number of Google searches per day of crypto-related search terms.
- *Sentiment data:* A measure of sentiment on the crypto markets using Twitter as a dataset and using some machine learning to qualify sentiment.

Advanced Metrics

Many advanced metrics are exposed through blockchain analysis tools, which we identify and describe below. There is so much data that can be obtained from blockchains; seeing that data over time can create significant trend data that you, as an investor, can leverage. Here are just a few that could be incorporated to provide an added layer of sophistication to fundamental analysis.

> *Bitcoin days destroyed:* This measure of the transaction volume of Bitcoin is calculated by taking the number of bitcoins in a transaction and multiplying by the number of days since those coins were last spent. This is used as a better metric to value economic activity;

thus, one bitcoin that hasn't been spent in 100 days (1 bitcoin × 100 days) counts as much as 100 bitcoins that were just spent yesterday (100 bitcoins × 1 day).

Liquidity coverage ratio (from Messari): A ratio of real daily volume/daily dollar value of newly mined crypto assets, where the real daily volume eliminates fake and wash trading from the metric. From that, a liquidity coverage ratio is obtained for a given blockchain network. This gives you a sense of whether there is enough exchange liquidity on a daily basis to handle new liquidations. Low liquidity coverage ratios may lead to steadily grinding lower price in individual markets.

UTXO age analysis: Basically an accounting system used in various blockchains like Bitcoin. *UTXO unspent transaction output* (UTXO) is the technical term for the amount of digital currency that remains after a cryptocurrency transaction. Basically, it is the unspent currency at the end. Every transaction creates a new UTXO, and the age of that UTXO tells in which block that transaction was first included. Analyzing UTXO age can give a savvy investor an idea of when that bitcoin was last transacted and, in aggregate, can give a window into historical and pricing patterns.

NVTG ratio: The ratio of NVT (network value to transaction value) to growth compares to the price/earnings-to-growth ratio in equities. A lower value indicates a better value. This is a relative valuation ratio as well.

Technical Analysis

We've covered the new domain of analyzing blockchain data. That was fundamental analysis. Now, we'll look at technical analysis just like an investor would be used to for stocks, currencies, or commodities. Each asset class always has technical analysis (TA) of price function. The six most important indicators in TA, in my opinion, are: price trend, support/resistance levels, trending with higher highs or lower lows, using moving averages, daily volume, and RSI.

Basic Indicators

Technical analysis is used to make price predictions based on past price trends in an asset. There are several metrics used, like moving averages. Shorter-time moving averages, like a 20-day moving average,

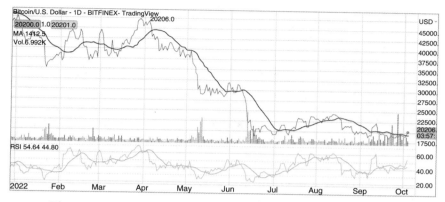

Figure 20.3 Example of Technical Analysis of Price Chart

will be more sensitive to price changes while longer-time averages, like a 200-day moving average, give longer trend information. Each can be used for predicting price trend over different timeframes. Below I outline several fundamental indicators you can use to help in beginning technical analysis (for an example, see Figure 20.3).

Technical analysis helps an investor enhance their approach. The objective is to look for trends in price and find patterns based on past price history. A lot of time can be dedicated to this, so it's important to think about how much time you want to put into your investing process. I think an investor should be putting at least 10 hours a week into their crypto portfolio research and analysis if they are going to manage their portfolio and use technical analysis. Otherwise, they should simply dollar cost average, which we talk about at the end of this chapter, or leave the crypto investing up to a professional on their behalf. The main areas of interest in basic technical analysis of price charts are:

1. *Overall trend:* Are prices increasing or decreasing over a period of weeks or months?

2. *Support and resistance levels:* What are the levels of support or resistance in price?

3. *Buying and selling pressure:* Are there more buyers or sellers?

4. *Trading volume:* How much conviction/how much trading is there compared to the past?

5. *Relative strength indicator* (overbought or oversold or neither): Is the asset overbought or oversold short-term?

Moving Averages

- Simple moving average (SMA)
- Exponential moving average (EMA)

Trading volume (Vol): Measures daily trading volume. A higher transaction volume means an asset is more liquid and therefore easier to trade in larger-size blocks. Higher transaction volume also means there's more conviction for trading at a certain price than if it traded at the same price with lower transaction volume.

Relative strength indicator (RSI): Shows whether an asset is overbought or oversold for a period of time. If there has been heavy selling of an asset, the RSI will indicate that it's oversold by being lower, like 30, and, conversely, overbought if higher, like 70. An RSI of 50 means it's neither.

Price trends tops and bottoms: One of the most critical indicators that I follow is price chart bottoms and tops and whether they are higher or lower than previous numbers. This pattern allows an investor to see if a price trend is continuing up or down or whether a trend reversal might be in place.

- *Higher highs (HH):* Indicates that a new higher high has been put in a price chart pattern.
- *Higher lows (HL):* Indicates that a new higher low has been put in a price chart pattern.
- *Lower lows (LL):* Indicates that a new lower low has been put in a price chart pattern.
- *Lower highs (LH):* Indicates that a new lower high has been put in a price chart pattern.

Trendline Support/Resistance: Looks at moving averages or chart patterns. It helps an investor glean whether a future price may run into support or resistance at certain levels. Suppose there was an accumulation at a certain price in the past. In that case, there's a good chance it might have a similar accumulation in the future because where traders enter or exit positions does influence where they may do a trade in the future. For example, if you chart a level of $10,000 in bitcoin and that level used to be a level of resistance, but bitcoin finally broke through and traded up to $25,000, when it falls or reverses, the $10,000 level may be a level of support on the downside. Conversely, if there was a level of support in the past, that may be a level of resistance in the future.

Trends

- *Uptrends:* Where the moving average line slopes up, indicating the trendline, and the price is making higher highs.
- *Downtrends:* Where the moving average line slopes down, and the price is making lower lows.
- *Consolidation:* Where price oscillates between two parallel horizontal trendlines.

Advanced Indicators

Any curious person with a wee bit of patience for math can glean financially useful insights from basic technical analysis. I recommend getting comfortable with all the basics before applying advanced indicators and metrics. They aren't necessarily better.

- *Bollinger Bands (BBs):* An advanced statistical chart that measures price and volatility of an asset over time. With BBs, a trader is looking to see if the bands are widening or tightening and then where the actual price trend falls within the band. There are entire advanced strategies built using BBs.
- *Trend Patterns*

  - *Reversal:* A trend pattern that shows a change in prevailing trend.
  - *Pennant:* A *continuation* pattern drawn with two trendlines that ultimately converge.
  - *Flag:* A *continuation* pattern drawn with two parallel trendlines that slope up or down.
  - *Wedge:* A *continuation* pattern drawn similar to pennants, but both trendlines are moving in the same direction, up or down.
  - *Triangle:* A *continuation* pattern marking a trend with an entry point, a profit target, and a stop loss. If trading (distinct from investing), all trades should have these three identified *before* a trade is initiated.

- *Cup and handle:* A bullish *continuation* pattern with an upward trend that has paused but then continues. The "cup" is the trend reversal and move higher, then the pause, then the "handle" is the continuation higher.
- *Head and shoulders:* A *reversal* pattern that can appear at market tops or bottoms.
- *Double top/bottom:* A *reversal* pattern signaling where the market has made two unsuccessful attempts higher or lower.

Charting Tools

1. *Trading View*

    TradingView is one of the most comprehensive tools on the market. It's good for novice users as well as the most advanced. You can do so much with this tool (see Figure 20.3). One great feature is that you can create templates that you can publicly share.

2. *Yahoo! Finance*

    Yahoo! Finance has been around a long time. It provides the basics and is easy to use. If you're just getting started, this might be one of the easier tools out there to use and it's free.

3. *Crypto-Trading-Focused Tools*

    a. CryptoWatch: A tool with good drawing tools for charting and predicting future pricing trends.

    b. Cryptrader: A good tool that connects to multiple platforms and exchanges for real-time data.

    c. Coinigy: A good tool for novice traders.

If Nothing Else, Dollar-Cost Average

As an investor, you'll want to consider how much time you want to devote to investing. Many/most people may not want to devote too much time. If you don't want to put in all the effort to track and analyze fundamental and technical data, you should follow the simple method of dollar-cost averaging (DCA).

Dollar-cost averaging is a buying strategy where an investor buys a certain amount at a standard, consistent time interval – for example, buying $1,000 of $BTC every month. When the position goes up, the investor accumulates performance gains. When the position goes down, the investor can accumulate more of the asset at the time of the buying. For example, when buying at the chosen interval, the $1,000 investment into $BTC at $10,000 buys more than when $BTC is at $15,000. This systematic approach removes emotion from the buying process. It's shown over time to provide better results for investors than when they try to time the market bottom with a specific guess. I suggest that if you're not going to invest a lot of time with charting or technical analysis, you dollar-cost average instead. It's still a systematic process and it'll help guard against mistakes driven by fear or greed.

21

Crypto as Diversification in a Total Portfolio

All total portfolios are looking for diversification of noncorrelated assets, which would include U.S. stocks, developed stocks, developing stocks, alternative assets (like gold, real estate, and commodities), bonds, cash, and crypto. In this chapter, we'll look at using crypto as a small percentage of a total diversified portfolio. We will also address how smart investors deploy crypto through hedging, buy and hold, and active versus passive strategies. As famed investor Jim Cramer says on his CNBC show *Mad Money*, "Diversification is truly the only free lunch." We don't agree with a lot of what Cramer says, but on this point we are truly aligned.

Two of the best books I've read on portfolio diversification are David Swensen's *Pioneering Portfolio Management* and *Unconventional Success*. In those two books, he talks about how he changed the endowment fund model to add more alternative asset classes into the total portfolio he was managing for Yale University and how he achieved market-beating returns. The key component is diversification. Investors want to add asset classes that have lower correlation to one another to improve risk-adjusted returns – and it works.

Diversification is helpful because different asset classes react differently to market dynamics. For example, stocks (an asset class) react differently to inflation or economic growth than bonds do. The same goes for real estate. The appreciation of real estate (an asset class), especially residential real estate, will be affected differently by rising interest rates than stocks are. That's because the appreciation of residential homes is primarily affected by the rate of the 10-year Treasury, the rate basis of most mortgages. Home prices can go up when rates go down because it is the monthly payment that most people are using to factor in their decision making. If incomes rise, people can afford to pay more for homes because their income is rising. However, when rates rise, that severely affects how much the monthly mortgage payment will be. A 1% increase in the interest rate can affect the monthly payment significantly. In comparison, stocks aren't nearly as affected by rates and businesses. This is why diversification of asset classes and the target percentage allocations for each is so important for generating optimized risk-adjusted returns.

Safe-Haven Assets – Gold and Bitcoin

A safe-haven asset is an asset that is expected to hold or even increase in value during times of market turbulence. Gold and some selective equities like utilities have generally been seen as safe-haven assets when markets tumble, and more and more we are seeing bitcoin demonstrating this behavior. We've been watching bitcoin for quite a while, and we see bitcoin shifting into safe-haven behavior when:

- VIX is up (the fear index)
- SPY is down (risk assets as measured by the S&P 500)
- Then, if GLD is up (trading like a safe-haven asset)
- Then, when BTC is also up (also trading like a safe-haven asset)

We started with bitcoin trading like a safe-haven asset in 2019 less than 20 days. Then by 2020, it was 53 days. In 2022, it's traded for 20 days as a safe-haven asset by June, and I wouldn't be surprised if 2023 was higher than 53 days. We believe that as the years go on and as bitcoin becomes more widely adopted, it will trade more and more like a safe-haven asset.

Generating Alpha – Market-Beating Returns

Harry Markowitz created the idea of modern portfolio theory (MPT) and introduced that concept in "Portfolio Selection," an article first published in the *Journal of Finance* in 1952. Markowitz was the first to talk about an investment portfolio and asset classes; he won the Nobel Prize in economics that year for his innovations with MPT because he devised a method to mathematically match an investor's risk tolerance to reward expectations through an ideal investment portfolio. Many know that in MPT there are three ways to generate *alpha*, simply market-beating returns: *portfolio construction, asset selection*, and *market timing*. A market will have volatility or risk and generate a certain return. Risk is the same as volatility. If a market or asset has more volatility, it carries more risk. Market risk is known as *beta*. Investors looking for outperformance will need to affect improvement in one or more of these three areas. Most novice investors focus on market timing, but that's the least valuable over a long period. Most alpha is generated through portfolio construction and asset selection. I want to talk about how investing in bitcoin will help in portfolio construction.

There are several dimensions to portfolio construction that help generate alpha. We know that three event-driven components largely generate an investment portfolio's performance:

1. The annual global economic growth percentage and the rate of change of that growth;
2. The expected inflation and the rate of change of that inflation; and
3. Interest rates and the rate of change of those interest rates.

These are the input functions of the event-driven aspect of managing a total portfolio. Bitcoin provides a few unique characteristics when combined in a complete portfolio. One is that it offers more diversification because it reacts differently to growth, inflation, and interest rate changes than other asset classes, such as stocks or bonds. We know this by looking at correlation over a long period of time. Many times, it can act like a risk-on asset, but many times it does not.

In 2020, bitcoin traded over 50 times (meaning 50 days of the tradable 365 days that year) like a safe-haven asset, which we defined earlier in this chapter. We calculate a safe-haven asset as when a volatility index, such as the ^VIX Index, is up and risk-on assets, for

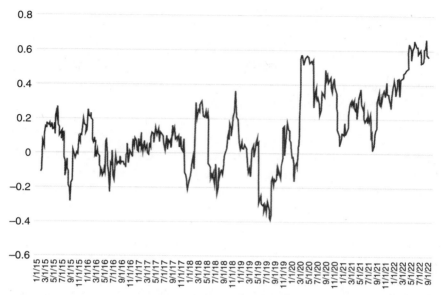

Figure 21.1 Correlation of $BTC to $SPY, the S&P 500 Index

example, the 500 largest stocks with the highest market capitalization like the S&P 500 Index, are down, and $BTC is still up (see Figure 21.1). Many times, gold acts like a safe-haven asset if/when investors were losing faith in U.S. Treasuries (USTs). So, if you looked back in 2020, we measured 53 days of the whole year where bitcoin traded like a safe-haven asset. That's a nice feature in one of your total portfolio's positions. I mentioned this in my first book, but the 60/40 model portfolio, where 60% of a portfolio is invested in stocks and 40% is invested in bonds, is dead! That strategy no longer works for several reasons; therefore, it's critical for today's investors to diversify so that not all of their portfolios behave the same way. There may be big days like March 12, 2020, when everything goes down (except volatility and interest rates), but there are many days where the correlation between bitcoin and stocks works in investors' favor.

Bitcoin also provides different convexity, a portfolio's exposure to standard market risk. It's not an asset that is affected by interest rates, although it does have an indirect relationship to interest rates – or inflation or economic growth, for that matter. A couple of factors affect bitcoin as an asset: an investor can generate yield by holding bitcoin by lending, just like any foreign/fiat currency. An investor could lend out their bitcoin and earn something like 3% to 5% in yield. So, investors may want to think about that income compared to a "risk-free" (LOL) UST. And suppose interest rates stay in a range. In that case, bitcoin has the opportunity to continue rising in price because it is an innovation with an increasing adoption rate – progressing through its innovation cycle (see Figure 11.1 in Chapter 11).

Bitcoin also reacts to inflation a bit differently. Bitcoin reacts more to monetary inflation than consumer price inflation. Monetary inflation relates to central banks and the money supply, whether the central bank is increasing the circulating supply of currency. Price inflation relates to prices rising in the economy. So, if the Fed and other central banks print more and more money, then bitcoin does better pricewise because it's a scarce asset. Just check the Federal Reserve's own website and see the almost-perfect indirect relationship between the price of bitcoin and M2 money supply (which is the money supply, including consumer and bank credit).

Near-infinite money is chasing finite resources and chasing scarcity. We know this because in the past decade, fine art, rare wines, and rare cars have outperformed the S&P 500 substantially by something like 173%. Right now, it's making more sense in terms of risk/reward for an investor to invest in scarcity over productivity. For example, here are forecasts and estimates for the beginning of Q4 2022 for the three major global macro factors—*global growth*, *expected inflation*, and *interest rates*: when things are good, growth is higher than real return on bonds, which is interest rate minus inflation. At the time of this writing, this is not the case. In general, you're losing money as inflation eats away purchasing power. *The headwinds are strong!*

In Q4 2022, the three macro factors are:

1. Expected growth 1.4% (for 2022 and beyond)
2. Expected inflation 8.3% (for 2022 and beyond)
3. Interest rates 3.7% (for the 10-year UST)

Global economic headwind then is −3.2% (Growth − Real return, with real return being Rates − Inflation).

Add to this the fact that the USD is the world's reserve currency and it's strong against all other fiat currencies. This creates recession-producing deflationary pressure.

Looking at these three metrics you can tell that if growth is 3% and expected inflation is 7%, then companies will have a harder time generating profits. So, suppose you're a lazy investor, or just a rational one. In that case, you can easily see that it's going to be, at least in terms of risk-adjusted returns, an easier or better investment to invest in something scarce versus trying to do the calculus to figure out how productive something is.

Bitcoin is also affected by growth. If the economy is growing, then bitcoin will progress faster through its adoption cycle (see S Curve). As more and more people invest with bitcoin or accept bitcoin, the price of bitcoin will go higher because it is a network good. Network goods have network effects. Network effects follow Metcalf's law in that it's nonlinear, meaning the value proportional to the network good is in relation to the number of users. We discuss this in greater detail in the *Age of Autonomy*® book.

Bitcoin is also a very reflexive asset, which is to say, if it goes up, it goes up a lot, and if it goes down, it goes down a lot. Having reflexive assets in a portfolio adds an extra dimension so that you do not have to deploy as much capital to get an outside return. It's almost like having leverage (same but different). The way you capture value inside a reflexive asset is by the duration it's held. If you hold bitcoin for over three years, then you're going to (or most likely going to) generate positive return, at least as history has shown.

Therefore, it makes perfect sense to include some percentage of bitcoin in a total portfolio. It's a scarce asset. It's the cleanest way to invest in scarcity because it's one of the only assets in the world with a precisely known quantity that's treated by the investment community with financialization—meaning the financial industry is building exchanges, derivatives, and futures on it. Bitcoin clearly adds real benefit to a diversified total portfolio. The amount to invest in bitcoin is up to you as the investor. So, how much? The answer is definitely not 0%.

Measuring Risk-Adjusted Returns

It's all well and good if you can generate 70% in one year; however, how much risk did you take to generate that return? An investor who can take less risk to generate that kind of return is better off. We can calculate risk-adjusted return by a Sharpe ratio or a Sortino ratio. These are slightly different, but their intention is the same: to calculate and communicate a risk-adjusted return (see Figure 21.2). If you look up a mutual fund on Morningstar or Yahoo! Finance, you can see that each has a Sharpe ratio

Sharpe Ratio	Sortino Ratio
• Identifies risk as total volatility	• Identifies downside risk specifically
• Uses expected or known rate of return in calculation	• Uses average rate of return in calculation
• Better used on generally lower-risk investments	• More suited for higher-risk investments since it better accounts for that added risk

Figure 21.2 Difference Between Sharpe and Sortino Ratios

and/or a Sortino ratio. A Sharpe ratio of 0 means that your returns match a "risk-free" return, like a U.S. Treasury. Yes, the industry still thinks of a Treasury as a risk-free asset, but if you've read my first book you know that a Treasury has gone from a risk-free return to a return-free risk. A Sharpe ratio of 1.0 is considered acceptable or good, and a ratio 2.0 or higher is excellent. A Sortino ratio, created by Frank A. Sortino, is similar to a Sharpe ratio, but it accounts more for downside risk. This is going to give you a better understanding of an investment or investment manager because upside risk should be good, right? So, the Sortino ratio takes into account the standard deviation of the downside, not the general standard deviation like the Sharpe ratio. Suffice it to say that either one of these ratios will give an investor a much better understanding of an investment's performance than just looking at its return because it indicates how much risk was taken to achieve said return.

Adding Bitcoin to a Total Portfolio

Because of bitcoin's volatility and low correlation to other markets, like stocks or bonds, adding it as diversification in a total portfolio is valuable. The best way to manage a volatile asset is through holding duration and position-sizing. If you're adding an extremely volatile asset into a total portfolio, you'll want to make sure to hold it for three years or longer and keep a smaller position than, say, your stock or bond allocation. You're not going to add bitcoin as 30% of your portfolio. But a 2%, 3%, or 5% allocation might make sense.

I was on the road with Ric Edelman a few years ago when he was putting on a Digital Asset track at several investment conferences. One of the conferences was TDAmeritrade's LINC Conference. Ric had an outstanding presentation that walked through what having a 1% allocation to bitcoin would do in a total portfolio. Even if bitcoin went to 0, it wouldn't greatly affect the performance of the total portfolio. And, if bitcoin really performed, it could add value in the returns.

In Ric's presentation, he demonstrated that adding a small position into bitcoin greatly improves a total portfolio's risk-adjusted returns. That's due, in part, to the fact that bitcoin has a 3+ Sharpe ratio if you hold it over three years. Adding small positions in other crypto assets just extends the same concept. It's important to note that the higher the volatility of a digital asset, the smaller the position size may be in a crypto portfolio. Having a crypto portfolio that may be 5% of a total portfolio and having 5–10 digital assets in that crypto portfolio may well be the best way to improve a total portfolio's diversification and risk-adjusted returns. And remember: the goal would be to hold these digital assets for three-plus years. Unless you're spending significant time researching and managing your digital asset portfolio, I wouldn't recommend having more than 5% to 10% allocated to digital assets, and bitcoin would be the highest allocation inside that crypto portfolio.

22

Savings, Borrowing, Income Strategies, and Taxes

They say there are two things that are certain in life and one of these two things is taxes. Since we can't avoid them, we're going to round out this section by diving right in while, at the same time, exploring concepts such as the benefits crypto provides via saving and borrowing.

Taxes

Taxes are pretty simple. Pay them. Do not fall into the trap of thinking that crypto is untraceable and anonymous, because that's just not the case. Exchanges such as Coinbase know who you are, they know what you have traded, and the law states that any gains made on the trade of any crypto asset are taxable. Let's say that Jane buys one bitcoin at $18,000. The price appreciates to $25,000, and she decides to sell it to buy a different asset, such as Ethereum. From the perspective of the government, it doesn't matter that Ethereum is still a crypto asset. When Jane sells her bitcoin at $25,000, she has made a gain of ($25,000 − $18,000) = 7,000, and that gain is *taxable*. Gains also must be calculated on any transaction in which crypto is transacted at a higher value, including trading it for dollars, buying other crypto, or even using it to buy a cup of coffee or a car. Any time there is a real-ized gain, taxes must be paid on that gain. Calculating this is relatively straightforward if you use one exchange and are just trading crypto assets; however, if you use many exchanges, you will want to consider implementing third-party software such as CoinTracking, which is designed to calculate gains and losses across all exchanges that you use. (Author's note: We are *not* recommending any particular software pack-age. As players in this space change all the time, we recommend that you research and find out who are the established players in your region with a history and a proven track record.)

There is one more nuance here that can work to your advantage because losses are also calculated the same way, so our dear Jane can work the opposite situation. Let's say, for example, that she bought her bitcoin at $25,000 and then the price drops to $18,000. By selling her bitcoin at that lower $18,000 price, she will have a *loss* of $7,000 that she can apply against her gains. Most importantly, unlike stocks, she can use this as a strategy. She can sell her bitcoin and immediately repur-chase it again at the same price, locking in the loss while still retaining her asset. You can't do this with stocks because of the *wash-sale rule*, which states that any time an equity is sold, it cannot be repurchased for at least 30 days. This is specifically to prevent tax loss harvesting, as described here. However, such a rule doesn't exist (yet) for crypto, so, until it does, have at it. Finally, and importantly, losses can generally only be used to offset gains of a like type, which is, in this case, crypto, so please do not think you can take a colossal crypto loss and then use it to offset your employment income. Instead, because you can carry losses forward, think about it as a way to lock in losses to offset your future crypto gains. As always, this is not tax advice, and laws do change, so our best recommendation is to check with your tax advisor before implementing any tax strategy.

Saving

Your dad, mom, uncle, sister, or someone you dated in college probably told you at some point that the way to make money is to have your money work for you. Ultimately, however, getting your money to work for you often entails risky investments, long-term lockups, or complex structures that aren't for the faint of heart. A bazillion books have been written regarding saving money, ranging from tips and tricks to motiva-

Average CD Rates: 2010 – 2019

After the global financial crisis, CD rates fell to their lowest point in U.S. history.
Toward the end of the decade, rates began rising, but fell again in 2019.

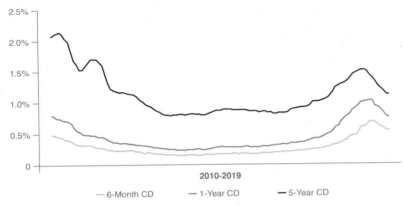

Figure 22.1 CD Rates, 2010–2019
Source: Bankrate National Survey.

tion to actual methods to make your money go further. We're not going
to touch that. Instead, we're going to discuss a unique opportunity that
exists in the world of crypto assets: the ability to generate yield.

Remember, if you will, the days of a savings account that earned
any meaningful interest. It's been a while. Even worse, certificates of
deposit – instruments where you commit to locking up your capital –
have returned less than 1% for a one-year CD and less than 2% for
a five-year CD over the past decade[1] (see Figure 22.1). These aren't
exactly inspiring numbers.

Well, there is another solution. Enter stablecoins. A stablecoin is a
crypto asset that is directly pegged to another currency in a one-to-
one relationship, generally a U.S. dollar. Because of this if you have
$100, you can convert it to 100 USD Coin and it is worth the same
$100. Once this is done, a world opens up, as many centralized and
decentralized vendors will gladly pay you to use your money. They
do this, just as banks have done for years, by offering interest against
deposited funds. How much is earned depends on the size of the
deposit, and the vendor. At the time of this writing, you can earn rates
as high as 12%. What is exciting about this is that you can do this
while keeping your principal in a *relatively* risk-free item that has the
value of a U.S. dollar. (Author's note: We're not doing this to discuss

the impact of inflation, the position of the U.S. dollar in the world, or the fact that its buying power is consistently less over time. We're simply going to focus on the fact that a dollar does not have the volatility that most crypto assets, at least now, do.)

With regard to that relatively risk-free comment, let's be clear: there are a few things to be aware of here. The first is that the U.S. government, among others, is really exploring regulation, and some lenders, for the moment, aren't offering this in the United States until there is absolute clarity. In addition, any time you have a counterparty (et tu, Celsius?), you have a risk that the counterparty could fail. We believe there is less risk in DeFi contracts, but as these are also new, there is always a chance that there could be a software problem that allows a breach. As the technology advances, however, we expect that over time regulation will be sorted out, central players will exist that provide minimal counterparty risk, and DeFi contracts will have matured to the point that, as well, the risk is minimized. This isn't magic, by the way. Entities can provide such great rates because, at least right now, demand for stablecoins far outweighs supply. We don't see this changing any time soon because stablecoins, since they are linked to fiat currencies, are poised to be the preferred way to transact in the blockchain world.

Borrowing

There is another way money can work for you in the blockchain world: borrowing against the crypto you own. This is called collateralized lending. Collateralized lending involves the process of, once again, depositing some principal in the form of a crypto asset, either in a DeFi contract or in an account at a counterparty like a bank or a lender. You can then borrow against this deposit. This allows you to gain access to liquidity – you can keep your asset while using the money. You may own, for example, $50,000 of a certain asset that you believe will be worth even more over time. Because of this, you want to keep it, but you also want access to cash. Voilà! Collateralized lending. How much you can borrow depends on your agreement with your lender and ultimately is a function of loan to value (LTV), which dictates how much you can borrow compared with the value of your deposit. So, for our earlier example, let's revisit Jane. If Jane has BTC worth $25,000 and deposits it with a lender that will give her 50% LTV, she can borrow $12,500 and use it for anything she likes. Now she has access to her money *with no taxable gains*. This, ladies and gentlemen, is one of the ways that the wealthy make their money work for them. They borrow against assets they own, which provides money they can use without incurring any taxes. Borrowed money is tax-free and can be used to take that vacation, buy more assets such as real property, or even buy more crypto assets, depending on one's risk tolerance.

LTV gets a little tricky with volatile crypto assets, however, so let's look at some risks. If you have X dollars deposited in the form of Ethereum, for example, and that Ethereum drops in price by 50%, you could be outside your stated LTV. In such cases, you may be called upon to deposit more funds or the contract or company facilitating the loan may sell some of the collateral to bring you back into a reasonable LTV, so always pay attention to the rules and do your homework! Also, as we learned from Celsius, there is risk any time you have a counterparty holding your asset, whether that's an exchange, a bank, or a lender. Borrowing against your crypto sure is an excellent option to have if needed, so that you have access to money while holding on to an asset that you expect to appreciate.

Income Strategies

There are several good ways to generate income with digital assets. Just like in traditional investing, you want to have strategies for capital appreciation and for income generation. With traditional asset classes, you may invest in a variety of assets that generate income like REITs, bonds, preferred stock, and dividend-paying equities. It's similar to investing in digital assets.

There are three main ways to generate income with digital assets. The first is to use CeFi or DeFi to lend out your digital assets and generate a yield. With CeFi, you can let the exchange lend your assets out on your behalf and there's generally not a particular duration. You can ask for your digital assets back, which typically takes two business days. With DeFi, there are several duration options, with each managed by a smart contract. The yield provided is typically better for longer duration just like with bonds or CDs in TradFi (traditional finance).

The second way to generate income is through staking of assets. If you own proof-of-stake (PoS) assets like $ETH, $DOT, or $SOL, you can generate a staking income by allowing your assets to be used as the collateral for a node validator. Remember that in PoS, the blockchain is secured by staked assets and the validator is putting up her assets to confirm the minting of a block has legitimate transactions. If the validator is wrong, they lose their staked assets for submitting an incorrect block. The income is generated not through lending but through transaction fees paid for managing transactions. This is interesting income because at present the IRS has stated that earning this income is not creating a taxable event.

The third way to generate income is by providing liquidity or market making services by providing a liquidity pool inside DeFi. A liquidity pool (LP) is typically two digital assets together submitted in a pool, for example, USDC:ETH. With an LP, inside DeFi like a service such as Compound, if DeFi users use your liquidity pool in their trade (in this example they are trading $USDC for $ETH), then you're providing liquidity in the marketplace and you will get paid a portion of the trading fees for providing such liquidity. This service is typically provided by big players in TradFi, but a user of almost any investment size can participate in this service in DeFi.

To summarize, there are 3 ways to generate income with digital assets:

1. Lend out your digital assets and generate interest payments.
2. Stake your digital assets, which help secure the blockchain network and therefore create staking yield payments to the staked asset holders that are paid by transaction fees generated through the use of the blockchain network.
3. Create a liquidity pool by providing two digital assets paired together, which allow liquidity for the buying and selling of those trading pairs in a DeFi application.

23

Investing and Retirement

Digital assets should be a part of a total portfolio. They are ideal assets for a portion of a retirement portfolio for the reasons we've already discussed in previous chapters. They provide diversification. Because they are volatile assets with price, holding digital assets for a longer duration decreases risk. Investing in both bitcoin and other digital assets can provide high risk/high returns in the portfolio as well as monetary inflation protection from the Fed's money-printing schemes. Finally, a savvy investor can use stablecoins to generate income similar to bonds in a traditional portfolio, oftentimes with much less risk. It's counterintuitive, but holding a U.S. dollar–backed stablecoin, like $USDC, is less risky than having a U.S. dollar in a savings account because the stablecoin is overcollateralized (i.e., more assets are held as collateral than the stablecoin's value in circulation) and backed by U.S. Treasuries. And, if the investor uses DeFi, they can remove any counterparty risk from the equation. Holding three different digital assets can produce a portfolio similar to a traditional portfolio that has stocks, bonds, and gold.

Right now, people are contemplating how to gain exposure to crypto inside their retirement accounts through vehicles such as crypto funds and direct token investment. A more practical solution is to have self-directed IRAs that hold digital assets directly. Crypto assets are bearer instruments without counterparty risk if investors can keep the digital assets directly inside a secure wallet. The smart investor of the future wants to avoid counterparty risk, and that's the beauty of digital assets executed on public blockchains. There are no intermediaries to add uncertainty or corrupt motives to your retirement planning. Think about the CeFi/DeFi historical example we talked about earlier. Those investors using DeFi instead of CeFi were not wiped out like the investors who used a CeFi firm like Celsius. Those Celsius investors are still waiting for the bankruptcy process to work out to see if they will get any of their principal back, and the answer is most likely that no, they won't. Crypto is like owning bearer bonds or physical gold. You hold it, and we have all heard the anecdote *Possession is nine-tenths of the law.*

Ways to Invest in Digital Assets in Retirement Accounts

There are several ways an innovative investor can get exposure to digital assets. The most common approach, investing in an indexed stock exchange–traded fund (ETF), is not currently possible. As of the time of writing this book, the SEC has approved a futures-based Bitcoin ETF but not a spot Bitcoin ETF. However, many other ways do exist. This section will outline ways an investor can invest using a retirement account.

Investing with IRAs

There are several ways to invest in digital assets using a retirement account. Several companies provide the option for an investor to use a self-directed IRA. Companies like uDirect and Equity Trust Company are among many that will help an investor set up a self-directed IRA and then from there, an investor can look to invest in digital assets directly. A self-directed IRA is required if an investor wants to invest directly. This is one reason why so many people would like a 40-Act-compatible (discussed later) fund for bitcoin, ether, and other digital assets.

Using Options and Futures Accounts

There are options for options investing in crypto (pardon the pun). Options are structured derivative products, available via the Chicago

Board of Options Exchange (CBOE), the only regulated provider in the United States. There are also other options contracts available by firms like FTX.US (formerly LedgerX), which provides a complete set of options on bitcoin and ether. All options trading employs leverage in the investment product since an investor is buying or selling a right to purchase or sell a fixed amount of tokens at a specific price (the strike price) by a certain date (the expiry date).

Bitcoin and ether futures are available on the Chicago Mercantile Exchange (CME). Futures contracts allow an investor to buy one contract equivalent to 5 bitcoins or 10 ether. This product will enable an investor to employ leverage as well as use a margin account. A margin account holds U.S. dollars as collateral against the purchased futures, and the margin account can have fewer dollars than the number of futures contracts held. Therein lies the leverage. Investing in futures contracts requires an investor to be accredited and able to get a commodity account.

Investing with Single-Asset Trusts

Single-asset trusts are a compelling way to get some exposure to the crypto markets. There are a couple of companies that provide these products. The benefit is that this might be a solution for you if you don't want to manage and store the digital asset. With these trusts, you'll need to be an accredited investor to purchase directly, although any investor can purchase units in the trust on the secondary market through a brokerage. Investors can buy units in these trusts and hold them now in a standard retirement fund, like an IRA, with an account at a brokerage firm like TDAmeritrade or Fidelity. This is much simpler than setting up a self-directed IRA, then investing directly with coins and tokens, although there are drawbacks to trusts because they don't expand or shrink the number of units that are circulating. Instead, all the outstanding units add up to a value that may be at a premium or discount to the net asset value (NAV) they represent, which is the value of all the coins held in the trust multiplied by the price per coin.

For example, if a trust like $GBTC or $ETHE were available to a nonaccredited investor through their brokerage account, those products might trade at a significant premium to NAV. As an investor, you'd be taking a risk both on the underlying asset's price move and the premium. If the premium fell dramatically, even if the underlying asset did not move, an investor could experience significant loss. I remember a time in 2020 when the Ether single-asset trust offered by Grayscale was *trading at a 400% premium to NAV*. At one point, if all the premium had been pulled out of the vehicle, investors could have experienced an 80% loss even if the underlying asset price went up or did not change!

Crypto Hedge and Venture Funds

Many crypto hedge funds focus on investing in liquid crypto assets. Our firm, Tradecraft Capital, manages such a fund. These investment vehicles are private and often exempt from certain regulatory requirements provided certain conditions are met. They are comprised of limited partners who invest in the fund and a manager who is responsible for the actual investments. A crypto hedge fund might employ many different investment strategies just like in the traditional hedge fund world. Some strategies include volatility, arbitrage, long-only, long-biased, long/short, quant, smart beta, discretionary, and opportunistic. Crypto hedge funds require investors to be qualified investors, which means they have a net worth of more than $2.2 million in assets, excluding their primary residence. Crypto hedge funds typically have a lockup of 12–18 months and are more liquid than their venture fund counterparts, although they often have longer-term investment horizons.

Crypto venture funds specialize primarily in early-stage venture investing within the crypto space. These funds invest in companies to get both equity and tokens in crypto enterprises. Venture funds typically have a 7- to 10-year time horizon with a 5- to 7-year lockup. Investors must also be qualified investors, just like with crypto hedge funds. This higher qualification for investors generally is required for investment vehicles like funds that charge higher fees while, generally, an investor could invest directly in a crypto startup and only need to be accredited, which means income of more than $200,000 per year for at least two years and/or a net worth of more than $1 million.

No "40-Act" Spot ETFs (Yet)

Currently, there are no spot ETFs that give exposure to spot bitcoin or any other crypto asset, although there is a futures-based Bitcoin ETF. Spot bitcoin refers to the actual coin asset versus some derivative investment products like futures or options, which are contracts and not the actual underlying asset. The term "40-Act" refers to legislation, the Investment Act of 1940, which Congress enacted after the 1929 stock market crash and subsequent bear market that lasted almost a decade.

Some trusts act somewhat like an ETF, but they do have drawbacks, as discussed previously in this chapter. There have been many attempts – from the Winklevoss twins to Van Eck to Bitwise Asset Management – to launch a spot Bitcoin ETF. From interpreting communication from the SEC, we're not going to see a spot ETF anytime soon. However, spot Bitcoin ETFs do exist in other countries like Canada though an investor would need a Canadian-dollar account with a brokerage dealing in Canadian stocks and funds.

While no spot ETF exists at the time of publication of this book, Grayscale Investments filed a lawsuit on June 29, 2022, against the Securities and Exchange Commission (SEC) for denying the conversion of its Grayscale Bitcoin Trust (GBTC) to a spot Bitcoin ETF. Since the SEC used the argument of a lack of investor protection, Grayscale Investments also lay out a reasonable argument, stating that the futures-based ETF that was approved is riskier to potential investors than a spot ETF.

Investing in Digital Assets

Whether you're investing in a retirement account or directly, the key is to invest in the digital assets themselves. Buy the tokens and coins directly and hold them. By doing this, you'll avoid massive risk, and you'll enjoy the benefits of digital asset investing.

Toward the end of 2022's crypto winter, there was the downfall of FTX. FTX was one of two of the big-daddy global, unregulated centralized exchanges where customers were able to buy and sell digital assets. FTX came crumbling down due to fraud and a whole bunch of reasons that we will all find out. But the main problem was easily avoidable if you weren't trying to participate in the new school of thinking bringing the old-school way of doing things. The whole point of digital asset investing is to not have counterparty risk, which those who trusted FTX with their funds and their digital assets learned the hard way. Lessons are expensive. Investors and customers alike lost billions in the collapse of FTX. But don't mistake that for digital asset investing. The people who invested in the coins and tokens and used decentralized finance (DeFi) to lend and borrow their digital assets did just fine. They got their interest payments that the smart contracts execute and maintain, and they kept on running 24/7/365.25.

FTX was a centralized exchange that allowed its customers to buy spot digital assets – that is, the actual coins and tokens – or to buy futures contracts called perps (for perpetual contracts). Perps are a new form of futures investment contracts in that they don't have an expiration date like all other futures contracts. Many sophisticated crypto investors were using these perp futures contracts to express a long position in a particular digital asset. For example, instead of going out to a centralized exchange and buying, say, ether (the digital asset of the Ethereum blockchain), customers would buy ether perps (futures contracts) and they would get to participate in investing in Ethereum. If $ETH went up $100, then the Ethereum perp futures contract would go up (roughly) $100. The perpetual futures markets mimic the spot market, but it is not the same.

Futures contracts, like perps of digital assets, are "paper" assets. They require a counterparty, and you don't own the actual digital asset. Digital assets are bearer instruments, and although they are digital, you can own/control them; they're yours. Relate to them more like gold or stock certificates or bearer bonds. You own them, you hold them, and you control them. You can take them and hold them on your computer in a digital wallet. You can lend them out if you want and generate interest income. You can stake them in a node/pool and generate income by being a holder of a particular digital asset.

For example, with ether, you can hold your ether in a wallet. You can pay for things in $ETH. You can stake your $ETH and generate staking yield whereby you'll get paid for securing the Ethereum blockchain network.

The future potential is unlimited – and you'll want to participate in that future. Investing in digital assets and holding them directly is the key to success. They belong in a total portfolio with other active investments.

24

Looking Ahead

"Beam me up, Scotty" is a quote that is etched in the heart of every science fiction fan. The seminal *Star Trek* from the sixties is well known and well loved, and this quote has become part of our cultural lexicon. Importantly, this show predicted many things that are a part of our everyday life right now – things that seemed outlandish at the time. Let's start with the communicator, a flip-phone device that allowed our beloved crew to communicate with each other over vast distances. Clearly with cell phones we have that now. Then, of course, there was the ability to speak to a computer and get information. Siri and Alexa have checked that box as well. Meanwhile, on the ship's bridge, Lieutenant Uhura had an earpiece in her ear which allowed her to hear conversations, communications, and information directly and privately. Yup, thank you, earbuds, we've got that too. Of course, the transporter allowed the crew to move vast distances instantaneously. (Okay, okay, we don't have teleportation yet, but we're pretty sure scientists are working on it, and given the rest of the predictions that the show made it would not surprise us at all if teleportation is someday a reality.) The point of all of this is that things that seemed far-fetched and made *no sense* 50 years ago are now commonplace today. The future, it would seem, is often not as far off as it seems. We can ignore it or step into it; the choice is ours.

Up until now we've mostly been unpacking and explaining core aspects of the world of crypto and blockchain, but in this chapter we're going to look ahead to the future that is unfolding and provide a preview of the impact this technology may well have.

The Future of the Metaverse

Today technology around the metaverse is still young, although there are multiple commercially available virtual reality headsets that allow us to experience alternative worlds. What is important is that we will be able to operate *inside* of a virtual world and, although young, this technology is *much* farther along than you may expect. During the pandemic, I could strap on a headset, beam into a virtual world, and have a conversation with family on the other side of the country. Our avatars were blocky and the environment was crude, but the experience was eye-opening and the technology was much more advanced than I had anticipated. Competition to create "the" metaverse is fierce, with major corporations striving to dominate. At the same time, blockchain upstarts are also pursuing their own vision. Who wins is not important, although we expect that, like most things, it will ultimately end up in a duopoly, with a couple of metaverses being ubiquitous, similar to how Apple and Samsung have ostensibly chopped up the smartphone market. The point is, sooner than you realize, we'll be able to engage virtually in much the same way we do today and we expect we'll quickly evolve from the blocky avatars today to slick, lifelike personas that get closer and closer to being indistinguishable from reality. Just as the Matrix films represented a virtual world that our heroes were trying to get out of, before long we'll have virtual worlds that everyone is trying to get in to!

Play in the Metaverse

For many, the metaverse is perceived to be a playground and, certainly, socialization and gaming will be a compelling use case. Imagine putting on a headset and being able to sit around the table with your family from all over the world and have a conversation – or play a game of cards – or see a concert together. We already have the beginnings of this kind of interaction today. Expanding this concept, imagine being able to travel to a foreign land, maybe Iceland or New Zealand, and wander, experiencing the countryside as if you were there, with all of the detail, including touch, smell, sight, sound, and even taste. Or participate in a *Dungeons and Dragons*™-style role-playing game as if you were actually *in* the game, with so much detail that it seems like it is actual reality. This extends to everything you might imagine. We will be able to experience virtual amusement parks, jump out of airplanes, race cars, even travel to other worlds (as best as they can be imagined), all without leaving the comfort of our couch. Consider sports as well. E-sports are a huge institution – in some cases as big financially as regular sports. It's perfectly logical to consider that, in a future metaverse, virtual teams can play each other with virtual fans experiencing the game just like they were there. Of course we have a way to go before this happens – but we see this as inevitable. The point is, we can experience a digital world – and people in it – just like it is the world that we are used to.

This brings us to consumerism, noted by the fact that many luxury brand companies have already jumped in. Adidas, Nike, Louis Vuitton, and others have all made large investments in having their digital products available in the metaverse. These, of course, are digital goods generally represented as NFTs, and these brands are counting on the fact that people are going to want them just as they do in reality today, because the blockchain breakthrough allows us to own these digital objects. So, in the future, you'll be able to activate your goggles (or glasses, or contacts, or perhaps a teeny-tiny disk), go to your metaverse house, put on your authentic NFT Nike sneakers and perhaps an NFT Armani suit, and hit the virtual town with your virtual friends in style! It's not all just about fun and games, however.

Work in the Metaverse

Recreation and play tend to take the lead in any new technology, but let's stop and consider the work implications of the metaverse. If we can meet virtually and play, why can't we conduct business? Videoconferencing has already demonstrated the ability to interact with people in a much more familiar way and conduct business much more intimately than just by telephone. Consider the metaverse to be the next level, where you will be able to take a virtual meeting with a colleague, client, or vendor and experience the meeting just as if you were sitting at a desk or around a conference table. Contracts could be negotiated, products purchased, and deals designed in a whole new way. The barriers of air travel halfway across the country or halfway across the world vanish as a consideration. For this reason, countries such as the UAE and Japan are sinking billions of dollars into this new technology, committed to becoming leaders and seminal waypoints in this new world. Similarly, banks like JPMorgan and Fidelity have already established their virtual outposts in Decentraland, a popular metaverse (at least at the time of this writing). The simple fact is that almost everything that can be done in reality can be done in virtual reality, and countries and businesses are moving forward to claim their stakes early.

Play-to-Earn Evolved

The metaverse application to gaming is obvious, whether you are sitting across from your opponent in a card game or chess match or watching your favorite Fútbol team (yes, soccer) from a virtual stadium where you have a front-row view. There is another twist to gaming, however, that has recently taken shape, driven by the blockchain break-through, which is play-to-earn. It functions exactly like it sounds and is happening today. Gamers, just by playing, can earn items and, indeed, money (crypto assets) that have value in the real world, not just in the game. While this may sound like a strange lark or an episode of *Black Mirror*, this is happening, today.

The concept is quite simple. Players log in and, by completing tasks inside a game, they can earn crypto assets. These assets reside in a player's wallet and, like any crypto asset, can then be transferred to external wallets or exchanges and then exchanged for actual cold, hard cash. This is the breakthrough. You see, in conventional gaming, anything earned is only granted given the purview of that video game. A gamer can own the item, whether found on a path, bought with in-game money, or acquired because of "leveling up," only because the video game says so and only while playing that game. Because of block-chain technology, however, the assets reside in cryptographically secure wallets and can get transferred out. An asset is not owned because the game says you own it; it's owned because you *actually own it*.

Like many new technologies, the future of this needs to be ironed out. The play-to-earn phenomenon got absolutely huge in the Phil-ippines in 2021 and 2022, and gamers were legitimately earning a livable wage; however, the constant game play, market swings, and new technology challenges ultimately made this untenable. Nevertheless, the fundamentals of this type of technology exist, and the ability to take something virtual into the real world has now been prototyped and what is important to take away here are the concept and opportunity.

The concept of something from the virtual world (fake money) being able to become something in the real world (real money) has the potential to change everything.

The Future of Sovereign Data

One of the great impacts of the world of Web 3.0 considers the fact that we can own our own data. Data is held in cryptographically secure wallets, and each wallet is controlled by a person. Wallets can be attached to applications, websites, and stores, and data can be transmitted only with the consent of the owner of the data. Let's explore how this might look.

If you've made it this far, you now understand what happens when a bitcoin is sent from person to person. We all know that your money can be transmitted only with your consent, but this gets far more interesting when applying the same principles to data. Let's unpack the concept touched on earlier, that all of your sensitive personal data could be stored in an NFT that you and only you control. This token cannot be changed without your permission and, importantly, it cannot be used or even read without your consent. It is not stored or controlled by any third party so it cannot be hacked, reducing ID theft, nor can it be monetized or ever used without your permission. You may choose to let third parties read subsets of the data, such as your driver's license number, Social Security number, or birthdate, but not every piece of data about you needs to necessarily be released and none of it is controlled by anyone but you. Now, you may actually choose to share your data and maybe even sell your data to certain companies for their use, but this is always and only with your consent. Health records are an obvious example. Complex laws have been written basically as a solution to the fact that so much of your health data is in so many hands. In fact, it's so spread out that sometimes it's even hard for you to gather all of it. What if, instead, you had an NFT of all of your health information? As long as you can prove that it is your data, which you can with your private keys, you can share it with whomever you want. By the way, this doesn't mean that you can modify your record as desired. This NFT could be set up so that only licensed doctors (with your permission) could modify it and, importantly, every modification would be trackable. Importantly, you also don't need to rush around to many doctors and insurance companies filling out forms asking them to release *your* data to *you*. You own your own data. You control your own data. Period. As with many other aspects of new technology this whole thing needs to get fleshed out properly, but the potential exists now, so it won't be long before this becomes commonplace. This will also, however, require a change in mindset and increased personal responsibility, but ultimately we see this as a good thing as well.

The Future of Money

We've spent so much time talking about the technology that we'd be remiss if we didn't talk a little bit about the future of money. While Bitcoin jockeys to be the reserve asset of the digital world we encourage you to think of it more like gold. It's a reserve asset of limited qualities that becomes a store of value. Transactions in the future between two people will be done via digital assets that represent the monetary tools with which we are most familiar. Of course, we're speaking of the dollar, the euro, and other fiat currencies.

Stablecoins, which are representations of a government-backed currency such as the dollar, gain all of the benefits of blockchain technology. Stablecoins are backed 1–1 with the underlying currency, so if you have 100 USDC, you can exchange it for $100. Stablecoins allow us to transact as peers in the same way that we do cash, but with the benefits of transparency, immutability, and decentralization. With cash getting ever more scarce, we see stablecoins as the future of transactable money.

Of course, governments do seem to like some sense of control, so they have their own answer, central bank digital currencies (CBDCs). You will certainly be hearing a lot about these in the future. The digital dollar, noted earlier, or currencies like the digital yuan are already gaining strides in China. We have to point out that these are not, at least today, blockchain-based implementations. These are digital representations of a currency we already know and love – but in a digital format. The distinction here is that CBDCs will have a counterparty that is in control. Just like Visa really has the final say-so on what is on your credit card statement, the government will have the final say-so on your digital dollars. It is important that they are not conflated with cash because, unlike USDC stored in your wallet, any digital dollar ultimately is granted use by Uncle Sam. Of course, the convenience that they provide will promote their use and this really isn't an issue for most people, but just like some prefer cash today, some will opt for the blockchain counterpart.

The important takeaway here is that the money of the future will for the most part not be physical in any way. This gives us additional benefits not only of convenience, but the ability to transact something of value in both the physical and virtual worlds, blurring the line between realities. If this sounds far-fetched, know that this prediction isn't really one of the future; it's already happening today.

The Future of the DAO

When we look back into the past we see that the concept of a company is not really all that new. We can trace the concept of individuals banding together as a legal entity as far back as Rome's Collegium from 49 BC,[1] while in the modern era many look to the East India Company, set up by British merchant adventurers and granted a royal charter of Queen Elizabeth I in 1600,[2] as the grandfather of all corporations. Rather than debate this, one thing that is generally accepted is the concept of a modern organizational structure in which we generally have an executive, a managing partner, or CEO who is accountable for ensuring that the company functions and is the ultimate decision maker for day-to-day operations. This executive in turn reports to a board, a small group of individuals also focused on the company's well-being who will vote on corporate matters and provide direction. This has been the go-to structure for getting things done and, while there are variants such as limited liability companies (LLCs) and partnerships, they all generally result in one or a few individuals ostensibly being in control of that entity. The point being, it's been a while since we've had anything really innovative or new in the world of legal entities, and we certainly don't have entities today that are governed by everyone involved.

A decentralized autonomous organization (DAO), as we learned in Chapter 5, takes the concept of decentralization found in blockchains and applies them to an organization. A DAO has no central authority. Instead, a DAO is managed by governance tokens, and those who hold them get to participate in how that organization is going to function. DAOs, like blockchains, are run by software that is publicly visible and verifiable – everyone knows the rules of the game and is considered by many to be the ultimate in shareholder empowerment. Furthermore, there is no one person or small group of people that stand to get paid if the company goes well, as all monies earned are distributed to the token holders.

DAOs are going to change everything, because they are not subject to the whims, desires, or biases of one (or a small group) of individuals whose actions often change to ensure that things turn out in their own best interest. Never have we seen such a glaring example of this as the implosion of FTX and Celsius. In both of these cases, decisions on governance were ultimately made by their respective CEOs. Because Celsius was a centralized play at common DeFi concepts, let's explore what this could have looked like as a DAO. Alex Mashinsky was CEO of Celsius and, as we have learned given its bankruptcy, his interests and choices weren't necessarily in the best interest of Celsius' users. Imagine, however, if a company like Celsius was a DAO that did basically the same thing – collateralized lending and yield earning.

Just because we can, we're going to call this fictional DAO Fahrenheit. Let's go on to suppose that Fahrenheit issued crypto assets called FAHR to everyone that deposited funds into the company and that these FAHR tokens were used to vote on governance. Those who are directly involved using Fahrenheit's products and services would then be participants in the rules and initiatives for Fahrenheit. We're not saying that this would have worked flawlessly but I don't think it's a stretch to say that it certainly couldn't have turned out much worse and, importantly, customers of Fahrenheit would have a real voice.

DAOs also open up the opportunity to have expansive two-sided marketplaces like Uber and Airbnb that function *without the need of the actual company, Uber or Airbnb!* Instead of a corporation, we simply need smart contracts – software that pairs up each side: drivers with riders, property owners with renters, and so on. This opens up a whole new world where buyers and sellers of almost anything can interact directly, without a central organization. Platform businesses, which are two-sided marketplaces, have shown to outperform and win against competition. One of the best books to read about this is *Platform Revolution* by Jeffrey Parker, Marshall Van Alstyne, and Sangeet Paul Choudary. Companies like Uber and Airbnb proved out the model and blockchain technology now makes it easier than ever to create a two-sided marketplace.

The concept of a DAO is still very new and, look, there are plenty of bugs to be worked out. There are some cases where centralization may well beat decentralization and vice versa. It's also very likely that we'll see some hybrids of this in the future. There are naturally a ton of questions about efficiency, operations, and so on that, quite frankly, aren't resolved yet and that we aren't going to tackle in this chapter. Ultimately, however, what we want to leave you with is that the out-cropping of the blockchain revolution is that we have the ability now to have self-governed organizations that are transparent and genuinely working in the best interest of their customers/users/constituents while reducing human bias. We have groups acting in concert to do things that are in the best interest of the group, and that is powerful.

The Future of Companies

Let's extend this concept and really look at the future of companies, because the structure of companies will change, too. Of course, we will still have corporations and limited partnerships and the legal enti-ties established in case law and overseen by the various regulatory and government authorities that provide their legal rights. It's how people come together and how that might be upgraded that will change, all to meet a more dynamic market.

Companies will always have owners, management, and labor. What may change in the future is how groups of people organize to meet common goals and objectives. For example, in the future, Uber (we're just picking a name out of a hat here) may not consist of one primary legal entity with departments of people working under like customer service, operations, finance, technology, partnerships (drivers), and business development (demand, those who seek rides). There may be one primary legal entity that becomes a decentralized autonomous corporation (DAC) and then multiple DAOs that report to the DAC. Each DAO will have its own set of goals and objectives, with a management team as a part of the DAO whose primary pur-pose is to guide that DAO to meet its objectives. They in turn recruit labor to join the DAO and work on its behalf to serve the goals of the organization. There may be token-based economies inside each DAO that drive the incentive structure to deliver on whatever goals are set forth within the DAO. This would allow resources and talent to pool much more dynamically. As well, by using an economics-based incentive structure for each group (DAO) under the one company DAC, there is a mechanism to align incentives between owners, man-agers, and labor.

Practical Examples

Most new technological revolutions start with the adoption of new clusters of innovation. The first big push in the adoption cycle is to re-create something we can already do but do it a lot more efficiently (or, better, in several ways). This time around, most of the focus with crypto has been to implement traditional financial services in a decentralized way and to view tokenized assets like stocks in the past – to invest in them and trade in them. But the big step into the future isn't about doing what we can already do. It's about being able to do something new or to do something so differently as to bring about a paradigm shift.

With blockchain technology, peer-to-peer transactions allow us to respond to the market much more dynamically. And that's what's going to happen. More markets, interacted with much more dynamically. We would like to walk you through two scenarios that almost everyone can relate to. This peek into the future may show what the world might be like in the years to come. How humans organize to produce in an economy, the methods, tools, and practices, is going to shift wildly.

Getting a Job (Contract)

What will the job market look like in the future? For one, it's going to become more dynamic than it is today. We're already on that vector. Forty years ago, a person was most likely going to stay at one company for most of their career. That's certainly changed over the past few decades. The average worker now stays at a company less than three years.

In the future, everyone will have an agent, like I have a literary agent. But this agent will be an AI agent, scouring the market to see all the job contract offerings available and presenting them to you in the order of your choice. Perhaps you want to see the potential job contracts available sorted by the highest fee first or by the probability of being awarded the contract. The process will be more gamified, almost like playing a character in *Dungeons & Dragons* or one of the role-playing character (RPC) games out there. Instead of hit points or strength, your character will have skills, experience, and passions. Your (AI) agent will be out there working on your behalf to find your next job contract. University degrees will become less pervasive as the cost becomes harder and harder for the average person to afford. Skills and credentials will become more commonplace. And those skills and certifications will be managed on a blockchain. Past work experience will be posted on a blockchain as well, so your work history and provenance can be immutably tracked. Finally, you'll want to feed your AI agent your passions – the things you want to do and where you'd like to take your career.

The order in which you take on new work or take on learning new skills will become more market responsive. AI and blockchain technology together will increase our capability to meet market demand. And it's this new model that will assist everyone in developing their skills to their passions to get awarded work that most effectively matches what they want to do with what they are good at and what experience they bring to the table. The job market will become more dynamic in nature.

Making an Investment

As we've stated earlier in the book, the trend to tokenize assets and bring them onto a blockchain provides vast new capabilities. When it becomes easier to form capital, it's the application of that capital formation that can add to productivity. Just like in earlier periods of history, the ability to create collateralized loans allowed businesses to become more productive. This concept is merely extending in the future with the ability to form capital and tokenize it. We see this in the United States, where it has made it easy to start a company. Since it's easier to start a company in the United States than in, say, France, more companies are formed, and more productivity can be generated. We've heard that there's something like 40 steps to the process of forming a company in France, where bureaucracy and red tape abound. By streamlining the process to form a charter, more people can form companies and more productivity can occur.

It's the same with capital. If, through technological innovation, it becomes easier to form capital and perform simple financial services, like collateralized loans on assets, more people can participate with the functions that make productivity easier, and the more productivity we're going to have. It's the trend of tokenization that provides this new capability. We see this today but it's just in its infancy.

Every DAC and DAO can create tokens and create an economy that generates value. That value can be captured by the token asset and then any and all financial services can be utilized. Exchange services, insurance services, derivatives to manage/mitigate risk, and fractionalization of ownership all contribute to the potential optimization of productivity. Think about the way online trading opened up Wall Street to everyone on Main Street. Fifty years ago it was difficult to buy a share in a company. Today, kids do it on a regular basis. That kind of change is going to happen due to these new technological breakthroughs.

If a company has inventory but needs a loan to obtain some working capital to land the next round of sales, getting the loan becomes much easier if the company has the ability to represent their inventory, and the ownership of that inventory, via tokens. The tokens represent the inventory as an asset and the company could get a loan on those assets. What's important is that it makes an illiquid asset liquid, which opens up significant flexibility for those who choose to hold the asset. It may work the other way around, too. You may have heard of invoice factoring/AR (accounts receivable) financing. Through this process, companies can represent their accounts receivable and all incoming revenue and get a loan on future income to speed up their growth prospects. We can already do factoring and inventory loans now; they just become much easier, cheaper, and faster to do in the future due to the flexibility of a tokenized asset.

Importantly, both of these products become available to everyone. Just as crowdfunding opened up once-rarefied air of investing to those with more modest means, any tokenized capital opens up the opportunity of participation to the same group. Capital at the personal level will become an important part of the multiple streams of income required to lead a middle-class life in the future. Everyone will need to get better at obtaining and keeping assets to generate income on their behalf. Just like we have AI agents on the front end looking for our next job contract, we may well have AI asset manager agents managing our assets in products much like the ones described earlier to produce income on our behalf. You will no longer need to be a millionaire to have access to millionaire opportunities.

The Technology Exists Today

We'll wrap this up by noting that it's the technologies that exist today that make all of this possible. The first is the tokenization of assets, as we've discussed in previous chapters. The second is the ease with which a two-sided marketplace can be implemented. Both are possible due to blockchain technology – we just have to see it come to fruition.

Yet these are just a few markets and marketplaces that show what the evolution might look like. It's the dynamic nature of markets that will shift and those who can respond and adapt to the ever-changing world will be the ones to capitalize on it. It's the adoption and application of technology that drives this process. Those who can adopt the new technology and apply it are the ones who will win out against the competition. Those who don't will go the way of Blockbuster.

A New Long Wave Economic Cycle Has Begun

Toward the end of 2022, OpenAI released a project called ChatGPT. There are some great TikToks explaining why it's so powerful.[3] ChatGPT is an AI platform where the user simply asks questions or has a conversation with the AI. It's a natural-language user interface that feels much more "human" than typing into forms on a web page. And it's powerful. Unbelievably powerful. Let me explain.

As a user, you go to the OpenAI website.[4] You create an account by entering your name and cell phone number (and in doing so you do give up your privacy). You are now provided a prompt where you can ask questions and give instructions in a natural language format. Something like, "Write me a 500-word essay summarizing the book *The Great Gatsby*." And guess what? It spits out a 500-word essay summarizing the book! No shit. It really does.

So, what are the ramifications of a free tool that does so much? The Age of Information is dead. It's matured. A new long-wave economic cycle is beginning. I call it the Age of Autonomy® and I write extensively on the new technological revolution that's upon us. You can read it in my first book, *Crypto Investing in the Age of Autonomy*.[5] Long-wave economic cycles are driven by technological revolutions. We've had five in the past 200 years.[6] From the Industrial Revolution to electrification, to railroads, to oil and automobiles, to the Age of Information, we've seen cycles play out throughout history.

When a new cycle begins, it changes the nature of how economies work and how people generate income, and it changes them drastically. Many information workers are now going to be in the process of dying. If you're a radiologist, a software developer, a lawyer, or any infomation worker take note, because the global economy won't need as many in the future. Why do we need radiologists when there's an AI program that can read an X-ray better than humans?[7] Why do we need software developers when the average person can ask ChatGPT to write a program in Python that will build a website for them?, Why do we need lawyers when anyone can ask ChatGPT to read a contract, interpret its meaning and intent, and evaluate certain risks and parameters? The possibilities are mind-boggling. Now, that doesn't mean we won't need *any* doctors or software developers or lawyers, but it does mean we'll need fewer of them. It's going to change the game of the 40-hour workweek and going into an office and all the things we've built as standards for the Age of Information.

The future will look quite different, and I'm talking about a decade, not 100 years, from now. We're going to need to rethink how society functions. For if there are fewer information worker jobs and software is now producing a large part of the global work product, what does that mean for tax receipts the government gets to run the country with? The ramifications are large, vast, and wide.

That doesn't mean, though, that the future is bleak. For what can we be doing instead of rote processes that can be done by software? We can get more creative. And that could be quite an interesting future to be a part of. The people who are early to understand these big changes are the people who can profit and prosper from their newly gained insight. The first people who start using ChatGPT in the small businesses are the ones who will create vast amounts of monthly income that will outweigh any salary they were getting from their old job. You'll see. Better yet, you'll participate because now you're in the know!

What's Next?

Buckminster Fuller challenged us with his famous statement, "We are called to be architects of our future, not victims of it." We love this quote, as it sums it all up. With it, Fuller describes exactly the phase we are going through now with the advent of blockchain technology. The world is changing, and this train has left the station. Wants, needs, desires, goals, alignments and outcomes, collaborations and competitions are all going to be pushed way past what we can possibly imagine under the current circumstances and constraints. More will be at stake. Much more will be won and lost under the new paradigm.

So then, from our perspective there is really only one question to answer: Will we participate in the future that is in front of us? Or are we going to stand by idly while it thunders forward? Our intent in author-ing *Crypto Decrypted* is to empower you to be participant because this is happening whether you like it or not.

Remember that the human imagination can be quite big. How big? Well, we'll find out together, won't we?

Notes

Chapter 1: What's the Big Deal About Blockchain?

1. John Battelle, *The Search: How Google and Its Rivals Rewrote the Rules of Business and Transformed Our Culture* (New York: Portfolio, 2005).

Chapter 2: Bitcoin, the First Application of a Blockchain

1. https://bitcoin.org/bitcoin.pdf.
2. https://www.forbes.com/sites/jasonbrett/2020/04/26/why-chris-giancarlo-considers-a-digital-dollar-mission-critical-for-the-world/?sh=55b74ec43c41.
3. https://en.wikipedia.org/wiki/Savings_and_loan_crisis#Consequences.
4. https://www.cftc.gov/LearnAndProtect/AdvisoriesAndArticles/understand_risks_of_virtual_currency.html.

Chapter 3: What Makes a Smart Contract Smart?

1. Tharaka Hewa, Mika Ylianttila, Madhusanka Liyanage, "Survey on Blockchain Based Smart Contracts: Applications, Opportunities and Challenges," *Journal of Network and Computer Applications* 177 (2021), https://doi.org/10.1016/j.jnca.2020.102857.
2. Tharaka Hewa, Mika Ylianttila, Madhusanka Liyanage, "Survey on Blockchain Based Smart Contracts: Applications, Opportunities and Challenges," *Journal of Network and Computer Applications* 177 (2021), https://doi.org/10.1016/j.jnca.2020.102857.

3. Shuchih Ernest Chang and YiChian Chen, "Blockchain in Health Care Innovation: Literature Review and Case Study from a Business Ecosystem Perspective," *Journal of Medical Internet Research* 22, no. 8 (August 2020): e19480. Published online August 31, 2020, doi: 10.2196/19480.

4. https://www.hospitalrecruiting.com/blog/7624/smart-contracts-in-healthcare/.

Chapter 4: What Is DeFi?

1. https://www.businessreview.global/finance/619f863ce2b85d6c370 67f43.

2. Global Findex Database: https://www.worldbank.org/en/publication/globalfindex/interactive-executive-summary-visualization#.

3. https://www.ey.com/en_us/financial-services/how-financial-firms-can-jump-start-digital-asset-strategies.

Chapter 5: The Metaverse, NFTs, and Web 3.0

1. https://worldart.news/2022/05/07/how-nfts-benefit-the-art-market/.

2. https://fortune.com/2022/04/01/citi-metaverse-economy-13-trillion-2030/.

3. https://en.wikipedia.org/wiki/Social_Credit_System.

Chapter 6: Myth – Regulation Will Kill Crypto

1. Pantera Capital, December newsletter.

2. Larry Hite, *The Rule* (New York: McGraw-Hill, 2019).

Chapter 7: Myth – Crypto Is a Bubble

1. https://apnews.com/article/inflation-economy-prices-jerome-powell-839eaf55d57958b96fe18f9bc0884397.

2. https://www.pcgamer.com/us-regulators-say-multi-billion-dollar-crypto-lender-celsius-was-operating-like-a-ponzi-scheme/.

3. https://www.nytimes.com/2022/09/13/technology/celsius-network-crypto.html.

4. https://www.usatoday.com/videos/news/health/2021/08/24/covid-misinformation-fda-warns-ivermectin-covid-treatment/5578920001/.

Chapter 8: Myth – Crypto Is Bad for the Environment

1. The Office of Science and Technology Policy (OSTP) was established by the National Science and Technology Policy, Organization, and Priorities Act of 1976 to provide the President and others within the Executive Office of the President with advice on the scientific, engineering, and technological aspects of the economy, national security, homeland security, health, foreign relations, the environment, and the technological recovery and use of resources, among other topics. OSTP leads interagency science and technology policy coordination efforts, assists the Office of Management and Budget (OMB) with an annual review and analysis of federal research and development in budgets, and serves as a source of scientific and technological analysis and judgment for the President with respect to major policies, plans, and programs of the federal government.

2. https://www.nytimes.com/2022/02/25/climate/bitcoin-china-energy-pollution.html.

3. https://www.channelchek.com/news-channel/could-cryptocurrency-become-a-catalyst-for-renewable-energy-projects.

Chapter 9: Myth – Crypto Is a Fraud

1. https://www.justice.gov/opa/pr/jpmorgan-chase-co-agrees-pay-920-million-connection-schemes-defraud-precious-metals-and-us.

2. https://www.sec.gov/news/press-release/2022-78.

3. Ibid.

4. SEC-CFTC: "On April 24, 2019, the United States Attorney's Office for the District of Oregon announced an indictment against two Nigerian citizens, Onwuemerie Ogor Gift (aka Onwuemerie Ogor) and Kelvin Usifoh, on one count of conspiracy to commit wire fraud, eleven counts of wire fraud, and one count of conspiracy to commit money laundering. The indictment alleges that the defendants engaged in a scheme to defraud whereby they solicited investments of bitcoin through certain websites that promised investors a 20–50 percent return on investments, 'zero risk' and instant withdrawals. The indictment further alleges that, despite the claims on the websites, the defendants told victims to deposit more bitcoins in order to receive the proceeds of their investments and never returned any funds to the victims. The indictment specifically alleges that the defendants are affiliated with three websites: wealthcurrency.com, boomcurrency.com, and merrycurrency.com" (https://www.cftc.gov/LearnAndProtect/AdvisoriesAndArticles/watch_out_for_digital_fraud.html).

5. https://www.sec.gov/oiea/investor-alerts-and-bulletins/social-media-and-investment-fraud-investor-alert.

6. https://www.ftc.gov/news-events/data-visualizations/data-spotlight/2022/06/reports-show-scammers-cashing-crypto-craze.

7. https://www.fbi.gov/news/stories/pennsylvania-affinity-fraud-ponzi-scheme-092321.

Chapter 10: Myth – Crypto Empowers Crime

1. https://blog.chainalysis.com/reports/2022-crypto-crime-report-introduction/.

2. https://www.forbes.com/sites/davidblack/2022/03/11/cryptocurrency-fuels-explosive-growth-of-crime/?sh=7bd78ac6618a.

3. https://www.nytimes.com/2021/06/09/technology/bitcoin-untraceable-pipeline-ransomware.html.

Part Three: The Breakthrough

1. https://www.youtube.com/watch?v=5ca70mCCf2M.

Chapter 13: Peer-to-Peer Models

1. Magnus Andersson, Anders Hjalmarsson, Michel Avital, "Peer-to-Peer Service Sharing Platforms: Driving Share and Share Alike on a Mass-Scale," research paper, presented at the 34th Annual Conference on Information Systems, Milan, 2013.

2. Ibid.

3. Michael Gowan, "Requiem for Napster," *PC World*, May 18, 2002. Archived from the original on April 26, 2014, retrieved June 13, 2013.

4. History.com, "2001, March 06: The Death Spiral of Napster Begins," *Inside History*, https://www.history.com/this-day-in-history/the-death-spiral-of-napster-begins, accessed October 12, 2022.

5. S. P. Choudary, G. G. Parker, M. W. Van Alstyne, *Platform Revolution: How Networked Markets Are Transforming the Economy and How to Make Them Work for You* (New York: W. W. Norton, 2016).

Chapter 15: No Permission Required

1. Global Findex Database, https://www.worldbank.org/en/publication/globalfindex/interactive-executive-summary-visualization#.

2. http://www.wsj.com/ad/article/mlf-women-around-the-world-face-hurdles-to-financial-inclusion.

3. https://www.fdic.gov/analysis/household-survey/index.html#:~:text=An%20estimated%204.5%20percent%20of,the%20survey%20began%20in%202009.

4. Global Findex Database, https://www.worldbank.org/en/publication/globalfindex/interactive-executive-summary-visualization#.

5. https://borgenproject.org/how-poverty-effects-society-children-and-violence/.

6. https://www.pewresearch.org/internet/2019/03/07/mobile-connectivity-in-emerging-economies/.

7. https://www.economist.com/special-report/2017/11/10/what-technology-can-do-for-africa.

8. https://www.alliedmarketresearch.com/micro-lending-market-A06003.

Chapter 16: Digital Scarcity

1. https://www.pennlive.com/entertainment/2019/11/star-wars-toy-from-1979-sold-for-world-record-price-by-central-pa-auction-house.html.
2. https://www.bobafettfanclub.com/bounty/toys/anh/anh_rocket/.
3. https://www.entrepreneur.com/money-finance/the-strong-case-for-wine-as-an-alternative-investment/378676.
4. https://www.investing.com/studios/article-1012.
5. https://www.cnbc.com/2022/06/18/the-worlds-most-valuable-sneakers-from-nike-dunks-to-og-jordans.html.

Chapter 18: Liquid Venture

1. https://www.wsj.com/articles/SB10000872396390443720204578004980476429190.
2. https://www.statista.com/statistics/617136/digital-population-worldwide/.

Chapter 19: Signals versus Noise

1. https://www.denverpost.com/2022/09/21/colorado-accepts-cryptocurrency-taxes/.

Chapter 22: Savings, Borrowing, Income Strategies, and Taxes

1. https://www.bankrate.com/banking/cds/historical-cd-interest-rates/.

Chapter 24: Looking Ahead

1. https://en.wikipedia.org/wiki/Collegium_(ancient_Rome).
2. https://en.wikipedia.org/wiki/East_India_Company.
3. https://vm.tiktok.com/ZMFsWfFA2/.

4. https://chat.openai.com/auth/login.

5. Jake Ryan, *Crypto Investing in the Age of Autonomy* (Hoboken, NJ: Wiley, 2021).

6. Carlota Perez, *Technological Revolutions and Financial Capital: The Dynamics of Bubbles and Golden Ages* (Cheltenham, UK/Northampton, MA: Edward Elgar, 2002).

7. https://www.cnn.com/2022/11/29/health/heart-attack-stroke-x-ray/index.html.

Additional Resources

Here are some additional resources:

Thought Leaders to Follow

- Andreas Antonopolous: https://aantonop.com/
- Saifedean Ammous: https://www.saifedean.com/
- Nic Carter: https://niccarter.info/
- Chris Dixon: https://cdixon.org/
- Ric Edelman: https://dacfp.com/
- Chris Giancarlo: https://www.chrisgiancarlo.org/
- Joshua Hong: https://about.me/joshua.hong and https://www.mind.ai/
- Travis Kling: https://www.kanaandkatana.com/
- Caitlin Long: https://caitlin-long.com/
- Dr. Pippa Malmgren: https://pippamalmgren.co.uk/index.html
- Anthony Pompliano: https://www.anthonypompliano.com/
- Jake Ryan (author): https://www.ageofautonomy.com/ and https://jakeryan.substack.com/
- Kyle Samani: https://www.kylesamani.me/
- Michael Saylor: https://www.michael.com/
- Tom Shaughnessy: https://delphidigital.io/research
- Laura Shin: https://laurashin.com/
- Nick Szabo: http://unenumerated.blogspot.com/
- Michael Terpin: https://transformgroup.com/
- Erik Townsend: https://www.macrovoices.com/

Tools and Research

- CoinMetrics: https://coinmetrics.io/
- DeFiLlama: https://defillama.com/
- Delphi Digital: https://delphidigital.io/
- Glassnode: https://glassnode.com/
- Luke Gromen: https://fftt-llc.com/
- Macrovoices Podcast: https://www.macrovoices.com/
- MetaMask: https://metamask.io/
- TradingView: https://www.tradingview.com/
- Zerion: https://app.zerion.io/

Top Crypto Funds as Thought Leaders to Watch

- A16z Crypto: https://a16zcrypto.com/
- Multicoin Capital: https://multicoin.capital/
- Pantera Capital: https://panteracapital.com/
- Tradecraft Capital: https://www.tradecraft.capital/ (our fund management company)

About the Authors

Jake Ryan is an author and CIO at Tradecraft Capital, a macro-themed crypto fund focused on the next long-wave economic cycle. His first book, *Crypto Investing in the Age of Autonomy*, published by John Wiley & Sons in 2021, is a *US News & World Report* Top 7 Book on Crypto and DeFi.

In addition, Jake has been the keynote speaker at top AI conferences and is a frequent speaker on the crypto circuit. He's also a contributor at Bloomberg Radio, *Newsweek*, and *Harvard Business Review* (HBR). He is a special contributor to the Digital Assets Council for Financial Professionals (DACFP).

Jake is also an advisor to several VC-backed startups as well as two VC accelerators and a PE firm. Prior to Tradecraft, he ran a specialized software engineering firm for 20 years. Jake earned a computer science degree from the University of Texas at Austin. He is the first author of published work in applying AI to cybersecurity, which has 750+ Google Scholar citations.

James Diorio is the CEO of Tradecraft Capital, which manages a macro/thesis-driven blockchain fund. He has been at the forefront of technology and innovation throughout his career, and has over 30 years of experience as an executive, serial entrepreneur, technologist, and advisor with depth creating and growing successful enterprises.

It was in 2018 that James took a deep dive into the blockchain space. Intrigued but with little true understanding of this technology, he spent a full year studying and attending conferences and events worldwide to get a broad perspective and appreciation of this technological breakthrough before fully embracing it. After becoming an early advisor to Tradecraft Capital where he helped refine the Age of Autonomy® thesis, he ultimately was invited to take the executive reins.

With a perspective based on education and understanding, his career has always been purpose-driven with an emphasis on empowering groups and individuals and, importantly, on ensuring that friends and colleagues understand the importance of "why" as it relates to any venture, be it personal or professional.

James has advised, coached, and mentored individuals as well as technology and blockchain startups and was co-founder of the Autonomy2040 conference where he was a moderator, contributor, and event facilitator. A technologist at heart, James holds a degree in computer science from University of California, Santa Barbara.

James is also co-founder of the Bella Organization, a nonprofit created in honor of his late daughter, Bella Diorio, and focused on impacting highly functioning teens on the autism spectrum. James currently lives in Austin, Texas, with his life partner, Sofia Koo.

Index